Praise for *Differentiating for the Young Child*

"The authors build a strong case for the WHY of differentiated instruction, and then go on to fill the pages with enticing examples of the HOW of differentiating instruction for each major subject area. Their presentation of lesson planning as a journey is a powerful metaphor that has the potential to transform classroom teaching! I loved the book! It was great fun!"

Sharon Easterling, Executive Director
Delaware Valley Association for the Education of Young Children

"Wrapped around a telling metaphor of a learning journey, Smutny and von Fremd provide the tools and the templates for differentiation for learners. Rich in practical ideas, rigorous in its applications, this is a 'must-have' research-based resource for differentiation for the young child."

Robin Fogarty, Professional Development Consultant
Chicago, IL

"At last, a practical book that is tailored to the early years and focuses on the how to's of differentiating curriculum and instructional delivery."

Jim Grant
Staff Development for Educators, NH

"The authors have done a remarkable job! I found the five-step sequence and the journey analogy absolutely brilliant. Even more profound is their ability to show how standards and district requirements can still be met, yet in a more developmentally appropriate way."

Patricia A. Phipps, Executive Director
California Association for the Education of Young Children

"The authors teach us to teach better. They use teacher voices, classroom stories, and solid foundations to guide the reader's thinking. Practical examples and specific guidelines make the book very useful without resorting to templates or gimmicks!"

Carol Ann Tomlinson, Professor
University of Virginia

"Whenever anyone asks me for advice on parenting and educating young children, I refer them, without hesitation, to Smutny and von Fremd. Their very special talent is in helping adults nurture and cherish the creativity and learning joy that is so intrinsic in young children."

Susan Winebrenner, Author
Teaching Gifted Kids in the Regular Classroom

To E. Paul Torrance, who saw the "different drummer" in every one of us

Differentiating
FOR THE
Young
Child

Teaching Strategies Across
the Content Areas (K-3)

Joan Franklin Smutny
S. E. von Fremd

Foreword by George S. Morrison

For information:

Corwin Press, Inc.
A Sage Publications Company
2455 Teller Road
Thousand Oaks, California 91320
www.corwinpress.com

Sage Publications Ltd.
6 Bonhill Street
London EC2A 4PU
United Kingdom

Sage Publications India Pvt. Ltd.
B-42 Panchsheel Enclave
Post Box 4109
New Delhi 110017 India

Printed in the United States of America

Library of Congress Cataloging-in-Publication Data

Smutny, Joan F.
  Differentiating for the young child: Teaching strategies across the content areas (K–3) / by Joan Franklin Smutny, S. E. von Fremd.
    p.cm
Includes bibliographical references and index.
ISBN 0-7619-3108-2 (cloth) — ISBN 0-7619-3109-0 (pbk.)
1. Education, Primary—Curricula. 2. Individualized instruction. 3. Cognitive styles in children. I. Von Fremd, S. E. II. Title
  LB1523.S59 2004
    372.21—dc22
                                            2004003700

This book is printed on acid-free paper.

04 05 06 10 9 8 7 6 5 4 3 2 1

Acquisitions Editor: Robert D. Clouse
Editorial Assistant: Jingle Vea
Production Editor: Diana E. Axelsen
Copy Editor: Gillian Dickens
Typesetter: Ruth Cottrell Books
Cover Designer: Tracy E. Miller
Graphic Designer: Lisa Miller

Contents

Foreword

Providing for the needs of all young children is a hallmark of early childhood education. However, meeting the needs of all children is a goal that is elusive for many teachers. That is, until now. Joan Franklin Smutny and S. E. von Fremd provide the profession with an intelligent, readable, and highly useful book on how to differentiate the curriculum for young children with the goal of meeting a wide range of learning needs.

Differentiated instruction is a wonderful means of providing for the learning and social needs of all young children. Teachers use a variety of methods, materials, and activities to make the curriculum more responsive to the abilities, challenges, learning styles, and interests of students. Through the strategies of differentiated instruction and a wider range of learning options, children of all backgrounds stand a better chance of reaching their potential, achieving at high levels, and becoming successful in school and life.

Differentiated instruction is frequently likened to a never-ending escalator that enables students to continually learn at higher and higher levels. Unfortunately, many teachers don't know what it is, why they should implement it in their classrooms, or how to manage a learning environment based on its philosophy and ideas. These can become barriers to changing practices or even attempting to implement the principles of differentiated instruction.

This book responds to the need for a user-friendly navigation system for primary teachers on their journey toward a more differentiated classroom. In addition to being an excellent resource and companion, the book acts as a guide for good teaching. After all, differentiated instruction is at the heart of all good teaching. Writing in an engaging and inviting style, the authors provide practical information and step-by-step instructions, guidelines, examples, and figures. All of these will enable primary teachers to begin to apply the strategies of differentiated instruction to their own classrooms.

Differentiating for the Young Child shows how to use the special abilities, problems, learning styles, and interests of students to determine what children should be taught. It guides primary teachers in modifying their curriculum to meet student needs and create appropriate learning environments. The book also gives readers the essentials of assessing learners and their learning as a means of establishing a firm foundation for teaching. The authors understand that teachers who know their students well will be able to successfully implement differentiated instruction. They stress the important teacher role of engaging children in active learning, encouraging them to play a major role in their own learning, and helping them become responsible, independent learners.

It is refreshing that Smutny and von Fremd emphasize the visual and performing arts as a means of differentiating the curriculum and learning. They demonstrate how to use the arts as a basis for learning across the curriculum and for engaging students in a holistic way in the process of learning. Through examples, teacher stories, and concise suggestions, they create a clear picture of how to apply the principles of differentiated instruction to all curriculum areas. Their examination of the role of assessment is particularly valuable in ensuring that students receive the education they need in all subject areas.

This important book will be useful to all primary teachers who want to do a better job of teaching and who are authentically interested in ensuring that all of their children learn joyfully and well.

—George S. Morrison
Professor, Velma E. Schmidt Endowed Chair
College of Education
University of North Texas
Denton, TX

Introduction

If children grew up according to early indications, we
should have nothing but geniuses.

—*Goethe*

Jimmy brought an armful of books to his first day of first grade. During a free activity period, he sidled over to a couple of children constructing a bridge and asked if they wanted him to read a Frog and Toad book. One of them agreed and sat quietly by his side as Jimmy read and dramatized one of his favorite stories.

In the same class sat Saha, whose family moved to the United States a month before she started school. She knew English but could not understand American accents very well. She shrank into her seat and scribbled the sounds of English words in Arabic script. When flipping through the books on a nearby table, she instinctively opened one from the back.

Russell had so much energy that he zoomed wherever he went. Some people in the school thought he had an attention deficit problem, but his teacher did not agree. His family had moved six times in the past 3 years seeking work, and Russell needed time to get used to the rhythms of school life. At the moment, all he seemed ready for was running around the edges of the classroom.

Desiree entered first grade with the idea of becoming a potter. She brought her own clay to class every day and asked the teacher when she would learn how to make pots and also statues of her favorite animals. She had no interest in reading or math and spent most of her time making the other children laugh.

During the primary years, children express a wider range of differences than older learners. As a general rule, the younger the age group, the more dramatic the variations within the group and the more likely that differences in tests or in the performance of any task reflect differences in developmental level. Add to this the influence of culture, special ability, and language, and you have a classroom, such as the above, where the range of knowledge and understanding in any given subject can span at least several years.

So how do we begin to teach such children? What does a teacher do in a grade where every child is supposed to finish the year reading at a certain level and yet at least a third of the class is bilingual, four children have special problems, and two are already reading? Is it possible to teach essential reading strategies to Russell, who can hardly sit still and barely knows his alphabet; Saha, who painstakingly sounds out words in an Arabic script; Desiree, who would rather do pottery; and Jimmy, who is already reading books at third-grade level?

The first response must be to know what these children are bringing to the table—their special abilities, their struggles, their loves, their particular state of development—and to craft each lesson around them. *Differentiating* instruction literally means beginning with the differences of the child and adjusting the curriculum accordingly. For young children, significant changes take place within each year of the primary grades. One month, you may find a child struggling with the most basic math concept; then the next month, he suddenly masters it. The strategies used to differentiate the curriculum give primary teachers tools for responding to these leaps and halts in development and also with other situations such as the growing number of bilingual and culturally different students in American classsrooms today.

A central purpose of *Differentiating for the Young Child* is to help primary teachers respond to the learning needs of an increasingly diverse student body while also navigating the demands of their curriculum (including state curriculum standards). Most primary teachers live under the constant pressure to deliver specific content each year to all students regardless of their learning needs and backgrounds. But they also recognize the developmental needs of young children and have already figured out ways to adjust instruction accordingly. The question is, How can we better balance the demands of state standards and district requirements with the needs of the children before us?

Using the original definition of *curriculum*, which means "to run" (Latin *currere*), this book approaches differentiating in the form of a journey. Thinking of teaching in this way makes sense when we consider what happens in the process of planning and executing a journey. Let us say that you have decided to organize a journey for 20 young children.

Two of them show up without shoes; 5 have shoes and boots but no sweaters for the cold nights. Three feel nervous about traveling by car and want to know if they can get out now and then to walk around. Two want to get there as quickly as possible. Questions immediately arise in your mind as you plan:

- How prepared are my children, and what do they need to complete this journey?

- What sights and experiences do I want all of them to experience no matter which route they take?

- What routes would best serve their needs (some may need a direct route, whereas others will benefit from a longer itinerary)?

- What should be the means of traveling (car, bike, foot, etc.)?

- How will you know if the journey did what you intended?

Differentiating for the Young Child presents a five-step sequence for your journey:

Step 1: Know the travelers (children).

- Are they prepared for the journey? What skills and abilities do they have?

- What differences from cultural background, life experience, and home life influence their ability to embark on this journey (i.e., learn)?

Step 2: Determine the destination (learning goal).

- Where do you want the children to be at the end of this journey (i.e., what do you want the students to understand or to be able to do)?

- What learning standards and curriculum goals will this journey address?

Step 3: Identify proof or evidence that they have reached the destination (i.e., understand what has been taught).

- What behaviors and comments would tell you that the students understand?

- What products, performances, constructions, and experiments would express understanding of the concepts, skills, and information taught?

Step 4: Plan the journey.

- How should the journey begin (how should the subject be introduced)?
- What teaching strategies should be used?
- What learning activities?
- What resources?
- How will the students be grouped?

Step 5: Reassess and adjust according to new needs and changes.

- What are the criteria for knowing that the children have reached the destination (understood the concepts and processes involved)?
- What measures (e.g., observation, questioning, rubrics) will give you the information you need to know if the child is on track or if he or she needs further adjustment?

As you travel through this book, think about your own needs and those of your students. The first chapter ("Preparing for the Journey of a Differentiated Classroom") explores the most important elements of a differentiated classroom: (a) an understanding of the students (their needs, strengths, habits, challenges, culture, etc.); (b) identification of the most essential concepts, knowledge, and skills in the curriculum that will give teachers the flexibility they need to make adjustments; and (c) a classroom environment and resources that will enable children with different needs and abilities to learn in unique ways.

The second chapter ("Assessing Primary Learners") clarifies the "why, what, when, who, and how" of assessment vis-à-vis young students. Because understanding the students is the cornerstone of "differentiating," the chapter illustrates how student assessment determines what will be taught. It includes strategies for preassessing students, such as testing, observations, portfolios, and parent consultations, and describes how to measure their progress during and after a unit through further observations, rubrics, and questioning.

The third chapter ("Strategies for Differentiating the Primary Curriculum") offers a summary of the different strategies you can use as you improve the fit between your curriculum and the students in your class. It has suggestions on how to prepare the children to take on more responsibility than they might be used to and shows how these strategies apply to different learning situations and student needs. It asks: What needs to be differentiated? In some cases, you need to vary the pace and level of the assignment. In other situations, a student or group may benefit from a difference in learning style, from integrating content with other disciplines, and from creative processes. The chapter also includes information on different grouping strategies—cluster, interest, tiered—and independent study.

The fourth chapter ("Using the Visual and Performing Arts to Differentiate the Primary Curriculum") is a guide for using the arts in a differentiated classroom. Too often, the arts are associated with enrichment and are rarely used to create significant growth in young children. This chapter applies the visual and performing arts to the four subject chapters (language arts, social studies, science, and math). It shows how the arts can be the *process* by which students explore, conceptualize, synthesize, or analyze content or the *products* that embody the learning they have done in a unit. The chapter has examples within the four general subject areas and a guide for assessing the suitability of specific art forms for assigned work.

Chapters 5 through 8 use the five-step sequence for traveling through the vast and various terrain of language arts, social studies, science, and mathematics and for "differentiating" the journey. They begin with what is *essential* (concepts, processes, and skills) in each of these subjects as a guide for selecting suitable learning goals for young children. To use the journey motif, we might ask the following: What mountains must all children scale? What rivers do I want them to dip their toes into? What forests must they pass? Each of the subject chapters clarifies (a) what the students are bringing to the table (abilities, learning styles, culture, etc.), (b) what the destination is (a topic related to some essential concept or skill), and (c) what evidence (products, behaviors, etc.) will prove that they understand it. The fourth step involves planning a sequence of learning activities that lead children to the "destination" you have identified, using a range of resources, grouping students appropriately, and making adjustments where needed. The fifth step in each of the chapters offers a number of ways teachers can gauge student progress and make adjustments after or during units. This is critical for determining whether students are getting what they need. Examples of the process draw all of these elements together.

The authors have not planned out every step you need to take to apply the principles of differentiation to your classroom. We believe that teachers know best how to incorporate new ideas into their classroom and that to nail down every step may defeat our purpose. What we have done is present the key elements of a differentiated classroom as simply as possible and in a way that, we hope, will inspire you to move in new directions. You can best determine what ideas to synthesize into your own planning and what may have to wait until a later time. We only hope that the structure and ideas we have presented will help you meet the diverse needs of young students.

Finally, let it be said that teachers of young children play a crucial role in the future success of their students. Without some measure of love for learning, few children can thrive in any real way. Working for approval or the attainment of good grades cannot carry students to the deeper realms of learning as can the "sense of wonder."

Rachel Carson (1965) puts it best when she writes,

> If I had influence with the good fairy who is supposed to preside over the christening of all children I should ask that her gift to each child in the world be a sense of wonder so indestructible that it would last throughout life, as an unfailing antidote against the boredom and disenchantments of later years, the sterile preoccupation with things that are artificial, the alienation from the sources of our strength. (p. 54)

Because the primary grades influence all the years that follow, young students who have been inspired, curious, and intrigued in their first encounters with new learning draw on this foundation into the middle and upper grades. It is in the earliest years that their sense of themselves as learners first emerges. It is in the earliest years that their love of learning is awakened and, through you, extended. So let the journey begin!

Acknowledgments

No book is ever written alone. Without the pioneering work of Carol Ann Tomlinson, Susan Winebrenner, Grant Wiggins, and Jay McTighe, we could not have developed a structure for this volume. They have charted pathways for generations of teachers yet to come!

We are indebted to Nora Ruckers and Dorothy Massalski, whose insightful suggestions proved invaluable during the rewriting and editing process. Janet Bartell, Carol Creighton, Annie-Jo Fridgeirsson, Karen Morse, and Nate Stoffregen also contributed a variety of helpful materials during the early stages of the book.

To write a book, one always needs friends. At the Center for Gifted, they were Cheryl Lind, Jenni Rinne, and Edie Myers. Sandy Berger, whose own contribution to education has influenced thousands of teachers, shared insights when needed.

The expertise and patient support of Robb Clouse, Jingle Vea, Diana Axelsen, and others at Corwin Press could not have been greater. They exemplify the highest standards in publishing and provided encouragement and guidance throughout the process of writing this book.

A special thanks to the primary teachers who have shared their classroom experiences with us and to the primary children who never cease to amaze, inspire, and touch our hearts.

Corwin Press gratefully acknowledges the contributions of the following people:

George S. Morrison
Professor, Velma E. Schmidt
  Endowed Chair
College of Education
University of North Texas
Denton, TX

Judith Smock
Teacher
Clark Elementary School
Erie, PA

Jann H. Leppien
Author, Associate Professor
College of Education
University of Great Falls
Great Falls, MT

Deborah E. Burns
Author, Curriculum Coordinator
Cheshire Public Schools
Cheshire, CT

Cathy Burdette
Teacher
Dodge Elementary School
Mobile, AL

Joseph Staub
Resource Specialist Teacher
Thomas Starr King Middle School
Los Angeles, CA

Jeanne H. Purcell
Author, Consultant
Gifted and Talented
Bureau of Curriculum and
  Instruction
Connecticut State Department of
  Education
Hartford, CT

Patricia A. Phipps
Executive Director
California Association for
  the Education of Young Children
Sacramento, CA

Susan Winebrenner
Educational Consultant
San Marcos, CA

Sharon Easterling
Executive Director
Delaware Valley Association for
  the Education of Young Children
Philadelphia, PA

Jim Grant
Founder, Executive Director
Staff Development for Educators
Peterborough, NH

Carol Ann Tomlinson
Professor of Educational
  Leadership, Foundations & Policy
University of Virginia
Charlottesville, VA

Robin Fogarty
Professional Development
  Consultant
President
Robin Fogarty & Associates, Ltd.
Chicago, IL

About the Authors

Joan Franklin Smutny is founder and director of the Center for Gifted at National-Louis University. She directs programs for thousands of gifted children from all socioeconomic and cultural backgrounds—age 4 through Grade 10. She teaches creative writing to children in her programs and courses on gifted education for graduate students. She is editor of the *Illinois Association for Gifted Children Journal*, contributing editor of *Understanding Our Gifted* and the *Roeper Review*, a feature writer for the *Gifted Education Communicator*, and a contributor to *Parenting for High Potential, TEMPO*, and *Chicago Parent Magazine*. She has authored, coauthored, and edited many articles and books on gifted education for teachers and parents, including *Teaching Young Gifted Children in the Regular Classroom* (1997); *The Young Gifted Child: Potential and Promise, an Anthology* (1998); *Gifted Girls* (1998); *Stand Up for Your Gifted Child* (2001); *Underserved Gifted Populations* (2003); *Differentiated Instruction* (2003); *Designing and Developing Programs for Gifted Children* (2003); and *Gifted Education: Promising Practices* (2003). In 1996, she won the NAGC Distinguished Service Award for outstanding contribution to the field of gifted education.

S. E. von Fremd is an independent scholar, writer, and editor with a background in education, cultural studies, and dance. She performed with the Never Stop Moving Dance Company in Chicago under the direction of Reynaldo Martinez and taught creative dance and theater to children in the city and surrounding areas. Her interest in creativity and culture eventually led her to do a doctorate in performance studies at Northwestern University. This included a year's research in Uganda, where she focused on the role of popular theater and dance in reviving cultural identity and educating children and young people throughout the country. She has written several book reviews on African musical traditions, a monograph on the cultural legacy of Kenyan novelist Ngugi wa Thiong'o and Nigerian playwright Wole Soyinka, a monograph on refugees in Africa, and an article on the performing arts as a popular forum for education in Uganda. She has also given presentations on Uganda's creative artists under the reign of Idi Amin and on dance movements throughout the continent of Africa.

1 Preparing for the Journey of a Differentiated Classroom

Barbereaux School, Evanston, Illinois

There are only two lasting bequests we can hope to
give our children. One of these is roots,
the other, wings.

—Hodding Carter

Every student who walks through the door of the classroom brings special gifts to the learning table. He may have unkempt hair and stare down at his shoes, or she may speak another language and hop around the room like a grasshopper. But each one has some hidden strength that enables her to learn. In preparing to differentiate, you have to find out who your learners are—what abilities, interests, and experiences have shaped them. In addition, you must honor the unique developmental needs of young children.

During the toddler years and even beyond, children learn by exploring their environment; they finger, touch, taste, and shape whatever they can get their hands on (Morrison, 1997). Gradually, their explorations become more focused as they seek to understand the world around them through more systematic experiments. As higher level thinking advances and they enter school, young primary students create and improvise with any materials at hand, inventing the world from their own imagination (Belgrad, 1998, p. 373).

It is this constructive behavior of young children that has become the foundation of teaching in preschool, kindergarten, and, to some extent, the primary grades (Cohen & Jipson, 1998, p. 405). Drawing on the work of Piaget (1977, 1980), a "constructivist" or "developmental" model evolved, based on how children *construct* their understanding of the world through continuous contact with and adaptation to their immediate environment. This constructivist model not only responds to the unique learning needs of young children but also stimulates growth in their reasoning and thinking ability (Cohen & Jipson, 1998, p. 406).

Teachers play a key role in anticipating students' learning needs and guiding the process of thinking, applying, and inventing. Vygotsky (1962) and Feuerstein (1980) theorized that teachers need to become active *mediators* in the learning process and lead development, rather than just provide contexts that may stimulate it. They design learning experiences that are slightly ahead of the child's development but within reach of his ability and understanding, thus stimulating cognitive growth.

This kind of educational program for young children emphasizes play, exploration, risk taking, and creative problem solving. Children advance at their own rate and teachers use learning contracts and planning sheets to assess strengths and weaknesses and to monitor each student's progress.

> In the developmentally appropriate classroom, the role of the teacher has changed. Formerly, the teacher was someone who told and imparted all of the knowledge. Now the teacher is one who extends, engages, questions, affirms, and challenges children as they are constructing knowledge. (Cummings & Piirto, 1998, p. 383)

Many primary teachers already have features of a differentiated classroom in place: ways to discover the learners' special abilities and characteristics, a variety of work areas in the classroom, a diversity of resources, and an active class of eager students who are used to doing different things. If this is your case, you already have a strong foundation to create a supportive environment for differentiating. On the other hand, if your school emphasizes direct instruction in the primary grades, introducing new changes may take more time. In this case, you can integrate the strategies of differentiated instruction more gradually, beginning with those areas where your students have the greatest need.

KNOW THE CHILD

Differentiated instruction grows from your understanding of the children before you. As the second chapter will show in more detail, assessing your students' talents, learning styles, and other attributes provides the means to make the changes they need to grow. Here are some examples from a kindergarten class:

> Alma is a bilingual child who grew up in the United States. She speaks Spanish to her parents and English to other relatives. She knows many stories told by her grandmother. Some are family stories; others are tales that come from the village where her parents grew up.

> Brendan spent a great deal of his childhood hanging around his father's garage because his mother had to work. Sometimes, his father let him carry some of his tools, and when he wasn't playing outside, he would sit on a tall stool and watch his father fix the cars that came in. His father pointed out a lot of things while he worked, and Brendan came to know a lot about car engines.

> Simon has traveled all over the United States. During the summer, the family packs up their tent and visits a new forest, mountain, or coastline. Simon's mother taught him a lot about birds and plants on these trips, and on the second day of school while looking out window, Simon spontaneously yelled out, "Yellow-bellied sapsucker!"

> Madeleine has two dogs, three cats, a couple of rabbits, and a tank full of fish. One day at school, she released the gerbil from its cage. When her teacher finally recaptured the animal, she asked, "Madeleine, why did you do this?" She whispered, "He had to find his friend." The teacher hadn't told the children that one of the gerbils was returned to its original owner the day before because she didn't think anyone would notice right away.

Each one of these children has special strengths gained from the lives they have lived so far. Alma has a wealth of stories—a wonderful source for literacy. Brendan understands engines and through this has a developed ability to construct things and improvise with a variety of objects. Simon brings his observation of the natural world to the study of science, and Madeleine's experience with animals has given her a sensitivity to and knowledge of other species.

Becoming aware of specific skills, experiences, and abilities that young children carry within them opens the door to new teaching options. Instead of focusing most energy on what the students lack, teachers become more familiar with what they have, how they work, what materials they gravitate to, and what they most enjoy doing. These are the tools that enable the children to extend their knowledge and also strengthen skills when needed. Unlike remedial instruction, differentiating actively draws on students' interests, experiences, and abilities.

Educator-anthropologist Luis Moll believed that discovering the hidden strengths (the knowledge, skills, and abilities) of bilingual communities should guide the education of their children—an approach he called "funds of knowledge" (Moll, 1992). In an effort to break away from the deficit approach to bilingual students, he did an ethnographic study of the Mexican American communities that fed into some of the barrio schools in Tucson, Arizona (North Central Regional Educational Laboratory, 1994). He discovered that the families and communities possessed a great deal of expertise on such subjects as agriculture, economics, mining, and science. Those with rural backgrounds shared what they knew about cultivating plants and animals and ranch management; others knew mechanics, carpentry, masonry, and electrical wiring. Many in the communities had entrepreneurial skills and knew specific information about archeology, biology, and mathematics.

Most schools knew little of these "funds" of experience and knowledge and therefore could not create meaningful bridges between the children and the curriculum. Bilingual children, Luis Moll argued, need to be able to use the strengths that have come to them within their first-language community to overcome the limitations they experience in their second-language community. This principle applies to all students, as all bring hidden "funds" through which teachers can make meaningful connections to the curriculum.

Preparing for the journey of a more differentiated curriculum, therefore, involves finding out the best way to get the most useful information about your students. Young children come to you with little formal schooling and a wide variety of home situations, cultural environments, and community learning experiences. Working with parents and community members (see Chapter 2) will enrich your approach to differentiating as you will have a much clearer sense of where your students have come from and what resources, processes, and catalysts for learning will develop their latent abilities. Many of you already do this. Here are three examples from primary teachers:

I make the most of the moments when parents come to pick up the kids. I will jot down a few things I noticed in class and get the parents talking. Over time, I find out a lot and they will now volunteer information that helps me understand why their child reacts a certain way to an activity in class.

—*Second-grade teacher*

Over the first month or two, I sit down with a parent from each family and we talk about their child. They bring something the child has done and I explain my philosophy and how I like to work with the students. This helps me because I can then call on them later when I need support for a project or I can suggest ways they can help their kids at home.

—*Kindergarten teacher*

The biggest enemy of education, I feel, is television! I start the year with a letter to the parents (in both Spanish and English) requesting that they try to limit television viewing on school nights. I ask (nicely!) if they would work with me on a book list and other projects. Some parents resist, but I've found that many are grateful and admit that the whole family needs a break from the monotony of television.

—*Third-grade teacher*

In the course of the school year, I've had about 15 parents in my room. At the beginning of the year, I try to find out what special areas of expertise the kids' parents have and I keep a file. When we move on to a new topic, I look in the file to see what parent might have a special skill or interest that relates to what we're doing. This has created a greater sense of community between my classroom and the families, and I've learned a lot more about the kids this way.

—First-grade teacher

The more you can learn about your students, the more you can differentiate. Because differentiating adjusts the *content* of a lesson or unit (what they are to learn), the *process* (how they are to learn it), and the *products* (what results they are to produce), you obviously have to know your students well to determine what kinds of changes they need.

CHANGES TO CURRICULUM		
Content	*Process*	*Products*
Does the level and pace of the content match his ability and interest? Does he fall behind in any area? Does he finish assignments quickly and well?	Does he learn more by doing (i.e., through experiments, building, constructing, designing, etc.) and less by listening to information? Does he show his greatest gifts in creative processes and open-ended assignments?	Does he have a hard time relating to the materials, the products he needs to use to express what he knows? For example, a bilingual child may still have trouble writing a report but may have a thorough and comprehensive understanding of the subject.

UNDERSTAND THE JOURNEY

Differentiating enables children to draw on *their* learning preferences, life experiences, and special strengths to advance through the curriculum.

Although you would certainly find a wide variety of approaches to differentiating from classroom to classroom, consider the following general-principles as you prepare your own curriculum, students, and classroom.

What the teacher does:

- The teacher identifies essential content (knowledge, concepts, skills, proficiencies) that he or she wants everyone in the class to master.

- The teacher begins instruction with student differences and modifies the curriculum based on the most important content within that curriculum and individual learning needs.

- The teacher assesses individual student achievement and the effectiveness of differentiated curriculum as she or he teaches (rather than at the end of a unit).

- The teacher adjusts content, process, and products (materials) in response to student learning profiles, strengths, problem areas, and interests.

- The teacher employs a range of strategies for differentiating the curriculum such as learning stations, curriculum compacting, tiered instruction, interest groups, cluster groups, creative activities and materials, and so on.

- The teacher maintains a high level of flexibility in modifying aspects of the curriculum to create maximum growth and learning for each student.

What the students do:

- Students actively participate in their own learning and make choices within structured assignments and activities.

- Students move flexibly from one level of complexity to the next, and from one kind of process to the next, rather than following a lock-step sequence.

- Students gradually assume more responsibility for their own learning and take an active part in such tasks as setting up and storing materials, arranging chairs, and forming groups for assigned work.

- Students participate in their own assessment and become knowledgeable about how they learn, what they do well, and where they need more practice.

- Students focus more on their own growth and work than on how they compare with other students.

Here are several examples of teachers who adjusted their curriculum in different ways.

> Because of the different kids mainstreamed into my room, I usually have quite a range of skill and ability—anything between 2 years below grade level to at least 2 above. Differentiating helps me deliver the curriculum so that I can be sure everyone is getting the important stuff and getting it in a way that works for them. One of the strategies I use regularly in math is separate learning stations where the kids take new information and apply it at different levels of complexity and with different kinds of materials. At the beginning of the year, I familiarize the kids with the three stations. The first one has a lot of manipulatives, drawing paper, rulers, pencils, etc. This is where students prove the math facts and rules they've learned and show their partner why their solution to a problem works. I give them suggestions for how they might demonstrate their answers. Another station is for practicing computation where they need more help. Materials at this station could be worksheets, computer programs, and other supports that help the students become more confident. In the third station, children do math-related projects, which tend to be long-term, and they have the option of working alone or in small groups. I work out their projects with them, depending on their individual interests and learning needs.
>
> —*Third-grade teacher*

> A pattern I developed with my kids was to begin with direct instruction and then branch off into creative applications. For kindergarteners, this worked really well. The class had been learning a number of different words from a series of stories we'd read together. On index cards, I wrote a number of words from these stories (one on each card) and mixed them up in a basket. The children took five words each and also selected a picture from a large stack of prints I keep in a box. The print gave them a setting. I asked them to think up

a story using the five words and the picture they had chosen. After some time, I had volunteers tell me their story while I wrote it down on the board. Other, more advanced kids wrote theirs; still others accompanied their story with sketches of their own. This experience gave everyone a chance to invent a story using words I wanted them to use and understanding more about what goes into a story. Creativity is a great differentiating source because of its flexibility. Everyone at every level can participate, and they can go as far as their ability and ideas allow.

—Kindergarten teacher

Last year, I had a gifted child who came from such substandard schools that he was more like a first grader in terms of skill and knowledge. I started off by creating a list (with him) of all the things he could do and what he was good at. I explained that this list was his "engine" for moving ahead. In every unit, I figured out the areas where he would have trouble, and when the rest of the class was practicing a skill or working on problems together, I would take him aside and instruct him. I would then give him an assignment related to what the other students were doing but simplified, with reinforcement in skills where he needed extra help. With the parents' active support and a lot of encouragement from me, the child progressed rapidly and soon caught up with the rest of the class. Differentiating gave me the tools to deal with a situation that, in the past, might have resulted in this child being placed back a year.

—Second-grade teacher

IDENTIFY WHAT IS ESSENTIAL IN YOUR CURRICULUM

An important step in differentiating the curriculum is to identify the essential concepts, knowledge, and skills of subject areas. The reason for this is clear. A narrower goal (e.g., teaching children a vocabulary list from a specific book) does not give you the flexibility you need to adapt assigned work as does a broader goal (teaching children how to identify what's most important in a text—an essential reading strategy). The latter gives you many options: assign books at different levels of complexity, ask students to read different kinds of books (nonfiction, science fiction, fantasy, biography, etc.), or allow different ways to express what they think the main idea of a book is (art, theatrical event, essay, diagram).

Because the curriculum typically exceeds what you can teach in a given year, you have to make choices. Think carefully about what you want all students to learn—concepts, skills, information, and thinking strategies. What enduring knowledge, concepts, and skills do you want to leave your students with by the end of a week, month, and year? What topics and units will enable your students to explore essential concepts and knowledge?

The following are four useful criteria for selecting the most essential content (Wiggins & McTighe, 1998, pp. 10–11):

1. To what extent does the idea, topic, or process represent a "big idea" having enduring value beyond the classroom? In other words, what fundamental concept undergirds this lesson? For example, a unit on the relationship between people and the oceans would focus, in different ways, on the interconnectedness of ocean ecology—the big idea.

2. To what extent does the idea, topic, or process reside at the heart of the discipline? To learn science, young children need to do science, not just read or think about it. In a language arts class, students write stories, poems, and essays; interpret literature through movement and theater games; and discuss ideas in favorite books. Learning correct rules of grammar, usage, and spelling are inherent in this process but not goals in themselves.

3. To what extent does the idea, topic, or process require uncoverage? Think about those areas of a subject that students often find difficult. What central concepts in math require more time and reinforcement? Do the reading activities you've designed help them grasp what's most important in a story, a poem, or a book on butterflies?

4. To what extent does the idea, topic, or process offer potential for engaging students? A key concept or idea may hold no interest for students, however essential it is to a subject. You need

to choose interesting topics that connect to a big idea and provide access to meaningful exploration and discovery. For example, you can teach about double-digit numbers through story and simulations.

As you review your curriculum, ask yourself two levels of questions—"essential" and "unit" (Heacox, 2002). Essential questions involve overarching themes, concepts, and principles. An example might be, "What is a folktale?" Unit questions evolve from this broad question and target specific information, concepts, and skills. An example would be, "Where do folktales come from? Why are they called folktales? How are they different from other stories?" Often, these questions tie in with curriculum standards. Keep the number of questions relatively low (no more than five) and write them in simple, child-friendly language. These questions not only guide you but also create a conceptual structure for the students to follow.

Differentiating the Learning Curriculum Plan

Level I: Essential
(themes, concepts, principles)
A single, broad question

Level II: Unit
Tied to Learning Standards
(specific information, concepts, skills)
Five clear, student-centered questions

I kind of like sitting down with a notebook, flipping through books, and figuring out what I want my kids to understand about science or reading or whatever. I often start by asking myself, "What is science really about anyway?" Then words will come to me that get me started, like patterns, cycles, forces. If I were to give advice, I'd say, don't just look at education books to come up with essential concepts and questions. Go to sources that will really inspire you. I hover around the stacks in bookstores or libraries, thumbing through nature books, books on astronomy. I go to cultural institutions (many of which have materials for teachers) like observatories, art museums, technology museums, aquariums, historical societies, and cultural organizations.

—Second-grade teacher

I think of essential content as the forest. The unit, a tree in this forest. If we were to go to a national forest, we would naturally want to know what forest we were in. So I see this part of differentiating as a way of saying to the kids, "This is the forest we're going to be exploring. And over here is a tree and we're going to learn about this tree. . . . Or here is a river and these are the things we're going to learn about the river." Sharing this with kids motivates them more because if they can see the big picture, they're likely to also see the value of exploring a smaller section of this forest. Before we get into a new unit, I often ask the kids what they'd like to learn, and it's amazing what they come up with. Last week, the students asked so many interesting questions about poetry (which we are studying now) that I had a pretty clear sense about what "big ideas" I wanted to focus on and how we would explore the different poetic traditions and literary conventions.

—Third-grade teacher

My school is always hammering away about state curriculum standards. These standards are pretty concrete. But there's a way you can look at these as a guide. I write down the ones I feel most apply to my grade and my students and then work back up to a "big idea." For example, in math we have this standard: "Demonstrate knowledge and use of numbers and their representations in a broad range of theoretical and practical settings." I ask myself, "What do kids need to know about numbers?" Then I consider things like quantity and size, and comparisons of quantity and size. From there, I might have as a key question, "How can you make a quantity larger or smaller?" This of course leads to addition and subtraction, fractions, and other mathematical concepts.

—First-grade teacher

DESIGN THE LEARNING ENVIRONMENT

Most primary teachers have seen what a difference the learning environment can make in bringing a subject alive for young students. They understand that the environment is not just a place for learning but a medium for it. In the days of straight rows and worksheets, even children who did well in assigned tasks applied themselves to subjects that held no life for them. Teacher-directed instruction was the rule of the day. In large part due to the early influence of Maria Montessori (1964, 1966) and the emphasis she placed on "following the child" and the "prepared environment," as well as the work of Piaget (1977) and others, classrooms began to change.

As part of this historic shift toward a more child-centered classroom, differentiating also emphasizes the environment as a catalyst for learning—responsive to the unique needs of the children anticipated. This sort of classroom is as dynamic as the students and teacher who live in it, continually adapting to new needs and circumstances. In such a situation, you cannot always anticipate exactly what preparations will work best for your class. And this brings us to an important point that will simplify your life: You don't have to do all the work! One of your richest resources are the children and their families, as this teacher discovered:

> There wasn't much of anything in my school other than textbooks, paper, a few commercially made (and rather ugly) charts, and some scrappy art supplies. More overwhelming than this, though, was the sterile feel of the classroom. I ended up bringing things in from garage sales and my own home—a rug for one area I was creating for quiet reading and some stuffed animals from my own collection. I brought in colored things—anything—that would diminish the overall drabness of the room. One day I met one of the bilingual teacher aides and she said, "You don't have to do it all, you know. The kids and their families will help you!" I'm so glad I listened to her. I no longer supply everything I need. After putting key elements in place, I always have my students bring in things that they think will work well in particular activities. I am continually amazed at their resourcefulness and how they can figure out ways to use materials in so many different ways. Also, as far as color goes, this is no longer an issue. Now that the mothers know I love color, they

have contributed wall hangings (made by hand) and posters from their native Mexico.

—First-grade teacher

Children love to contribute to the environment where they learn; by doing so, they make the space their own and the classroom becomes a safe haven for them to grow. You have probably experienced this yourself. In a class about the environmental changes of autumn, a teacher might have students bring in different kinds and colors of leaves that have fallen from their neighborhood trees, rather than supply leaves themselves.

In the naturally open and creative environment of most early childhood and many primary classrooms, the tools for responding to different learning needs are already in place. The following design will help you think about how you can best prepare your classroom space and the materials you have. Who your students are, what they need, and the curriculum you are planning will guide you.

Visual stimulation

Arrangement and flexibility of seating

Resource areas

Independent use of centers

SPACE

Whole-class to small-group transition

Available resources reflect intelligence areas

Circulation from simple to more complex activities

Variety of materials and activities

Engaging ways to
begin your day

Clear behavior
standards and
expectations

Parental input
on students

ATMOSPHERE

Interest, engagement,
risk-taking demonstrated

Encouragement and
respect for students

Positive peer
relationships
fostered

Learning centers with materials
for different learning styles

Colorful and diverse
materials that are
modified frequently

Area for extended
activities to
promote higher
level thinking
and creative
problem solving

CLASSROOM

Space
for teacher
supplies and
resources

Small group work areas

Adequate spaces for storage
of long-term projects and portfolios

EXPLORE RESOURCES

If you're a primary teacher, you already know that resources are everything in a classroom for young children. To accommodate students' unique learning needs and styles, you probably have resource centers of your own. Some of them may have a variety of materials (e.g., books, art materials, displays, maps, games, construction materials) for exploring specific concepts in a unit. Others may be areas of the room where particular kinds of activities happen. An example of this might be a semi-enclosed quiet area with rugs and pillows where children can read, write, or sketch their ideas away from the bustle of the classroom. Or you might discover that you have a number of performers in your class who need a space, equipped with costumes, props, and construction paper, so that they can work on dramatic presentations, a mime piece, or a creative dance piece.

There is no need to have any more centers than the ones you really need. They will evolve naturally from your understanding of the children before you and from your work together. In this regard, Howard Gardner's (1993) research on "multiple intelligences" can shed light on those students in your class who may require different kinds of resources to progress in your classroom (see Smutny, Walker, & Meckstroth, 1997, pp. 33–37). Children from other cultures often need alternative ways to process new learning and express the strengths of their heritage. The following list offers some ideas on how you can create learning centers focused on specific "intelligences."

Linguistic Center—Linguistically oriented students learn best through the written word. They exhibit mastery in language (sometimes in a dialect) and often have a verbal wit and an ease expressing themselves verbally or on paper. A linguistic center should be located where it is quieter and have comfortable floor pillows, chairs, and tables.

Resources: Books; magazines; encyclopedias; dictionaries; paper for writing and drawing stories; books on tape; magnetic letters with board; spelling materials and games; alphabet games; sentence blocks with articles, nouns, verbs, adjectives, and adverbs; computer software for word processing and story writing; taped stories from oral traditions around the world; taped poetry.

Musical Center—Musically able students learn through rhythm and melody—by singing, humming, rapping, or tapping a pencil, foot, or finger. They often express a deep love for music, have an ability to compose catchy tunes of their own, and recognize a wide range of melodies easily.

Resources: Piano, keyboard and headset, other musical instruments, drums, rhythm instruments, cassette player and taped music, blank tapes for children's music, instrument picture cards.

Logical-Mathematical Center—Children with special abilities in the area of logic and mathematics are drawn to numbers and to discovering the logic and pattern of numbers. They often enjoy exploring other ways of calculating to understand how patterns work. They love logic and applying reason to solve complex mathematical problems.

Resources:

Math materials—felt board with felt objects and numerals; peg boards with colored pegs; pattern cards; puzzles; dice; number cards for sequencing and matching; math facts cards; number games and projects; tangrams; attribute blocks; Venn diagrams, graphic organizers, and matrices; codes to decipher; computer software for math activities.

Science materials—simple machines (e.g., pulley, gears), magnifying glass, microscope, telescope, mirrors, prisms, thermometers, models of planets, paper and pencil to record and draw data, computer software for computer-based science activities.

Visual-Spatial Center—Some gifted children gravitate toward the visual. They feel most at home in activities that involve seeing, representing, and manipulating lines, objects, and spaces. You might find them working out an idea in a diagram or sketching a word problem so they can "see" it and solve it. They are often the first students to notice any subtle changes in the classroom (a new poster, the addition of a few more desks, etc.) and prefer to sketch, diagram, or map out their thinking process.

Resources: Paints, paintbrushes, and easels; finger paints; clay; cookie cutters to make prints; markers; crayons; colored pencils; paper in various sizes and colors; scissors; scraps of ribbon, fabric, and yarn; glue, paste, and tape; old catalogs and magazines; pictures; photographs; mazes; picture puzzles; posters; camera and film; illustrated books, maps, charts, and diagrams; computer software (CD-ROMs) showing famous works of art or museum tours.

Bodily-Kinesthetic Center—Gifted children who learn best in a bodily-kinesthetic mode express this through hands-on activities and by doing. They enjoy touching, building, and moving and often express an exceptional gross or fine motor control—in sports, dance, or mime. They may be the class clown or the theatrical children who can't resist acting out the stories they tell or imitating (to perfection) the different people in their stories. They play roles that imitate real life and often solve problems and deal with abstractions using their imagination.

Resources: Trucks and cars, equipment and materials for crafts, large blocks, cardboard bricks, dress-up clothes, a variety of hats and props, masks, kitchen equipment, dishes, pots and pans, workbench and tools, puppets, stuffed animals, manipulatives to sequence, puzzles.

Interpersonal Center—Children inclined toward the interpersonal domain relate well to others and are leaders, organizers, and mediators. This doesn't mean they are necessarily outgoing. They may be the unassuming students who quietly diffuse arguments or anticipate problems in group projects. This center could be an area for group activities or even total group work. *Activities might include brainstorming, cooperative tasks, collaborative problem solving, mentoring and apprenticeship, and group games. It could also include biographies of great leaders from around the world.*

Intrapersonal Center—Students with intrapersonal intelligence tend to be introverts. They are often independent and have keen insight into their own thoughts, feelings, and personal growth. They know what they need and where their strengths lie, and they are equipped to deal with their emotions and personal goals. These students tend to be quiet and prefer working alone. *A center could simply be a couple of desks where students engage in independent assignments,* *journals, self-paced projects, problem solving, time alone, reflection, or computer software for word processing, or it could have a few relaxing chairs where children can listen to audiotapes or think quietly.*

Naturalist Intelligence—There are children who have a close affinity with the natural world. They have a deep sense of connection with both flora and fauna and demonstrate an extensive (in some cases, an encyclopedic) knowledge of certain species. Their responses to nature often embrace a poetic as well as scientific sensibility. They enjoy classifying and identifying species and exploring natural phenomena such as climate, ecological change, and environmental conservation.

Resources: Rocks; seeds; pots and soil for planting; garden area (e.g., potting soil in suit boxes lined with plastic); live animals; variety of leaves, fossils, and seeds; pictures of plants and trees for classifying and comparing; pictures of mammals, reptiles, birds, fish, and insects; plastic creatures; dinosaur models; paper and pencils for drawing and recording data; database software; bird feeders (hopefully, one outside); nests.

Structured experiences at a few centers such as these will give you a chance to observe where your students' strengths lie. Having a rich collection of materials that are suited to different learning styles also enables you to honor what is unique about the children and to create a bridge to new ideas and information in the curriculum. Knowing where you want all your students to be in terms of essential learning, you can use the environment and resources to design how they will get there.

LOOKING AHEAD

The next chapter is about assessment. This includes how you can find out the most useful information about your students as learners, how to monitor their progress while they are learning, and how to determine whether you need to make other adjustments at the end of a unit or lesson. Without knowing your students, you cannot really plan the most suitable activities for them. And without being able to determine if the changes you've made are benefiting them, you are teaching blind—

never a good position in a profession where accountability is a constant issue.

Below you will find an overview of the steps used in this book to differentiate in the four major subject areas (language arts, social studies, science, math). The diagram offers a useful and simple way to structure this journey:

THE JOURNEY OF A DIFFERENTIATED CLASSROOM

1. Who are my students?

Determine student readiness and preparedness for the journey by assessing

- Abilities
- Cultural traditions and strengths
- Learning preferences
- Special challenges

2. Where are they going to be by the end of this journey?

Identify what you want students to understand and master by considering

- Children's strengths, passions, and backgrounds
- Essential concepts, knowledge, and skills
- Curriculum goals
- Curriculum standards

3. How will I know when they've reached the destination?

Identify evidence of understanding, such as

- Behaviors
- Comments and discussions
- Observed processes
- Products

---

4. How do my students get there?

Design teaching strategies, learning activities, and resources through

- Catalysts for introductory activities
- Learning environment
- Adjustments in content
- Adjustments in process
- Adjustments in products

5. How do I monitor their progress?

Assess students through

- Ongoing observations
- Conferences with students
- Lists of criteria for peer evaluations
- Rubrics

Assessing Primary Learners

Barbereaux School, Evanston, Illinois

One must always tell what one sees. Above all, which
is more difficult, one must always see what one sees.
—*Charles Peguy*

In a longitudinal study, Torrance (1980) tells the story of Tammy Debbins, a talented first grader from the projects with an IQ of 177. Like many young children, Tammy had an imaginary friend. The school didn't understand this and never saw her potential. By third grade, Tammy's performance and creativity had become average. Torrance reported that Tammy never used her talents in high school or afterward and that her greatest frustration in life was that she wasn't "very smart" (p. 152).

It's easy for us to say that this school failed Tammy Debbins. But 30 years ago, most primary teachers would probably not expect—or even understand—a young child with needs so different from the other students. Nor were they exposed to the open learning environments that characterize many primary grades today. In this new century, primary teachers understand a great deal more about the unique and diverse learning needs of young children, and Tammy Debbins would stand a better chance.

For our purposes, the story of Tammy Debbins illustrates the danger of the "blank-slate" approach to assessment, where we see only the presence or absence of certain school-taught abilities. Like many young children, Tammy was a richly endowed being with a creative reservoir alive in her mind, needing only the right kind of nurturance and support to bring it all out. During the primary years, children develop in uneven, unpredictable ways; a particular skill or ability will seem absent for a while and then suddenly appear. Their interest in subjects evolves in a similar way. You're going along in your unit on geometry when a child suddenly makes a connection between the shapes he's learning and the patterns on the leaves he brought to class the day before. Here are a couple of observations by primary teachers:

> What makes younger kids different from older elementary is that a lot of things can affect how they perform at any moment. For instance, an older child will buckle down and do her best even if she's tired or the classroom next door is a little noisy. But a kindergartener or first or second grader can be thrown off by any number of things. If he's tired or not in the mood or bored, he might blow off an assignment or test. If she's taken by the nesting birds near the windowsill, she loses concentration. I had a child last year who knew how to divide with his eyes closed, but if he wanted to do something else he would just hand in the assignment with answers he just made up spontaneously so he could go do what he wanted. A fourth or fifth grader wouldn't do that.
>
> —*First-grade teacher*

> An advantage I've had as a second-grade teacher is my son. He was considered a poor reader until third grade, when he blossomed. Before then, he never liked books, never even liked being read to! He was like a woodland creature, always in nature, always asking me about insects and birds and plants he'd seen. Because of him I've developed the patience I think you need in primary school—patience to let the kids be where they are without labeling them as this or that. And to stay open because at any moment, a surprise may come and we have to be ready for it!
>
> —*Second-grade teacher*

The National Association for the Education of Young Children has a position statement on assessment that clearly describes *why* teachers assess students (rationale); *what* they assess (abilities, problems, learning styles, etc.); *who*, besides teachers, assesses students (resource teachers, aides, parents, children); *when* they assess (before a new unit, during, after); and *how* (what methods). As in the teaching of young children, the foundation of differentiating is assessment. You cannot adjust your curriculum to specific needs if you don't know what these needs are and what the students bring to the learning situation at hand.

From looking at the box below and on the following page, it becomes clear that the methods you choose to assess students depends a great deal on why you're doing it the first place and what you need to know about your students. This may seem obvious, but it's surprising how easily we can lose touch with our objectives. Here's an example from a third-grade teacher:

> I taught a class where each child turned in a short report on an animal or plant from a list of species in the Mojave desert. At first, I found myself making judgments on the basis of how well the kids organized their thoughts and wrote. Then I realized, "Wait a minute. What am I interested in here— how they write or what they understand about how this species survives in the desert?" Writing is important, but in this case, it may not tell me what the children *understand,* which then led me to consider some alternative ways for the kids to share their research. I particularly remember Jamie, a girl with terrible penmanship who often wrote in incomplete sentences. When I asked her questions, she was animated, eager to share her understanding about scorpions and drawing sketches and diagrams to illustrate her points.

ASSESSMENT FOR YOUNG STUDENTS IN A DIFFERENTIATED CLASSROOM

1. WHY?

A. Reveals a need for adjustments for the child

B. Gives teacher information to support child's learning and development, to plan for individuals and groups, and to communicate with parents

C. Supports child development and learning and does not threaten safety or self-esteem

D. Supports parents' relationship with their child

E. Is an essential component of a teacher's role

2. WHAT?

    A. Child's learning and development in all domains—physical, social, emotional, and cognitive

    B. Demonstrated performance during real, not contrived, activities

    C. Child's overall strengths and progress

    D. Projects child can do independently and those he can do with assistance

    E. Samples of student work, descriptions of performances

3. WHO?

    A. Teacher is the primary evaluator, gathering data from a variety of sources to respond to child's unique needs

    B. Teacher aides and resource people share observations, hunches, and insights

    C. Child engages in self-evaluation

    D. Collaborative process involving child and teachers, teachers and parents, school and community

4. WHEN?

    A. Integrated throughout the teaching day

    B. Regular and periodic observations of child in variety of circumstances

    C. Information on child systematically collected and recorded at regular intervals

    D. Information shared regularly between teachers and parents

5. HOW?

    A. Informal and ongoing observations of child learning in all domains

    B. Regular interactions with child in a wide range of situations

    C. Use of methods that reflect real life of classroom and the child's natural learning process

    D. Recordings and descriptions of demonstrated performance in real activities

    E. Use of a variety of tools and processes—arts, stories, taped readings, performances, self- and peer evaluation

    F. Recognition of cultural diversity in learning styles, strengths, and challenges

WHY ASSESS IN A DIFFERENTIATED CLASS?

In the old days, assessment focused on grading students, and this meant comparing the ability and achievement of students against each other and, in the case of standardized tests, against a state or national norm. But as primary education became more child centered (which isn't to say that it's less concerned about content), assessment came to be seen as a process that should serve the needs of the child and her teachers and parents rather than the reverse. Given the heavy burden many teachers feel in the area of assessment, it's important for you to make assessment something that *serves you and your students.* If it's very time-consuming and feels irrelevant to your needs and those of your students, then something is wrong.

Ask yourself why you're assessing your students. This may sound like an obvious question, but asking this periodically can sometimes lead to important discoveries. You may realize, for example, that there's a better way of measuring your students' ability and achievement in a particular domain than you thought of before. Or, you may discover new reasons to assess that hadn't occurred to you before you had the students you now have, and this may lead to a new approach. Or, you may realize that you're assessing too much (you don't have to assess everything a child does!); knowing why you're assessing will help you identify when you need to do it and when you don't. In a differentiated classroom, assessment should result in significant benefits for students, teachers, and parents.

Students. Assessment should create the greatest benefits for the students. As the previous chart illustrates, one of the most obvious benefits is that it reveals the need for curriculum adjustments for the child. If a child uses phrases and constructions directly from her first language, the teacher can, through assessment, determine what kinds of experiences will harness her unique verbal gifts while still increasing her development in verbal and written English. This is just one example. Primary teachers have many students who can't process new information or concepts in a particular way (different learning style) or who find the pace out of sync with what they can do on their own (too fast or too slow). Assessment enables you to anticipate learning needs and to make changes for students or groups of students as new problems or circumstances arise.

In a differentiated classroom, assessment supports children's self-esteem and fosters healthy attitudes about the learning process. The absence of this can be seen in the case of Tammy Debbins at the beginning of this chapter. Nothing is so fragile in young children as their self-concept, and the primary grades often establish what a student thinks about himself as a learner. Unfortunately for some, this early sense can have far-reaching consequences. Two college students recall early experiences:

> I started kindergarten reading, and I knew I was ahead of other kids because both my parents and the kindergarten teacher talked about my reading ability. I was so little then! But I remember feeling so tense in first grade if I ever got a correction or anything wrong. I literally couldn't learn from my mistakes because I couldn't get past the fact that I had made a mistake. My stomach was in knots and I was only 7 years old!

> I had a really hard time in math. I was OK until we got to double-digit subtraction and then I was lost. I remember working with an older kid my mom got to help me at home, and I felt so dumb. As I look back now, I know I could do math if I found the right approach. But I lived with this incredible phobia about math, as though it were a mysterious subject that only an elite group can ever do.

Assessment should lead students to self-discovery and self-acceptance. It should help young children understand what they're good at, what they love doing, how they work best, and what they may need more help on. Differentiating steers students away from comparing themselves with others or from situations where they might feel inadequate. Giving children appropriate assignments (challenging but within their reach) is an example of this. Assessment, where a child reviews his own assignment and works with the teacher and peers on ways to improve on or correct what he has done, helps the child focus on *learning*, not on a grade or judgment of his mistakes. Ideally, assessment should help young students become comfortable with the natural process of making mistakes, understanding where they went wrong, and correcting them.

Teachers. Assessment has obvious benefits for teachers. The more they understand what their students need in different areas of the curriculum, the better they will be able to respond. Also, being accountable for their students' achievement, they have to be able to talk knowledgeably to parents and other concerned adults. If they understand how specific children work best, where they need to grow more, and what kinds of activities might help them at home, teachers can share this information with parents, which will then benefit the relationship between parents and their children.

In my experience, assessment never really stops. I'm always observing how my plans are working out for students—who's struggling on the sidelines, who's bouncing on his seat to move on to the next thing, who's completely left out. I'm always asking myself, "What's the best way to do this? What am I missing? Why didn't this work? Or, what did I do right this time?" I keep track of my process because it's the only way that I can remember what worked, what didn't, and why.

—Second-grade teacher

Assessment also benefits other teachers, resource people, and aides who help in the classroom. A process that encourages the main teacher and others to share observations and insights puts all the adults in a better position to help the students.

Parents. Parents know a great deal about their children but may not always know what to make of certain behaviors or inconsistencies. Assessment in a differentiated classroom generates a lot more information for parents than report cards. The impact on the child can in some cases be significant.

We had a family move into our district who had suffered a lot of financial trouble for some years. I'm not sure how long. Anyway, the father usually came to school to pick up Josie, and he seemed worried about his daughter's struggles with reading. He also struggled with reading, he said, and he didn't want his daughter to have the kind of life he had. She was only 7 years old! The father didn't really understand how important reading experiences are in developing a child's love of books. I remember feeling that what I said to the father at that moment could make all the difference in how he saw his daughter. I assured him that she was *not* a slow reader; she just needed more reading experiences, and he could begin that process by getting a library card for her. We developed a friendship over time, and he enjoyed taking his daughter to the library.

—First-grade teacher

Today, when more young children from other cultures are attending our schools, parents are in even greater need of information. Many of them come to U.S. schools with their own cultural expectations of their children, of what schools teach and do, and how one is to treat teachers. For example, many other societies hold teachers in such great esteem that they are disinclined to ask questions, even when they have legitimate concerns.

WHAT DO I ASSESS?

An ocean of data washes over you daily as you teach. As a teacher, you're already in the habit of sifting through these data, though you may not always know at what point you noticed a particular characteristic in a specific child. In differentiated instruction, you may not see more in your students than you did before, but you become more *aware* of what you are seeing. To reiterate the quote by Charles Peguy at the beginning of this chapter, "One must always see what one sees."

Use a Wide Lens

Knowing what to assess and where to look, of course, enables you to "see what you see." Teachers assess their students' physical, social, emotional, and cognitive growth in a number of domains. Through a variety of methods (see "How Do I Assess My Children?" section, beginning on page 38), a more detailed portrait of students' general strengths, culture, preferences, special talents, and difficulties gradually emerges. This portrait continues to change and grow as daily interactions give you a deeper understanding of the children.

The following are notes that teachers have made to themselves:

> Marta worked on her drawing again today. It's definitely helping her handwriting, which has been such a frustration for her.

> Since Timothy's such a drama guy, I thought he'd do well in the simulation we did. It didn't go so well, mostly because he bossed everyone around. But he's got incredibly creative ideas; I just need to work with him on how to work with the other kids.

> Hai Ping discovered negative numbers. When I asked what you would have if you subtracted five from zero, everyone said you can't do it. But Hai Ping, who had been playing around with money, said, "You would owe five and then

when you get more money, you pay the five back and keep
what's left over."

Insights such as these enable you to become more precise in the
kinds of adjustments you make for individual children. They become the
features of the sculpted images you're creating of your students—the
details that enrich your interactions with them and lead to greater
growth.

The above insights are less common in a more traditional environment where teachers are peering through a narrower lens to measure
achievement. As the assessment chart shows, what you assess must
include abilities in a range of domains. Most primary teachers already
assess their students within a broad framework of ability, skill, and interest. Many of them also have children from other cultures who bring new
resources to the classroom, as well as knowledge and experience that
enrich the learning environment. One second-grade teacher did a survey
of her foreign students and realized that she had

- an East Indian girl with a knowledge of dance,

- a boy from Mexico who knew a lot about carpentry,

- two boys from Korea who were studying in a Korean martial arts
  academy,

- a girl from Nigeria who knew a lot about farming and crops,

- a Russian girl with experience in a special style of decorative art.

Look in Natural Settings

In a classroom of young students, assessment may occasionally take
the form of a test. But more often, assessment focuses on activities the
child is doing in real situations. A test is an artificial situation for young
students, and what you see often says as much about the child's response
to the testing situation as it does about what he can do. Observing students in *natural* contexts, you may discover why they do well in one
assignment but not in another. Certain learning preferences may surface
(see Kolb, 1984; McCarthy, 1990). For example, some students need to
know the big picture first—the forest they're exploring before focusing on
individual trees. Other students enjoy examining the trees, looking them
over, noting their characteristics, and sizing them up as part of getting
acquainted with the forest.

Josh doesn't do well thrown into an activity without prior introduction. He has to know what's being presented, and then he can relax and go with the flow.

Shari loves the surprise, the chaos of just being in a situation where she has to figure out what the new activity will be about.

—Notes from a third-grade teacher

Some students need very specific goals about what they will produce; others prefer an open-ended assignment where they can create or play around with an idea.

Barry asks a stream of questions whenever he gets an assignment. Should I use this paper? How long should it be? Should I do it this way?

Simone jumps in without hesitation. She thrives in situations where she can take an idea and go off on another tangent. In fact, keeping her on track is sometimes a problem in more structured situations.

—Second-grade teacher

Some children learn better by working with others who have similar interests; they thrive on sharing ideas and feeding off each other's enthusiasm and energy. Others prefer going off into a corner where they can think quietly and work without any interruptions or interference.

James works well with Steve, Jason, and Meryl. He shares his own ideas more freely in a small group than in front of the class. And the reception he gets from the other kids has given him more confidence.

Lakesha seems to do better by herself. Since she has no real problem participating in a group, I see no need to push her into it. She tends to go for more "far-out" ideas that the others don't like. A different drummer!

—Kindergarten teacher

These are just a few of the insights you might gain in your daily work with students. In fact, hundreds of observations wash over teachers in the course of a year—some of them noted down, others barely remembered. Differentiating harvests the insights and hunches you have about your students so that you can apply them to your curriculum plans.

What to Assess in a Specific Activity

Let's say you're teaching a kindergarten class on vowels and consonants and you want your students to understand the characteristics of each and how they differ. Before teaching, you need to first consider the children themselves. What are their environmental needs (noise/quiet, resources, seating arrangements), learning styles, special strengths, and interests? Then, you need to think about what the students could do that would demonstrate their understanding of a basic concept. Depending on your teaching style and your students' learning needs, this evidence could be any of the following:

- Children identify letters as vowels or consonants based on what their mouths, teeth, and tongue do—they say how vowels "feel" and what certain consonants remind them of (e.g., "S is like the hissing sea," etc.).

- Children create specific physical movements to express different consonants and contrasting movements for vowels.

- Children sing the different vowels.

- Children write/paint, draw simple words without vowels, and share with partners who have to guess what the words are (supply vowels).

- Children write their names without vowels and try to pronounce them.

- Children describe, draw, and dramatize what vowels and consonants are like. (One primary teacher reported that her student said, "Vowels are like the sandwich meat and the bread is like the consonants.")

- Children tell a story about a vowel who decided to leave the alphabet and what happened.

- Children choose 10 words from a book they love and identify which letters are vowels and which are not.

WHO ASSESSES THE STUDENTS?

Classroom teacher. Obviously, the regular classroom teacher assesses students most of the time. A primary role of the teacher is to continually measure how the students are doing with the activities he or she has planned. Is there a need for adjustment? If so, where? How? As mentioned before, this activity, which takes place more or less continuously in a variety of forms (see "How Do I Assess My Children?" section on page 38), lies at the heart of planning in a differentiated classroom.

Auxiliary teachers and aides/resource people. The main classroom teacher often coordinates the sharing of insights, stories, hunches, intuitions, observations, and concerns with other auxiliary teachers, aides, librarians, and specialists (anyone who has an impact on the child).

> It's difficult to find time to share information with other personnel in my building. We often exchange insights informally, while we're standing in the hall or walking to our cars. One thing that has helped this year, though, is an observation box where anyone from the librarian to the aide to even the school secretary can jot down something they saw, heard, or felt and slip it inside the box. We also started keeping more accurate records of what we've observed in our students and also which ones we haven't written much about at all. Some teachers focus on three or four specific kids a day to ensure that everyone gets the attention they deserve.
>
> *—Second-grade teacher*

> I always learn something from getting other people's feedback on my kids. I may not always agree with an assessment, but even when that happens, I end up discovering something new just by trying to understand another's perspective.
>
> *—Kindergarten teacher*

> Other personnel besides the main teacher can bring fresh eyes to a situation. There was a second grader I know I was able to help. He never passed up on an opportunity to distract the

other kids and draw attention to himself. It was so clear to me how intimidated and insecure he felt. For some reason, I clicked with this kid and ended up tutoring him in the library at specified times. His teacher and I were able to lift that kid up out of a situation that could have started him on the wrong foot. Since this experience, I've come to see how powerful a child's perception of himself or herself is.

—Librarian

Auxiliary people can also include parents and community volunteers. In districts with a lot of bilingual children, these individuals become indispensable sources of cultural and community information.

Parents. Parents are often the most realistic predictors of their children's abilities and needs, especially from birth to age 8. Family members can save you a great deal of time by tipping you off about their children's abilities, learning styles, and problem areas. Some teachers write letters and enclose forms asking parents to identify strengths. Other teachers request actual products or samples of writing, compositions, artwork, or science projects that demonstrate potential. Face-to-face meetings, of course, give you the most valuable information. More natural than filling out a form or responding to a letter in the mail, conversation can turn to a wide variety of topics and is generally more inclusive of the parents and their concerns. Even when you have specific questions to discuss, conversation has a natural, serendipitous quality that may reveal a few surprises.

Harry's parents were not what I expected. I somehow imagined them as arty, maybe even slightly hippyish. Poor Harry! Here was this free-spirited, artistic, sometimes rowdy child in a family the exact opposite—buttoned up, tidy to a fault, and, though kind and compassionate, completely baffled by their son. Ten minutes into our meeting, I already had a completely different take on some of Harry's problems in school.

—Third-grade teacher

When I told Mrs. Shernon that her daughter was having trouble with double-digit subtraction, she tossed her head back and laughed. I wasn't sure how to take this, and then she smiled at me and said, "Oh, I'm sorry, but you see, he tutors other kids in math and I happen to know that . . . well . . . he must have his own reasons for doing this because he most certainly does know double-digit subtraction." This was the biggest surprise I ever experienced talking with a parent. Parents can really help teachers understand what's going on with a child, and even though there may be a few pains in the bunch, the vast majority have been wonderful to me, and I make use of their knowledge.

—Second-grade teacher

Parents can provide helpful information about a child's home life and experiences and can also be another interpreting lens on her performance. If a student struggles to achieve in a certain area, a teacher may already have a plan for tackling the problem. But parents almost always have stories from the child's life at home that will shed light on the situation.

Students. Differentiated classrooms give children many opportunities to assess and understand themselves. Safe environments with a variety of workspaces enable students to advance at a pace and in a way that supports their growth. They move freely between different group activities so that they never develop a sense of being in a "slow" or "fast" group. They address problems through their strengths. They discover mistakes with other students or the teacher and learn how to correct them.

Children need to develop a healthy attitude about self-assessment—one that leads to discovery and learning rather than to self-criticism. This isn't just taught. Teachers nurture it by being affectionate and patient toward the children, as well as accepting and tolerant of themselves and their own errors. Teachers who feel free about themselves as learners can more easily put their young students at ease.

I was explaining to the children what we were going to do that day, and there was this dead silence in the room. I looked around. Marta slowly raised her hand and said, "Um ... we were supposed to do that on Friday." I laughed and said that I had skipped a whole day in my mind and that I needed them to remind me! A few of them giggled. It's good for them to see me goof up because then they know that making errors is just part of learning and life.

—Third-grade teacher

Giving young students positive experiences (see "How Do I Assess?" section on page 38) in evaluating their own work is fundamental to their growth, especially for those who have a tendency to be perfectionists. As they get older, the habit of self-belittlement and fear is more difficult to break.

WHEN DO I ASSESS?

In a traditional classroom, teachers usually assess students at the end of teaching a unit or lesson. In a differentiated classroom, assessment takes place before, during, and after teaching and through a wide range of methods. The reason for this is that you can't make informed decisions about what changes a child might need without a system for documenting their progress *as they work* and anticipating learning needs *as they arise.* Assessment should give ongoing feedback to the learners, as well as their teachers and parents, so that children receive the optimum support and resources to grow in all areas of the curriculum.

Preassess for Different Learning Needs

When beginning a new unit, you will need to know how much of the content your students already know, what skills they possess, and/or what gaps in knowledge and conceptual understanding they have. Without this information, it's difficult to gauge their progress or determine if their needs are being met. Your preassessments could cover a significant portion or just a part of a whole unit of study, include critical and creative thinking, target specific skills you want students to have, and give children different ways of showing what they know.

> If I want to be sure my students are ready for a new unit, I'll sometimes do a short activity that includes the concepts I plan to teach. For example, I might tell the kids to imagine that their classroom has $50 and they are bookkeepers in charge of keeping track of the money. Then, I create a story involving multiplication and division (introducing material that will be covered in my unit) and ask them to calculate. They can sit at a table with manipulatives if that helps them. They can draw or sketch. From their sketches, scribblings, calculations, etc., I can pretty much assess their skill and knowledge level.
>
> —*Third-grade teacher*

As a result of preassessment (whether in the form of a test, assignment, or introductory activity), you can gauge whether students have an exceptional knowledge, a basic understanding, a beginning knowledge, or no understanding or experience in the subject (Gregory & Chapman, 2002, p. 40). In some cases, preassessment isn't necessary. Many teachers find, as time goes on, that they have a good handle on the needs and learning styles of their students. Based on what the children have done in previous assignments, teachers can often anticipate what adjustments they need to make.

Assess While You Teach

More and more, teachers are realizing the need to assess children throughout the duration of a project rather than at the end (when it's too late for students to act on useful feedback). In addition to tests or assignments, you can accomplish this through student portfolios, self-evaluation, and rubrics (see next section). You can create a system for reviewing student performance and goals and adjust instruction as new needs arise.

HOW DO I ASSESS MY STUDENTS?

If you know *why* you are assessing your students, *what* abilities and skills you are assessing, *who* (besides you) should assess, and *when* you should do it (before a new unit, while the children are working, after the unit or lesson), knowing *how* becomes clearer. If the curriculum is a journey, assessment ensures that you have all the information you need to determine (1) how prepared the students are; (2) what background, skills, abilities, and special problems they may bring with them; and (3) what adjustments will be necessary to ensure that they reach their destination.

INFORMATION-GATHERING STRATEGIES			
Informal Interviews	*Direct Observations*	*Portfolios*	*Rubrics*
• Parent consultation • Child brings photo, favorite product, or object	• Main teacher • Resource teachers and aides • Parents	• Parent portfolios • Teacher and student portfolios (both contribute to them) • Multiple purposes	• Developmental rubrics • Summative rubrics

Gathering information on your students' abilities and learning styles doesn't have to become a lengthy process. Some teachers think they have to know a great deal about their students before they begin the year. They fill out elaborate charts they got in workshops or in books, pass out questionnaires to parents or students about learning styles, and write notes on the resources that different students use and what subjects and materials appeal to them. But they also wonder how they can possibly keep track of every student's preferences, strengths, and interests and how they can make the most of this information for what they have to teach right now.

> I see the value of spending some time in the beginning of the year getting to know students. But you have to relate it to some activity you're about to do. Last year, I had questionnaires for parents; I did interviews; I did it all and put it in a file. And there it sat unused for most of the year! I didn't have the time to sort it out and put it in a form that I could actually use.
>
> *—Second-grade teacher*

> We had an in-service focusing on learning preferences and how we could integrate Gardner's "intelligences" into our resource areas. It was a helpful session, but I remember thinking, "How does one teacher keep track of this information?" I felt kind of overwhelmed. We had charts and things to record observations and information, but it became another thing I had to add to my schedule.
>
> *—Kindergarten teacher*

> One thing I know from talking to other teachers in my city is that we all face a larger immigrant population than ever before. We don't have enough bilingual teachers to meet the demand, and many of us have a lot of kids who still need special help. I'd like information on how we can assess our bilingual and multicultural kids better.
>
> *—Third-grade teacher*

Part of the process of assessment is realizing *how much you already see and know.* As mentioned before, assessing students is, to some extent, about seeing what you're seeing. Practically speaking, you can only assimilate so much information about each of your students. To serve both the students in your class and yourself, it makes sense to relate your initial assessments to the content you'll be introducing to the class.

Informal Interviews

Think of the interviews as a chance to sit down with your students individually and assess how ready they are for what you have in mind for the beginning of the year. This is something you could do while the children are doing projects or working in groups. You could send a letter home to all the families notifying them of your desire to meet with their children and requesting that they find a few pictures they have made, project they might like to share, or family photographs that have a special meaning for them. Explain that the point of the interview is for you to become more acquainted with their children—their interests, personal likes and dislikes, unique strengths, and so forth. Ask them to share insights about their children and any suggestions that might help the "interview."

Although it is difficult to find the time to consult with parents, what you learn about their child will save you time later on. If the parents come from other countries—places where it is not the custom to confer with teachers—you may need to call instead of write and explain that you'd like to know a little bit about their child so that you can plan for her needs. Keep this simple. Like you, parents often have busy lives and may find a barrage of questions overwhelming.

> I usually send a note home with the kids to their parents welcoming them to my class. Then I ask, "Is there anything you want me to know about your child (his/her favorite thing to do, strengths, talents, problems, dreams, favorite foods, cartoons, imaginary friends)?" I usually get back about two thirds of these within the first week; the rest I call on the phone. This works for me. I can't sit down with all the parents, especially at the beginning of the year when we have so much going on around here. But this gives parents an opportunity to express whatever they want me to know and opens the door to our communicating through the year. And they

share a lot that I can use in the classroom. Having just one question means that they can say more.

—*Kindergarten teacher*

In the interview, you can use what the children bring to discuss what they love to do; a little of their history, culture, and family life; and what their hopes are for school. Draw up some questions that will give you information you can use in your lesson plans, but let the children lead you in the conversation. Children from other cultures can sometimes be very shy—both because they feel foreign and because they belong to a society where children don't generally have conversations with their teachers. As much as possible, focus on the object they've brought to show you and on topics that they feel free discussing rather than on them personally. Here are some examples from teachers:

Carmen showed me a Guatemalan shawl. She stared down at her feet for a lot of the interview, and so I just focused on the shawl and we talked about the colors and how her grandmother had made it for her. I asked her if she liked to make things and she nodded and finally began to mention some of the things she made at home. At one point, she pointed to the threads in her shawl and explained how her grandmother made the pattern. I like having the kids bring something in because when I jot down the name, the object, and a few notes, the whole thing comes back to me.

—*First-grade teacher*

I do my interviews while the kids are working. I take one aside and I do an activity with him or her. Michael sat down with me, and since we were going to move into language arts, I started telling a story and sketching the action (simple stick figures!). I would ask him questions like, "What do you think will happen next?" Or, "What would you like to happen?" He was quite imaginative and asked to do his own sketches. I try to sit down with each child, even if only for a brief while, and usually I focus on something we're about to do. I get a few insights, record them, and this sometimes gives me ideas on other kids.

—*Second-grade teacher*

Lizzie had no problem telling me all about her interests. Though she's only just turned 6, she told me that she's planning to be an actress. She said that what she wants to do in school is make up stories and act them out with the other kids (herself starring of course). A verbally gifted child—with an imagination that I better keep busy!

—Kindergarten teacher

In the second and third grade, you can often explore other questions and subjects:

- If you had a choice between building a model of an imaginary place or writing a story about it, which would you do?
- Do you like playing with numbers?
- Dressing up and pretending to be someone else?
- Doing experiments and explaining them to people?
- If you could change anything in school, what would it be?

Two important benefits result from these interviews. In the first place, you gain valuable insight into each child's strengths, interests, and personality that you can use immediately. In the second place, some special alone time with the children makes them feel valued and liked. Feeling valued and liked by a teacher has a significant influence on students' success in school. A second-grade teacher noticed this with one of her students:

At first I wasn't sure if these interviews were really necessary, but I've had little ripple effects from these interviews that I didn't expect. For example, one of my kids, Ben, proudly announced to me that he had gotten some information on a unit we were doing from his Russian grandfather—"You know, the old man with a pipe that I showed you at the beginning of the year!"

Observations

The most common way for teachers to assess children is through observation. Although observation sometimes has a reputation for being subjective and imprecise and therefore not a reliable source of information, in fact, the opposite is often the case. Focused and repeated observations of children over weeks of time yield more insight into how they learn than most tests.

> From the first-grade teacher, I already knew that I had a range of ability and skill in my room. In reading, I've been working with the kids on anticipating the plots of stories and getting them to look for clues in texts. I have a stack of sheets on my desk with the kids' names on and a blank space next to each name where I can quickly write down some observation or insight next to a name or two or three. These observations tend to be focused on specific things, rather than general observations. For example, I recently did a short exercise where the kids closed their eyes and I read most of a short story and then stopped. The text was printed out on a piece of paper for each child. I then had them imagine what they thought happened in the end. I asked questions. Why do you think this? Where in the story did you get that idea? What is it about the characters that made you think that they would act like this? I asked the kids to write out what they thought happened. They could also sketch their ideas and share them verbally. From this exercise, I was able to see which kids needed more advanced texts, which ones could benefit from drawing on other media (visual arts, etc.) besides writing to express their ideas.

> —*Second-grade teacher*

In this way, observations help this teacher plan for her students' needs and prepare for adjustments as she goes along. From what she has seen in this activity, she can now create different ways for her students to anticipate while they read (or listen). She can offer the option of writing, telling, dramatizing, or even sketching what they think will happen. As they work, she can continue to observe, focusing on their thinking process as they decide how the story will go. She may ask, "Are they just randomly picking an ending? Or is this an answer based on what the characters are *likely* to do or what has happened so far, or is it based on some other clues?" She can pose questions as she looks over their shoulders and observes what they're doing.

Most teachers have specific reasons for observing their students. They want to know the level of understanding and skill in the class and the kinds of needs that require a different approach to the lesson or unit they've planned. It helps to have guidelines for observations (Coil & Merritt, 2001, p. 84):

1. list the main learning objectives,

2. have clear observable criteria for achieving the objectives,

3. create a rating scale for judging the criteria (when appropriate).

An example of this follows:

NAME: _____

DATE: _____

Assignment: Write a fractured fairytale by changing a character.

Learning objectives:

- To understand how character affects plot.

- To learn how important character is to the suspense and conflict of a story.

Criteria: **Rating Scale (1–3):**

- The change in character results in a significant change in plot. _____

- The plot, though changed, has suspense. _____

- The composition is imaginative and vivid in its depiction of character. _____

Comments: _____
_____

Although the main classroom teacher may observe students for specific content-related behaviors and abilities, other adults in the school often make their own discoveries. Consider including input from auxiliary teachers and support staff. The music, art, or gym teacher, teaching assistants, float teachers, and one-on-one aides might share more freely if you had a small form (see below), where they could easily jot down something they saw and put it on your desk.

Here are a couple of examples:

Student's Name: *Mariela Diaz*

Date: *2/13/03*

Teacher/Aide/Staff: *Mrs. Henderson*

Context: *Working on a collage*

Behavior observed: *Mariela has an incredible design sense. I think collage gave her what she needed to use it. She cut out strips of images from magazines, sketched on paper what she wanted to put where, and then carefully glued the pieces on. She also included a lot of words, artfully placed among the images. Come and see it!*

Student's Name: Barry Longwood

Date: 9/8/03

Teacher/Aide/Staff: Mr. Harroway

Context: playground game

Behavior observed: Barry lets himself be bossed around by some of the more forceful kids. He hangs back sometimes and doesn't want to do what the stronger kids say. But he does it anyway. He needs help working in groups and not feeling he just has to obey orders!

Portfolios

One of the best ways to gather information on primary students is to use portfolios—collections of the children's work from home and in school. Parents, teachers, and students may all contribute to the collection. Portfolios work especially well for children who perform poorly on tests or have some other problem that makes their ability less visible. Portfolios of student work are common in many districts. In the case of young (K–3) children especially, examples of student work in a variety of school and home situations are by far the most reliable evidence of ability and learning styles.

Portfolios often include observations of parents. If you teach kindergarten and first-grade students, you will need examples of children's work from home and parents' stories (written or recorded) about them. These children have been busy learning for a number of years before coming to you, and the "classroom" has been their homes, playgrounds, nature preserves, gardens, cultural events, and local libraries. Children love bringing things to class and talking about them or depicting stories from their lives, showing photographs of a family adventure, or presenting a display of costumes and props for a play they staged with their cousins.

> Valerie whispered in my ear one day that she wanted to bring in a bear she had made by hand. Our class had set up a "museum" of kid creations, and every week we would feature five students (it was voluntary). They would bring in something they made or a picture or drawing of something they did or experienced. Next to whatever they brought in, they would write a little text about it. I learned a lot about my kids from this and would write notes of my own and stick it in their folders.
>
> —*First-grade teacher*

> When I think of portfolios, I think of those large black leather cases that artists use to keep their work. I don't know that I really understand what portfolios are in a regular classroom. But several years ago, I had my brother create these wooden pigeon holes—wide slats that are kid level and put together like a bookshelf—where the students can put things they're proud of. Then I have my file on them, and between these two, I feel I have a lot to go on.
>
> —*Third-grade teacher*

The value of portfolios is that they provide authentic assessment—evidence of witnessed behaviors and abilities. Such evidence is valuable in determining instructional plans, especially for children from kindergarten through third grade. A portfolio of work samples (from home and class) has the following benefits (Smutny et al., 1997, p. 10):

- validates your observations and hunches about a child;
- provides evidence of ability to challenge evaluations of a child based on tests;
- enables you to talk more decisively about your plans with parents, guardians, caregivers, and support staff;

- helps you evaluate the child's progress;

- guides you to a more child-centered and responsive curriculum;

- broadens your ideas and the choices you have to offer all of the children in your class;

- creates a source of pride and accomplishment for the child.

The portfolio is a collection of what a child *can* do. Its focus is on strengths and specific learning needs. For example, a gifted child with a reading disability may have teacher observations of his work on a science experiment, a painting he did at home, and an original solution to a challenging math problem. Another child who struggles to read may have an audiotape of a humorous and clever rap she created and sketches of her ideas about a short story.

Portfolios can also create meaningful partnerships between students and teachers as they make joint decisions about the contents of the portfolios, discuss student work in different categories, and project future goals and projects (see Burke, Fogarty, & Belgrad, 1994). You can design portfolios for a variety of purposes. For example, some focus on process, where you might have different drafts of a story that you and a child can review together. Others collect observations, student products, tests, and stories from different sources (teachers, the librarian, parents, and community people) that represent a reliable record of student growth in thinking, skill, and creativity. To be effective, student portfolios should have the following components (see Clark, 2002, p. 31):

- a clearly stated purpose so that students understand what is expected,

- evidence of links between course content and materials selected,

- a variety of products that demonstrate competency and growth in different areas,

- direct correspondence between concepts learned and classroom instruction,

- evidence of cognitive and creative growth in the learner through selected work (not just students' best work),

- students' selections based on their self-evaluation and understanding of themselves as learners with unique academic and emotional needs.

Perhaps the greatest value of portfolios is that they enable students to see their own progress and development over time. Children so often experience assessment as something other people do to them. When working with portfolios, it helps to sit down with your students individually and talk about their work. Simply reviewing products will not tell you enough. Ask children about their work. Don't assume that you know what a student is trying to do or whether or not it works. It may be that his idea is more interesting or sophisticated than his ability to express it. Uneven development is common in young children, and cultural differences may enhance this phenomenon.

Ask students specific questions about their thinking process, problem-solving strategies, and use of materials. Here is an example:

> I have a student named Saha whose greatest strength, I thought, was math. But when I reviewed her portfolio, I noticed that she'd added some interesting little sketches of an imaginary animal she called a "nayuni." I asked what a "nayuni" was and she said, "part lizard, part dog" and then added, "Do you want to see my nayuni stories? I have some at home." The next day, she brought in some stories that she dictated to her father, who entered them in the computer. Three things became clear: (1) she loved writing (something I never knew); (2) she had a wonderful sense of humor, which she hardly showed in class; (3) she wanted to do more creative work. I don't think I would spend much time on portfolios if I didn't go over them with the kids. I find out the most important stuff about a child's thinking process, strengths, and weaknesses; the way she views herself; and the learning styles she prefers.
>
> —*First-grade teacher*

Meeting with students about their portfolios helps them understand their own strengths and learning styles better. One of the sad realities of conventional testing and assessment is that students rarely gain any insight about themselves as learners. All they know is whether or not they mastered certain content and the grades they received. In many cases, students develop negative self-concepts as a result of assessments they neither understand nor interpret accurately. Children at every point on the ability spectrum need to develop a healthy approach to learning. Enabling students to understand themselves as learners—what their strengths and problem areas are, how they learn best, and what the evidence of their work means in terms of future goals and directions—is an extraordinary gift. It fosters a sense of self-acceptance and confidence that young children need to reach their real potential.

Here is an example of a form you can use (or adapt) to guide this process:

Name: _____

Date: _____

Project: _____

I: STARTING-OFF SCALE   (No/Sort of/Yes)

I liked the project I picked. _____
I got good materials to do it (books, art materials, science materials, prints, maps, etc.). _____

II. DOING THE PROJECT

I liked working on the project. _____
I found out things from different places (books, videos, Internet). The information gave me new ideas. _____
I worked on these ideas in ways that I liked (through notes, doing things, acting them out, etc.). _____

III. THE PRODUCT

I like my final product. _____
It came out as I imagined in my mind. _____
I have some ideas of how I would make it even better. _____

When children understand why they find certain tasks hard, how they learn best, and what steps they can take to build on their current level of achievement, learning loses its mystery, and they can avoid slipping into negative self-assessment.

Rubrics

Teachers often use a rubric or other planning device as a way of keeping track of learning goals and expectations and assessing students' progress at each phase of a unit. A rubric is a scoring guide. It helps you create a more accurate and precise way to assess projects and performances. You can design a rubric for a specific task or for an entire unit.

Children benefit because they understand what's important in the assignment and the criteria by which their projects will be assessed. Generally speaking, rubrics include the following:

- criteria,
- rating scale of points or stages for different degrees of mastery,
- descriptors that identify what each of these points or stages would look like in terms of the assignment.

You can design two kinds of rubrics—developmental and summative. A developmental rubric shows children the strengths and weaknesses of their work and helps guide the learning process. The aim is to provide immediate feedback that will stimulate growth and a higher quality product.

Here is an example:

SCIENCE UNIT: STUDY OF BIRD MIGRATION FOR ARCTIC TERNS

Criteria	Come for help.	You're on the right track.	Excellent work. Keep going!
Map of migratory route • **states labeled** • **arrows show route** • **breeding area and wintering areas labeled** • **legend designed**	Map doesn't show the route clearly. No states are labeled, and there's no legend.	Map shows the route clearly but is missing two of the other components.	Map has all four components and gives a clear picture of how the birds travel, where they winter and nest, and includes a legend.

Criteria	Come for help.	You're on the right track.	Excellent work: Keep going!
Two-paragraph essay on migration patterns for Arctic terns • **composition quality** • **cause of migration** • **description of route** • **times of year** • **distance**	Writing has many grammatical errors and is unclear. Doesn't explain why the terns migrate or describe one of their routes.	Writing is clear and grammatically correct but is still missing some information.	Well written and includes information on all points—causes of migration, route, times, distance.
Drawing of Arctic tern • **main parts labeled** • **markings**	Drawing is incomplete, has no labeled parts, and shows no markings.	Drawing has detailed parts but lacks either identification of these parts or the markings.	Drawing is carefully sketched with all elements complete.

A "summative rubric" assesses student performance at the end of a task. Most often, teachers create rubrics for tasks that are difficult to quantify, such as an independent project on reptiles or a map-making assignment. They include the following elements:

1. criteria,

2. a scale of different degrees or stages of mastery,

3. descriptors for assessing each aspect of the project or assignment and where it belongs on the scale.

Here is an example of a scoring rubric for a math assignment. Note that the rubrics you design depend entirely on the learning objective. In the one below, for example, the main goal is that children understand that addition always means an increase of some quantity (number, length, etc.), whereas subtracting is a decrease. The rubric targets this understanding in different ways.

Criteria	Beginner	Intermediate	Advanced
Dramatize adding and subtracting • **Use examples from stories provided** • **Identify process as addition or subtraction**	Can act out a scene read out loud by a partner but cannot always understand when the process is addition and when it's subtraction.	Can act out and identify which process is involved and explain it in math language ("Goldilocks subtracted one of the three bowls of porridge because she ate it.").	Can easily identify whether a process is adding or subtracting and can create new scenarios of their own and say what those are.
Use of manipulatives • **Perform addition and subtraction assignments through objects of choice** • **Explain to partner what is happening ("By putting this group with this group, I am adding," etc.)**	Using objects of her choice (e.g., marbles, pencils, rocks, etc.), the child can add one by one and subtract one by one when asked to do so.	Can put objects into groups and identify them as numbers while he's working (e.g., "here's five over here and four there, and now I'm adding them").	Can generate complex math situations beyond adding and subtracting simple numbers (e.g., subtracting a larger number from a smaller one).
Math symbols • **Translate different adding and subtracting actions into symbols** • **Create math situations from algorithms**	Can understand what actions he takes mean but needs practice writing it. Can sometimes translate written math into specific actions.	Can translate math stories into algorithms. Can turn most algorithms into real actions, and perform them.	Can take the process into more creative directions. Creates humorous scenarios and writes them out in algorithm form. Understands algorithms as stories and uses imagination freely.

The value in using rubrics is that you clearly establish in your own mind which criteria should drive your assessment, based on the learning objectives, the needs of the children, and the subject, and you avoid making judgments based on criteria that carry less weight than other objectives. A rubric also gives you evidence of where students are in a way that you can share with parents.

A differentiated classroom promises to reach many more students in our schools by responding to their unique learning styles, abilities, problems, and cultural and linguistic backgrounds. None of this will matter if assessment does not do the same. Students need to know that they are safe in the classroom, can take risks, and can expect clear guidance, support whenever needed, and a certain amount of individual attention. They need to become accustomed to assessments of their work that stimulate growth (rather than fear) and give them more freedom to participate in their own evaluation and future development as learners.

LOOKING AHEAD

The next chapter reviews the strategies of differentiating and the learning situations where they work well. Reviewing these strategies in one chapter will give you an overview of how they function in a primary classroom and help you decide what will best apply to your curriculum and students. The chapter explores strategies for adjusting the pace (for students who need to move ahead more slowly or more quickly), the level of difficulty, and the kind of activity (in response to learning style, interest, special strengths, or need).

Position statement from the National Association for the Education of Young Children (Bredekamp & Rosegrant, 1992, pp. 22–24):

1. Curriculum and assessment are integrated throughout the program; assessment is congruent with and relevant to the goals, objectives, and content of the program.

2. Assessment results in benefits to the child, such as needed adjustments in the curriculum or more individualized instruction and improvements in the program.

3. Children's development and learning in all domains—physical, social, emotional, and cognitive—

and their dispositions and feelings are informally and routinely assessed by teachers observing children's activities and interactions, listening to them as they talk, and using their constructive errors to understand their learning.

4. Assessment provides teachers with useful information to successfully fulfill their responsibilities to support children's learning and development, to plan for individuals and groups, and to communicate with parents.

5. Assessment involves regular and periodic observation of the child in a wide variety of circumstances that are representative of the child's behavior in the program over time.

6. Assessment relies primarily on procedures that reflect the ongoing life of the classroom and typical activities of the children. Assessment avoids approaches that place children in artificial situations, impede the usual learning and developmental experiences in the classroom, or divert children from their natural learning processes.

7. Assessment relies on demonstrated performance during real, not contrived, activities, for example, real reading and writing activities rather than only skills testing.

8. Assessment uses an array of tools and a variety of processes, including, but not limited to, collections of representative work by children (artwork, stories they write, tape recordings of their reading), records of systematic observations by teachers, records of conversations and interviews with children, and teachers' summaries of children's progress as individuals and as groups.

9. Assessment recognizes individual diversity of learning and allows for differences in styles and rates of learning. Assessment takes into consideration children's ability in English, their stage of language acquisition, and whether they have been given the time and opportunity to develop proficiency in their native language as well as English.

10. Assessment supports children's development and learning; it does *not* threaten children's psychological safety or feelings of self-esteem.

11. Assessment supports parents' relationships with their children and does not undermine parents' confidence in their children's or their own ability, nor does it devalue the language and culture of the family.

12. Assessment demonstrates children's overall strengths and progress, what children *can* do, not just their wrong answers and what they cannot do or do not know.

13. Assessment is an essential component of the teacher's role. Because teachers can make maximal use of assessment results, the teacher is the *primary* assessor.

14. Assessment is a collaborative process involving children and teachers, teachers and parents, and school and community. Information from parents about each child's experiences at home is used in planning instruction and evaluating children's learning. Information obtained from assessment is shared with parents in language they can understand.

15. Assessment encourages children to participate in self-evaluation.

16. Assessment addresses what children can do independently and what they can demonstrate with assistance because the latter shows the direction of their growth.

17. Information about each child's growth, development, and learning is systematically collected and recorded at regular intervals. Information, such as samples of children's work, descriptions of their performance, and anecdotal records, is used for planning instruction and communicating with parents.

18. A regular process exists for periodic information sharing between teachers and parents about children's growth and development and performance. The method of reporting to parents does not rely on letter or numerical grades but rather provides more meaningful, descriptive information in narrative form.

3 Strategies for Differentiating the Primary Curriculum

The Center for Gifted, National-Louis University, Evanston, Illinois

> *"Now, what I want is, Facts. Teach these boys and girls nothing but Facts. Facts alone are wanted in life. Plant nothing else, and root out everything else. . . . Stick to Facts, Sir!"*
> —*Thomas Gradgrind in Charles Dickens's* Hard Times

The tyrannical Thomas Gradgrind would be horrified by our attention to conceptual understanding and would most certainly respond to our attempts to differentiate with "Stick to the facts, Sir!" The old "stick to the facts" approach to teaching focused on memorization, and primary children sat in rows of small desks doing pen and paper work for long hours at a stretch. Today's primary classroom would be unrecognizable to Mr. Gradgrind, and he would probably regard differentiation as "soft."

Mr. Gradgrind aside, teachers do have concerns about differentiation. The first author has frequently heard comments like these:

> After spending all the time that differentiation demands, I wonder if this system will really give my students the skills and knowledge they need.
>
> —*First-grade teacher*

> My question is, If I have a kid who has trouble writing and I give him another way of expressing what he knows, how does this help his writing?
>
> —*Third-grade teacher*

> Differentiation is more work for the teacher, less work for the kids.
>
> —*Second-grade teacher*

> In my class, I have five limited English-proficient kids, three LD [learning disabled], and two gifted. I've tried to differentiate, but I can't cope with the chaos it creates in my classroom.
>
> —*First-grade teacher*

In different ways, all these comments express similar concerns: (a) the workload of the teacher and (b) the need to know that all students—regardless of their needs—will meet fundamental learning goals. Some teachers abandon differentiation because of the increase in potentially unmanageable activity. As the year goes on, they decide that the challenges of having groups of young children who are all doing different activities, engaging in animated (and increasingly loud) discussions, and creating piles of mess everywhere exceed the benefits. As one teacher put it at a workshop, "Differentiating demands a certain amount of self-control and cooperation that little kids are just beginning to learn. Thus, the teacher carries the burden alone."

The more you differentiate, the more independent your students need to become. This doesn't mean that younger children cannot function as well in a differentiated situation as older ones. In some ways, it may be easier because your students haven't been in school long enough to be used to a more teacher-centered system. But it goes without question that they will need experiences where they can practice following certain classroom routines, being respectful of other children, sharing materials, and putting away supplies. Because these are some of the skills most primary teachers work on anyway, they can use differentiating as an avenue for putting these skills to use.

The biggest problem I had when I differentiated a math activity focused on money (learning the value of different coins, how to make change, etc.) was dealing with the endless bombardment of kids' questions. I would be working with one group, and I'd have three of four other kids from other groups asking questions or complaining about a kid who wasn't sharing or whatever. I almost gave up; it just wasn't worth it. But the kids LOVED it. So, I developed a system. First, I gave each group a pile of colored Post-its (different color for each group). If there was a question or problem, they stuck the Post-it on the board, and if another group came along, they would put their Post-it underneath the one ahead of them. This meant that I would go to each group in order, and NO ONE would bug me while I was in the middle of instructing another group. That took care of that problem, and the kids like it because it's fair. Then there were other problems with the groups themselves. I had to make some adjustments. Some kids can work together in an activity (for example, we had a group where kids were practicing "buying" things from each other and giving change), and others may be better off sharing supplies but not interacting as much. I'm always trying to gauge what kind of group process individual kids are really ready for.

—Second-grade teacher

Once you know what you want all your students to learn in a unit and what unique strengths, experiences, interests, and needs they bring to the subject at hand, you can create some alternatives. Now, a host of practical concerns arise:

- How will students move around the room?
- What level of noise is acceptable?
- What is the best way to give directions when there are several or more groups doing different tasks?
- How should you arrange seating?
- What should your role be when students are working in different groups (or independently) on projects?
- When should you work with the different groups, and what should you do when students finish their projects early?

Thinking about these questions ahead of time will help you create ways to preserve the spontaneity and joy of learning without sacrificing all semblance of order.

Prepare the students. The more students understand how you plan to work with them in the classroom, the more they can contribute to the process. Right at the beginning, talk to them about different learning styles and the fact that we all have things we can do very well and other things that we find difficult. Introduce them to the idea that everyone learns differently and has their own special strengths, and give them time in class to explore theirs. If you or your students are used to a more traditional, teacher-directed learning environment, begin changes gradually and give them time to assume the responsibilities and experience the freedoms of a more child-centered classroom.

The receptivity of your students should determine the kind of alternatives you create. Some children come to school with experience that gives them an advantage in certain areas. For example:

> James comes from a family of 10. His whole life is about sharing with others and negotiating disagreements.

> Rebecca grew up in a small East African town where all the kids played in the neighborhood. Every day of her earliest years of life was spent playing games, acting out imaginary dramas, and helping her family cook, clean, and bargain at the market.

> Simone has only one sibling, 10 years her senior. She lives in a high-rise condo and spends a lot of time alone. She learned early how to amuse herself with art projects, reading, and science experiments.

When you assess students at the beginning of the year (see Chapter 2), you will discover which ones have had practice working with other kids, who's used to getting his way, who is self-directed and able to work independently, and who needs more support. The culture of a child's family also affects how well he acclimates to a differentiated classroom. Children who come from authoritarian homes may feel lost in an environment where they have choices. Others who have permissive parents may expect the world to accommodate to their whims. After the first few months of the year, primary teachers usually know how many choices their students can handle, when they will need specific direction, and when they can work alone.

Create kid-friendly routines. Differentiated instruction asks students to become more involved in their own learning than if they were in Mr. Gradgrind's "stick to the facts" classroom. The process requires rules that govern

- behavior in small groups and while moving about the room,
- noise level in the room,
- routines for arranging seats,
- routines for distributing and collecting materials,
- rules for asking the teacher or other students for help.

Obviously, each one of these is a large project in and of itself! But many young children can assume more responsibility than they currently do if the routines you create take into account the needs of the students in your class.

> The day before I was going to do a group activity, I worked out which chairs had to be moved and where the work areas would be. I had it all set up the first time the kids worked like this. Then I explained that when we work in groups, I would move the tables and they would put six chairs around the tables in these areas. I developed a routine where I would say, "What comes first?" Someone would say, "The tables!" I'd move the tables, and then they would move the chairs. Each child would move a chair the same place each time (regardless of which area he or she worked), and this prevented kids bumping into each other.
>
> *—First-grade teacher*

> Noise level is a constant challenge. What do you do if you have a group of kids preparing a dramatic interpretation of a story and other kids who are writing or doing a visual art piece? The only way I've been able to keep the volume down for students doing anything theatrical is to tell them that they have to keep their idea secret (a surprise for the rest of the class!). I also purchased a screen so that I could create a temporary divider on the far side of the room, and in this way it doesn't dominate the whole space.
>
> *—Third-grade teacher*

Share some responsibilities. If you're accustomed to the traditional teacher role, you may find differentiation overwhelming because you think you have to do more of the work than you actually need to. Ask yourself, "Are there any tasks or jobs I could give my students?" For example, you could assign a couple of children per week to distribute and collect all materials. As the first-grade teacher just quoted, you could have the children practice moving their chairs around in different formations so that they become accustomed to the process. You could have students with special abilities take charge of certain things (e.g., a child with technical skill could operate the video equipment when you use it or help with computer problems). When appropriate, you might also let a child with low self-esteem or a shy student be the person other kids go to if they need supplies.

Set up as much as you can ahead of time. The more you arrange ahead of time, the less you will have to think about when you're immersed in an activity that demands your whole attention. Think about seating arrangements and the supplies you'll need. Consider the practical needs your students will face completing assigned work. Here are some ways teachers have solved some of the logistical challenges:

> I post the kids' names for different groups (so they can find their own seats!).
>
> *—First-grade teacher*

> I put the instructions for assignments on large index cards numbered 1, 2, and 3 at the tables where the groups are to work.
>
> *—Third-grade teacher*

> I have stacked drawers with the students' names on where they can store unfinished work that they need to go back to at another time.
>
> *—Kindergarten teacher*

> My supplies are at kid level, labeled, and easy to put away; special supplies (e.g., compass, magnifying glass) they have

to sign a sheet so that the next child who needs it can find the one who has it.

—Second-grade teacher

I have a file cabinet of creative and interesting extension activities divided into subject categories. Any student who finishes early can go in there, select an activity, confer with me, and do it. One of my students goes in there at least once a week to get "story starter" ideas.

—Third-grade teacher

Provide clear directions. Many teachers find "work cards" (Heacox, 2002, pp. 96–97) a helpful tool. They can be the size of an index card or larger, and some teachers color code and laminate them for future use. These cards provide clear directions on assigned work for a group, pair, or individual and may also have criteria for quality performance and sometimes a checklist of all the steps students need to take. Work cards significantly increase students' autonomy and reduce the number of times they have to run to the teacher for guidance.

If you're teaching kindergarten, there are other ways to make sure your students understand what they're supposed to do. Have them repeat back to you what you said. Have them show you what the directions mean by demonstrating it (e.g., "You want us to use these cardboard shapes here to see if we can make a square and a rectangle"). You could also assign a student the job of explaining the process to other students; then, if they still don't understand, they can come to you.

Recording student progress and need. Plan ahead for all the different ways you will monitor student progress and need (see Chapter 2). Consider the use of observations, informal talks with the students, checklists, student portfolios, their own self-evaluations, and consultations with parents. With the suggested rubrics and observations described in Chapter 2, you can design a simple method of keeping track of student progress that best suits your teaching schedule and style. Some teachers have students fill out logs where they enter what they did each day and a couple of lines about what they enjoyed, what they feel they learned, and what they still need help on. They compare these with their own observations and with student work samples. In situations where time allows only minimal assessment, teachers could supply each area with a clipboard and chart to fill out quickly as they observe students' progress and work. These are easily collected on a daily or weekly basis. Regular, systematic assessment is the only way you can know when students need new adjustments.

STRATEGIES FOR DIFFERENTIATING YOUR CURRICULUM

Although some strategies (such as compacting, for instance) apply more specifically to some student needs than others, most of the strategies described in the remainder of this chapter can work in a wide range of teaching situations. The categories—"Pace and Level" and "Depth and Breadth"—demarcate two broad areas where you will make specific kinds of changes. They are not meant in a prescriptive sense (i.e., "If this child is gifted in this subject, then she needs compacting" or "If this child is a kinetic learner, he needs an independent study"). They provide a useful conceptual framework for discussing the different strategies teachers can use and their applications.

Strategies for differentiating any curriculum focus on three areas: content, process, and products.

DIFFERENTIATING CONTENT, PROCESS, AND PRODUCTS

Pace/Level	Depth/Breadth	Grouping
Compacting Learning stations Tiered activities	Integrated curriculum Response to learning styles Creative processes	Cluster groups Interest groups Tiered groups Independent study

Focusing on these three areas, you might ask yourself the following:

Content: What changes should I make to this assignment so that my struggling math students can work on the same concepts as the other children but in a more accessible form?

Process: What activities could my kinetic learners do that would reinforce the new science concepts we learned yesterday and prepare them for other applications?

Products: What alternative student products will prove that they have mastered the material I taught (poems, dramatizations, drawings, diagrams, models, experiments)?

Differentiate for Pace and Level

This section begins with the pace and level of student learning. During an activity where most students are working on the same content in a more or less similar way, it's easy to notice the child who completes assignments quickly or the one who dawdles behind, the one who has grasped a more advanced level of mathematics or the one who cannot apply the last concept mastered by the other students. Here are some examples:

When Sheena added up the numbers, she clearly didn't understand the process. If she had estimated the answer, she would have instantly seen that her answer couldn't possibly be right.

Mario whipped through the story so quickly, I knew he couldn't have really understood it. But he retold it all to me—in great detail!

James never finishes anything he starts.

Kim asks questions way beyond her years, like this: "How do you really know the history books are telling the truth?"

Pace and level apply particularly well to sequential areas of study, such as mathematics and science, but can also include areas of language arts and social studies that focus on skill development (grammar, vocabulary, research skills) or that demand analytical thinking. Bear in mind that the strategies listed below do not apply exclusively to those who need to learn at a faster or slower pace or at a higher or lower level of complexity.

Compacting

> Josh came to our school already knowing how to multiply. I felt that he would eventually need to go to another grade for math instruction, but until his parents, the gifted coordinator, and I could meet and work this out, I decided to compact the math curriculum. Before every unit, I would give him a range of problems to do from the new material. Based on his performance and my conversation with him, he would (a) work on whatever area of the new content he had not mastered, (b) move on to more advanced math assignments based on my network with the third-grade teacher, or (c) use the time to work on an independent project related to math.
>
> *—First-grade teacher*

Compacting involves identifying content and skills that you can accelerate or eliminate for advanced learners. The strategy evolved in response to the concern that gifted children were repeating content they had already mastered. If you have students who consistently finish their assignments early and look bored even when you're presenting something new, compacting might be the best option. You can give these children a pretest or some activity that will show you what they already know about the unit you are about to teach. Examples:

- They could tackle problems that require knowledge of fractions.
- They could write a paragraph using and identifying particular parts of speech.
- They could show how photosynthesis works by creating a diagram of the process.

To compact the curriculum for a child, you need to do the following:

1. establish what concepts, knowledge, and skills you want all students to master;

2. determine, on the basis of the child's preassessment, what you can delete and what you should adjust for his or her ability and understanding;

3. explore (with the child) what alternative project the student can do:

   - a more accelerated and more challenging version of the assignment,

   - another assignment in the same subject area but in the area of the child's interest,

   - an independent project in any subject in which the child has a special talent or passion.

After assessment, you can identify the areas where students need more challenge and where they may require more instruction or practice. One of the advantages of compacting is that it enables students to get the support they need where they need it, without hindering their abilities in other areas. This especially aids poor and minority gifted children, for example, who may be deficient in skills and knowledge but who desperately need opportunities to use their abilities. You could have a student participate in class when you're planning to review certain skills and then move on to more challenging work in areas where she excels.

Compacting applies to a range of students, not just advanced learners. You might have a student from another country, for example, who already knows most of the math planned for the first half of your school year. You might have a child who loves languages and wants to move ahead at a faster pace because he enjoys studying languages in his spare time, or you could have a child of an architect who's learned some drafting from her mother and whose visual thinking skills when it comes to lines, angles, and shapes outstrip her peers by leagues. Or you could have a child who comes from a culture of proverbs, witticisms, and trickster tales that have made him a quick and agile thinker in discussions about stories read in class.

Most teachers create a contract that specifies the project or task a child will do and the materials involved. You can include criteria, learning goals, and a timeline for completing assignments.

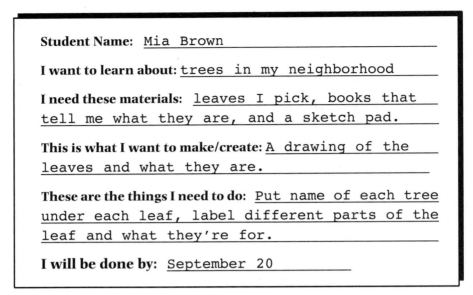

Student Name: Mia Brown

I want to learn about: trees in my neighborhood

I need these materials: leaves I pick, books that tell me what they are, and a sketch pad.

This is what I want to make/create: A drawing of the leaves and what they are.

These are the things I need to do: Put name of each tree under each leaf, label different parts of the leaf and what they're for.

I will be done by: September 20

Learning Stations

> Learning stations made sense to me. Because I teach kindergarten, I'm used to having students who span 3 years in terms of ability, experience, and knowledge. With learning stations in a language arts session, I once created three areas that focused on different clusters of words (depending on what they already knew). The first area was where kids could listen to a story told slowly, recognize words, and copy them down on paper—a listen-say-look-write process. The second area had piles of words typed on cards (one for each child), and they made short sentences, which they read to each other (e.g., "Bob has a mop and goes up to the top of his shop and says stop!")—a look-arrange-write process. The third area was for advanced readers. Students read a book of choice, chose words from the story to make their own sentences—a read-select-write process. In kindergarten, learning stations can help address very specific areas where children need practice and growth.
>
> —*Kindergarten teacher*

Stations are designated areas of the classroom where students can work on different tasks within a unit. These areas are often sequential, with each one representing a higher level of complexity than the one before it. Students can move freely from one task to the next as they master the material (they are not identified and locked into any particular "level"). You can create as many stations as are necessary for the different ability and achievement levels of your students.

In a math class, the stations might include the following (Tomlinson, 1999, pp. 62–64): a teaching station where students receive direct instruction from you at the blackboard or in a small group at the back of the room; a proving area where children explore the "why" behind their computations, using manipulatives and other resources for this purpose; a practice station for students who need more opportunities to go over the principles they've learned and how they work in different contexts; an applications station where children can test their understanding of real-world problems requiring mathematical reasoning and computation; and a project station that allows students to develop (with your help) independent math-related projects that draw on individual interests. Stations create a flexibility in the curriculum that gives your students the freedom to choose the level of challenge they feel ready for and a range of materials they can use to process and understand new concepts.

Tiered Activities

Like learning stations, tiered activities also ensure that all students work at a level appropriate for them. The idea behind tiered activities is that all of your students—regardless of the differences in experience, culture, skill, and ability—can focus on the same learning goal if this goal is broad enough (i.e., an essential concept or skill that all students need to learn). This means that if your broader goal is that students understand what American cities do to local environments and wildlife, and you are using bird migration in Chicago as an example, you can easily accommodate differences in skill, knowledge, and ability. You can keep this process simple by not creating more tiered groups than you really need. Here's an example:

Third-Grade Unit on Bird Migration

- Group 1 creates a map of the fall migration of a particular species along the Great Lakes and lists the dangers they face on the way.

- Group 2 selects one of these problems—the skyscrapers and towers that confuse nighttime migrating birds—and writes reports on the number of birds killed by skyscrapers and what can be done about it.

When you use tiered assignments, try to make the different activities equally interesting. Students will quickly see which group is more or less "advanced" unless you offer assignments different enough from each other to make the levels of complexity less obvious. For example, giving the same assignment for two groups but having one read a more difficult book than another will be transparent to most children. But if you're having the students explore point of view in a language arts class, you might divide the groups like this:

- Group 1 compares the point of view of two characters in a story, imagines being each character, and tells/writes and draws what they think about their situation.

- Group 2 chooses one character from two separate stories and analyzes how the two characters would respond if they switched stories.

Differentiate for Depth and Breadth

Although some strategies help students who need adjustments in pace and difficulty, others aid those who love exploring an interest in depth, who thrive in more interdisciplinary work, or who have nontraditional learning styles.

> Gaurav is my artist. He has a private set of colored pencils, which he keeps with him at all times. He doodles through math class, which can sometimes be irritating. He sketches me, the students, even the pigeons on the windowsill. Every spare moment he gets, he scurries over to the art supplies and draws.
>
> —*Third-grade teacher*

> Amy got her love of science fiction watching a horror flick with her older brother and realizing that the "monster" was like a praying mantis. I never saw her more animated than when I told her she could create her own creature based on what she recently learned about different animal species. She immediately began sketching and asked me if she could write a story about her "species."
>
> —*Second-grade teacher*

> Kendra's family was passing through difficult times, and Kendra sometimes came to school really tense. She loved the nature books in the classroom and found great peace thumb-

ing through the pictures. Elephants became her favorite animal, and I often have her bring elephants into whatever we're working on—whether it's math, science, geography, or whatever. Babar transfixed her.

—*Kindergarten teacher*

To achieve depth and breadth in the curriculum, teachers need to provide alternative ways for students to process new concepts and information. This often means integrating subject areas, using a range of materials (artistic, written, technology, science sources, graphs, maps, etc.), and giving students choices in how they demonstrate mastery— essays, charts, demonstrations, performances, and so forth. It also includes an emphasis on the creative process as a vehicle for children to discover the world around them through interpretation, imagination, and invention.

Integrating the Curriculum

Differentiated classrooms often integrate the curriculum, and if you're a primary teacher, you are probably doing this already. Few primary classrooms separate subjects in the way the older grades do, except to teach and reinforce specific skills and content. As you have no doubt seen in your own classroom, integrating subjects can create significant cognitive, artistic, and conceptual growth. Exploring the connections between science and art, for example, a kindergarten child can study the changes of the seasons represented in paintings. Or, a first-grade student can listen to stories about a great explorer as a way of learning about history. Here is an example from a classroom:

> In history class, a third-grade student became fascinated by the discovery of longitude. Her teacher structured an independent study project that enabled her to focus on the science of John Harrison's discovery.

Integrating the curriculum enables primary students to draw on the skills, ideas, and materials of more than one discipline. This process has the potential to create completely new insights and understandings than would happen if they limited themselves to one subject area. Here is an example:

> Second-grade Anil knew a lot about how buildings were constructed from his uncle, who had a construction com-

pany. He could tell the class about how the Back Bay area of Boston was once a swamp and how they had to drain it to build on it. When the class was studying about early settlers in Boston, his teacher had him look at pictures and text on the early villages of that time. He used his knowledge of construction to calculate how the Pilgrims made their buildings and then read about it. He made sketches and wrote a short report.

Responding to Learning Styles

Knowing the learning styles of your students is an essential part of differentiated instruction. Howard Gardner's (1993) work on "multiple intelligences" has inspired more teachers to consider a child's learning preferences while they plan curriculum. Rather than focus on a child's "deficiencies" because he has a hard time learning in a particular format (e.g., visual displays or verbal explanations), teachers today are more likely to find out how a student learns best and capitalize on that. Here are several examples:

- In preparation for an essay on a short story, Moira makes sketches of scenes she feels are important and uses them to expound on her ideas. (visual/spatial)

- A group of students demonstrate their knowledge of the solar system by staging the movements of four planets over the course of a year. (bodily/kinesthetic)

- Students compare two maps of the world (e.g., an old historical one and the Arno Peters map) and judge the accuracy in terms of relative proportions, sizes, and so on. (logical/mathematical)

- Pia needs to know the reason for learning things and the bigger picture of whatever facts her teacher presents. Her teacher once showed her how knowing the shapes and measurements of things (math) will help her identify trees, plants, and birds—an interest of Pia's. Pia has an easier time doing math when she can see math in the world.

- Josh retreats in group work. A quiet, thoughtful child, he's not inclined to interrupt other kids or argue for his own ideas. He thrives in independent projects where he can develop his own ideas and explore resources without having to talk to other people about it.

As you can see, how students learn does not relate solely to multiple intelligences but to other factors, such as group orientation and cognitive style. Examples of cognitive styles include the following:

Creative / conforming

1. Ali often hears a version of what the teacher asks, but this rarely bothers him. He generates a lot of ideas and delights in finding new and unusual ways of doing things.

2. Nika asks a lot of questions to make sure she understands what the teacher wants, and she tries her best to follow directions.

Whole to part / part to whole

1. Ben has to know the forest before he learns about the trees. In a class introducing geometry, Ben needs to experience the world of shapes—what they are and how they occur in the world—before he can explore details.

2. Tanya doesn't like preliminaries or introductions. She prefers to jump into an activity and gradually arrive at the big picture by exploring the specifics.

Nonlinear / linear

1. Jessica thinks like an impressionist painting. The dots do have an order of their own, and if you step back you can see the image. But for anyone working with her, Jessica seems to be leaping from point to point. She cannot follow one line of thinking exclusively.

2. Harry loves to follow clean, precise sequences. None of this leaping about jazz! He dislikes being interrupted and wants to follow one line of thinking to the end before abandoning it for another.

Inductive / deductive

1. Jerry loves the mystery of figuring something out by looking at many different pieces. For example, he'd rather figure out what makes a triangle different from a rectangle by looking at many examples than be told that triangles have three sides. If he knows the premise, the mystery is gone. He feels like a detective.

2. Amanda would rather know the premise of a thing first. She'd rather know that all triangles are three-sided and then figure out which shapes are and are not triangles from that premise. She feels comfortable using logical reasoning.

Easily distracted / long attention span

1. Neil is a child who will walk into a room with the intention of doing one thing and then quickly find himself immersed in something else. "If Neil didn't have a sense of direction, he would quickly lose himself," his mother says.

2. Wild horses could not pry Anna from her work. She loves school and learning new things. When she's working on a project that interests her, she can stay focused on it long after other students are begging the teacher to move on to something else.

As you know from your own experience, young children are often more sensitive to environmental situations than older ones. You will notice that some students need quiet; others, like Anna, function well in a bustling atmosphere (children who live in noisy homes may even need it!). Some are affected by temperature, but others seem oblivious. Some children are more flexible about routines, whereas others feel safer in classrooms that follow a regular routine.

Using Creative Processes

Creativity plays a crucial role in educating primary students. Few differentiated classrooms could meet their unique needs without it. Creative strategies apply to all subjects, whether it be calculating the perimeter of a rectangle, choreographing the formation of the clouds, interpreting a story, or exploring the landscape of the past. When applied appropriately at specific moments in a unit, creativity can stimulate cognitive growth in significant ways.

> Our children must have creative experiences in school, not to make artists out of them (although some of them may become artists), but to give them an inner resource that can survive any assault that comes along. I teach in the city, and if I do nothing else for my kids, I give them opportunities to imagine and create, create, create! Children—especially those from poor homes, unhappy families, or those who have come to our shores from war-ravaged countries—cannot create a life for themselves unless they can imagine it. I've seen lives change from creativity. I have four parent volunteers who said they wanted to be part of the projects we're doing in class. My kids learn all the things students are supposed to, but they learn it by creating it for themselves.
>
> —*Third-grade teacher*

Creative strategies take different forms depending on student needs and curriculum goals. A wide range of processes have been explored under the creativity category, though the four most widely known (Guilford, 1967; Torrance, 1969) are as follows:

- **fluency** (generating many ideas),
- **flexibility** (creating divergent and alternative ideas),
- **originality** (producing unique, innovative ideas),
- **elaboration** (extending, embellishing, and implementing ideas).

Creativity opens the door to discovery. It prompts children to look for ideas where they've never looked before, to find similarities between dissimilar things and differences between similar things, to explore new ways to make something or find new uses for a commonplace object, and to diverge from one kind of thing to make quite a different thing (i.e., creating a new object out of an old one—writing a fractured fairy tale).

> Valerie lived near a junkyard. Everyone in the neighborhood complained about the yard, but she loved picking around in the piles for treasures. Mostly, she collected colored wire and bits of tin. She began making small doll figures out of twisted wire and bottle caps, and after a while, she collected other tin sheets, plywood, small auto parts, and other objects for a miniature house and swing set that she wanted to make in her bedroom.
>
> *—Volunteer at the community center*

Valerie expresses the creative ability that E. Paul Torrance (1977) consistently found among culturally different and poor children. According to Torrance, the ability to improvise with commonplace materials is one of the distinguishing characteristics. You can draw on and nurture these strengths in your students by designing creative processes as an introduction to a new lesson, as a structure for problem solving, or as a way to approach a writing assignment. Related to the creative processes described by Torrance, the following strategies engage children in applications to specific problems:

- **brainstorming** (producing as many ideas as possible, using techniques such as the Scamper method [Eberle, 1996]);
- **metaphorical or analogical thinking**—exploring how two objects, ideas, or entities are alike with the objective of generating a new perspective, solution, and so on;

- **synectics**—applying analogies and opposites to the process of solving problems (Gordon, 1961);

- **visualization**—using guided imagery and other techniques to stimulate students' imagination and insight;

- **attribute listing**—changing an attribute or applying it to another thing or situation to generate creative ideas;

- **creative problem solving**—solving problems through fact finding, problem finding, idea finding, solution finding, and acceptance finding (Parnes, 1981);

- **role-playing**—using the techniques of creative dramatics to assume specific roles with the idea of solving a problem or gaining deeper insight.

Future chapters will demonstrate how you can implement creative strategies in a manageable way to achieve specific learning goals for gifted students.

Group Students in Different Ways

Differentiating instruction often involves either group work or some form of independent study. Curriculum goals and student learning styles often dictate whether you arrange your students in groups or create an independent study.

GROUPING			
Cluster	**Interest**	**Tiered**	**Independent Study**
Advanced learners work together on alternative assignments whenever their needs call for more challenging content. Clusters often stay together for the school year.	Students with a common interest work together for the duration of specific projects or assignments.	Students at a similar level of mastery work on assignments designed for this level. Students advance to more difficult assignments as they gain mastery.	Students work alone on a project using a learning contract. They may do paired work occasionally.

Grouping

This strategy enables you to put students together who have similar learning styles, abilities, and/or interests in order to tackle specific tasks. You can maintain these groups for a day or longer and then change the composition of groups as the needs change or as the learning situation alters. It's important to keep groups flexible so that they serve the changing needs of students.

Cluster groups. Generally speaking, you should cluster students who have mastered concepts and skills quickly. Gifted students don't get enough time to work with other gifted students, and, as services for advanced children rarely start until third or fourth grade, cluster groups may be their only opportunity to do this. Clustering not only puts advanced learners in a situation where they can greatly increase each other's learning, but it makes them less inclined to hide their abilities to get along socially. As you become acquainted with your students, you'll discover the ones who may need this arrangement and the areas in the curriculum where they most need it.

Interest groups. In the course of a project or assignment, you may discover that a number of students have a strong interest in some aspect of the subject you're teaching. In this case, even if you have a mixed-ability group, the high motivation and interest will carry them along and provide activities and resources that benefit everyone. For example, if you have three or four students who love nothing more than pouring over maps and measuring distances, you could incorporate a map-making and map-reading project that would accommodate the different ability levels in the group.

Tiered groups. As already explained, tiered instruction designs several activities where groups of students work on the same topic, skill, or concept but at varying levels of difficulty. You can devise as many groups as you like as long as you know how they will help achieve specific learning objectives. To avoid a situation where you have to monitor the groups, you might consider the following guidelines.

GROUP GUIDELINES

- Design assignments that the groups will be able to tackle with minimum input from you. They should provide enough challenge to stimulate and stretch the students but not so much challenge that they feel overwhelmed and need you constantly.

- Give each group step-by-step instructions and examples to guide the process.

- Create a clear set of rules to ensure fairness and a measure of order in the classroom. These rules should spell out how much noise is permissible and how students should treat each other (e.g., sharing air time, respecting each other's suggestions, not interrupting, not ganging up on a student, etc.). Establishing clear guidelines in this area will encourage children to participate.

- Be clear about what each individual student is responsible for—what he or she must do and produce by the end of the process.

If you are more accustomed to whole-class instruction than small-group instruction, then start out by grouping your students in a skill area and keep it short for the first few tries. Once you become more comfortable, try a longer process involving different resources. Some teachers in the same grade have also organized flexible grouping with each other. For example, two teachers could plan to group on the same day, with one teacher providing special instruction for those who need more practice or who are struggling with a particular concept, while the other teacher designs a task for those who are eager to move on.

As already mentioned, these techniques apply to a variety of learning situations—not just those where you want to create adjustments in the pace and level of challenge. The key to these techniques is the flexibility that enables you to adjust instruction and group composition as you assess the growth and needs of individual students. The value of designing activities that accommodate students in this way, of course, is that you can create a classroom where no child is kept back, where students with different learning styles can learn in groups that most benefit them.

Independent Study

Some students prefer to work alone. You can differentiate for a child who wants to do an independent study by creating a structure for the project to be undertaken, including the responsibilities and accountabilities of the student. Most teachers accomplish this through contracts and agreements that enable them to manage the process of preassessment, compacting, designing alternative work, and monitoring student progress. More information on this will come in future chapters. Contracts for independent study may aid in a variety of strategies such as compacting, tiered instruction, research projects, and creative work. Your main objective is to establish clear goals and directions and structure the project so that the student knows exactly what is expected of him and has a timeline for submitting work. The following guidelines may help students get the most out of an independent project.

INDEPENDENT STUDY GUIDELINES

- identify what students should know (facts), understand (concepts), and be able to do (skills) by the end of the project;

- identify a result in the form of a product (e.g., a poem, an experiment, a report, a map, or a combination of products);

- list expectations for content (what is to be learned), process (how it's done), and product (result that demonstrates learning);

- determine support you may need to give the student (goal setting, brainstorming, timelines, etc.);

- differentiate assignments based on student ability, mastery of subject, interest, and learning style;

- mentor the student when needed.

This process can be as in-depth and long term as is appropriate for your student and the project at hand. Although the students will need specific goals and directions, you do not have to structure every phase of it, especially if you're working with younger children. Here is an example of a more involved and structured contract for a project versus a less involved one. The children should fill these out with the teacher's support and feedback.

Sample Contract (Older Primary Child)

Name: _Brandon Kiefer_

This is what I want to learn (FACTS AND CONCEPTS):
1. *How to make a good plot for a story*
2. *The elements of plot: (a) good hook in the beginning, (b) suspense in the middle, (c) a climax, and (d) a strong ending.*

This is what I will need to do (SKILLS):
1. *Read two stories with good plots I like*
2. *Brainstorm some plot ideas of my own*
3. *Put my idea into each section of the plot to see how it works*

This is what I will create (PRODUCT):
A mystery story of my own with sketches

These are the things I have to do before I'm finished:
- use at least _2_ books and 1 other source to get information I need
- record the important things I learned by writing them down and one other way (diagrams, sketches, maps, etc.) _Drawings_
- brainstorm at least _3_ ways to do my project
- choose one way and do the project
- ask the teacher for help if I get stuck

I will complete my project by: _Friday_

Student's Signature: _Brandon Kiefer_

Teacher's Signature: _Mr. Garrison_

Sample Contract (Younger Child)

Name: ___Marisol Gutierrez___

I want to learn about: _the parts of a tree_

I will do this: _I will draw the different parts of a tree underground and above the ground and label them. I will explain what makes the trees grow._

I will finish it by: _Tuesday_

Student's Signature: _Marisol Gutierrez_

Teacher's Signature: _Mrs. Benson_

LOOKING AHEAD

In the chapters that follow, you will see different ways that you can apply the strategies just described to specific subjects and themes. There is no single way to differentiate in any given situation. At each point, you need to look at (a) the **child**—what he or she brings to the learning table in terms of special strengths, interests, and challenges; (b) the **content**—to determine its appropriateness for particular students; (c) the **process**—to decide what the children should do; and (d) the **product**—to identify the appropriate creation (composition, map, diagram, calculation, etc.) that will show what the children have learned. In making these decisions, you focus on the children's

- group orientation,
- cognitive style,
- learning style,
- preferred learning environment,
- interests.

Differentiated instruction is not an inflexible set of rules or methods. How you differentiate depends a great deal on your own teaching style and what you find most beneficial as you observe the class and the ongoing needs of your students. Chapters 5 through 8 include a number of examples from primary teachers that illustrate the variety in differentiated classrooms.

4

Using the Visual and Performing Arts to Differentiate the Primary Curriculum

Barbereaux School, Evanston, Illinois

The song of the brush.
                    —Chinese saying

Anyone who watches young children painting, drawing, imagining, dancing, miming, and singing understands the value of the arts to the growth of primary grade students. The arts become a fundamental means for constructing knowledge and exploring the world. Children from the preprimary level to the third grade need learning experiences where they can act on their environment by seeing, hearing, feeling, moving, touching, and sensing the materials around them. It is not an overstatement to say that creativity and the arts are essential to cognitive growth in young children.

Goertz (2003) envisions art instruction as the "fourth R" in education and argues that it increases the skills of observation, abstract thinking, and problem analysis:

> The artist visualizes and sets goals to find and define the problem, chooses techniques to collect data, and then evaluates and revises the problem solution with imagination in order to create. . . . The artist, in his or her creative process, requires a high-order thought process. (p. 460)

Experience supports Goertz' theory. Creativity and the arts enable children with different learning styles to apply their reasoning and problem-solving abilities in the curriculum (see Smutny et al., 1997). An example of this follows:

> I read a fractured fairy tale to my students called *Pondlarker,* a whimsical retelling of the frog and prince story. We talked about the frog's choice to remain a frog and the things about being a frog that led him to make this choice. Then, I gave them four choices for fairy tales (I had multiple copies in the room). They were to choose a character, imagine being that character, and tell the story from this point of view. (For example, tell *Little Red Riding Hood* from the point of view of the wolf or the grandmother. Tell *Cinderella* from the stepmother's point of view.) They could choose the main character if they wanted to and create an alternative perspective than the one we assume in the original story. They were allowed to embellish or invent in any way they wanted. We did one story together and brainstormed different possibilities so that the kids could get a feel for the process. This worked incredibly well. The children *loved* the idea of creating another version of a story. Many of them came up with really humorous retellings, and everyone in the class, I think, learned something about point of view. It's something they bring up on their own in other class sessions.
>
> —*Third-grade teacher*

The visual and performing arts can help you meet primary students where they are. From toddlerhood, they have been imagining adventures, imagining themselves as other creatures, inventing machines from materials they find around the house, dressing up in costumes, imitating the movements of animals, singing and humming to themselves, and drawing characters from stories they have heard. Entering school should not signify the end of such rich imaginative and cognitive activity but be a continuation and expansion of it.

Creating and improvising also have special significance among other cultural groups, and in places of poverty, young children's inner creative resources provide an endless source of interest and learning (Torrance, 1977). Here are two examples from other countries:

> A journalist in Kenya (wa Gacheru, 1985) described how young children in Mathare Valley fashioned cars—in artful detail—out of the tin and scraps they found in the neighborhood. Called "child engineers," most had never sat in a car or truck or even stood close enough to examine how they work. Yet they made autos with moveable wheels, steering wheels that maneuvered the front wheels, brakes, and other attachments. The local schoolmaster said that these "child engineers" surpassed their classmates because of their advanced creative thinking.

> In Uganda, a place besieged by civil war for two decades until the late 1980s, young children take part in the frequent dance and drama competitions organized throughout the country. The second author witnessed a moving dance history, choreographed by young children, about Uganda's emergence from bloodshed and ethnic conflict to an era of peace. At a young age, many children know two or three languages and a wide range of songs, proverbs, stories, and cultural dances.

These examples apply to many schools across America, where children from other cultures bring their own inner creative resources to the learning table. Using the arts to engage such students provides them with a way to experience their strengths and creates a bridge to the curriculum. Learning activities that integrate creativity and the arts lead naturally to complex, higher level thinking and enable children of all backgrounds to make significant and lasting discoveries (Smutny et al., 1997). They can also stimulate fruitful collaboration among learners as they test, invent, imagine, and interpret content in creative ways.

Many primary teachers have experienced the benefits of a more arts-infused curriculum, both in the cognitive and affective arenas. Some of the themes repeated by teachers are the following:

- Imaginative discovery

When I use the arts—whether it be a role-playing situation or combining paintings with authors' writings to inspire new ways of thinking—I almost always find that spark in the kids' faces. The spark of a new idea, some new way to see something that they hadn't thought of before. To me, the arts are a direct route to the child's imagination.

—First-grade teacher

- Divergent, creative thinking

I've used the arts a lot in math and science—two areas where kids can get stuck in rigid, formula-driven thinking. When we do this, the walls come down; new doors open. Just recently, they created short stories with the idea of creating math problems— stories that they also sketched out in sequences. From this, a number of students found different ways of solving problems.

—Third-grade teacher

- Invention

My students LOVE anything creative. I have large books of black and white photographs and paintings, which we use as story starters. They select several pictures at random, put them in a sequence, and then invent a narrative to string them together. Each photograph adds a dimension to the process. The kids love it, and it's something they can do independently when they've finished their other work.

—Second-grade teacher

- A sense of beauty and artistry

Most of my students live in concrete high-rises. They're surrounded by a world of brick and concrete, with only a television or maybe a Nintendo game to relieve their boredom. I think it's a crime that our kids are assailed by so much ugliness. Therefore, I have art, art, art all over my walls—at their level. Frida Kahlo is a big hit.

—Kindergarten teacher

- Depth of feeling

I know we need to be always thinking about academic goals. But how a child is affected—in his heart and soul—may influence his learning more than any other single thing. The arts draw on that subterranean area of a child that we educators tend to avoid talking about. In my experience, a child who is deeply moved and inspired can attain heights never imagined.

—Second-grade teacher

The arts enable young children to make personal connections with content by including the facility for feeling, intuiting, experiencing, and imagining. Young children are especially receptive to creativity and the arts. The world bombards their eyes, ears, nose, and taste buds with multiple and complex sensations. The beauty of Canadian geese flying south at dusk awes them; the pounding beat of the bass from a passing car radio shakes them to their bones; the gentle breeze that sends the fallen leaves into a half-hearted spin makes them want to leap into the air; the pelting rain against their skin feels like the whipping of an angry sky. Young children notice little things—mud squishing through their toes, the spicy smell of dinner cooking, the warmth of the radiator against their feet on a cold evening. A mother once shared this with a teacher:

> Yesterday I was reading *Seven Loaves of Bread* to my 6-year-old girl. We've read it many times before. She is reading now and wanted to read a page. Then let me read, then her, etc. At one point she paused and said, "Mommy, we should make our bread. I just think the feeling of kneading the dough would be so wonderful to have."

The arts can link the world of sensibility, feeling, and creating to the world of inquiry, reason, and investigation. As you prepare your units or lessons, consider the following questions:

- What fundamental knowledge, concept, and skill do students need to learn as a result of this unit?

- What kinds of adjustments do I need to make in learning style, level of ability, knowledge, and interest?

- Do my students need to use their bodies? Do something with their hands? Use their ears and eyes? Touch and feel things? Imagine they are someone else? Something else? Somewhere else?

- Which of the arts would best serve this purpose?

- When should they be used—as a catalyst in the beginning? As a process throughout the assignment? As a final project?

If you're about to teach a mathematics lesson, you might ask yourself, "What art form would work best for the learning goals of my math lesson (concepts, skills, thinking processes)? What would best serve my kinetic learners? My visual learners?" The guide below provides some ideas on the kinds of activities most suited to each art form.

ARTS APPLICATIONS

Music: counting, adding, measuring, evoking (mood, atmosphere), coordinating (sounds, themes), feeling, sensing, developing (theme, story)

Dance: measuring (line), shaping (pattern), exploring (force, velocity, gravity), miming (story, mood), interpreting (ideas, cultures, stories)

Theater: role-playing, impersonating, imitating, dramatizing (humor, mood, feelings, ideas)

Visual Arts: exploring images; reasoning spatially; analyzing distance, perspective, proportions, dimensions; evoking vivid details, shades of color, light

---

As an example, let us consider the experience of this teacher in a creative writing workshop for young children who wanted to integrate the arts (particularly visual art) with science and language arts by focusing on trees.

Most young children have a favorite tree. They are quick to tell me about that special tree in their backyard they learned to climb, the tree that holds the swing at their friend's house, or the large maples in the park where they play games. I show them pictures of different trees, and we talk about the needs of trees for light, minerals, and water. I have posters and paintings of trees on the walls all around the room—at their eye level—so that they can examine them closely. I ask them what they know about trees. What keeps them alive? Do they eat? Some children know that the leaves on the branches take light from the sun and make it into energy for their "tree bodies." We focus on other amazing facts about trees:

- the two main groups of trees (broad-leaves and conifers) and the differences between them;
- the kinds of places trees live—the poles, temperate zones, tropical areas—and how these climates affect trees (e.g., the huge barrel-shaped trunk of the baobab tree helps it store water and protects it from evaporation during the dry season);
- what happens to trees in different seasons (including dry and wet for tropical climates);
- what happens to trees during the night and in the day;
- insects and animals that depend on trees and that provide nutrients for them;
- people who live in the forest and depend heavily on trees.

I have a table with different kinds of bark for the children to feel, as well as a thick piece of a tree trunk where they can see the many lines indicating the years of the tree. After we've spent time exploring different trees, climates, and environments, the children choose a tree species and imagine they are that tree. I have many magazines, books, and posters, and we watch a video on forests and trees. I pose questions such as the following:

- What kind of land surrounds you? Woods? Rocks? Desert? Hills?
- What kind of bark and leaves do you have? How tall are you?
- What kinds of animals live around you? Inside you? Who crawls or hops on you?
- Are there other trees near you?
- What is the greatest need for trees like you?

The children respond by drawing, writing, and discussing their thoughts. For an activity like this, catalysts are critical. It's better to have too much stuff than too little! Thomas Locker's *Sky Tree Portfolio* (Locker & Christensen, 1995) has an extraordinary collection of posters of the artist's original paintings of a tree in different seasons and weather conditions. On the back of each poster, writer Candace Christensen (a teacher) has written some text on the science of the tree. For example, on the back of "The Summer Tree" painting, she writes, "All summer the tree bathes its leaves in the light of the sun. The leaves also take in air. The roots are actively absorbing water and minerals from the soil. The water, air and minerals meet in sugars. No human being or animal can create sugar out of air, earth and water. It must be interesting to be a tree!"

Teachers can create similar sorts of catalysts by finding pictures and paintings on their own and creating a simple text to accompany them. I try to give a lot of imaginative options for the children's work. Since my workshop is focused on creative writing, most of them write stories, autobiographies, or poems. But I did once have a dance student who wanted to create a dance history about a tree and wrote a script to go with it (which she had another student read while she moved). The possibilities are endless, and once you touch the creative potential of the children, they start coming up with new ideas to pursue.

In my experience, integrating the arts in this way enables young children not only to discover some new knowledge about a phenomenon such as trees but also to feel its beauty and artistry. An interesting process begins to happen. The students explore different ways of expressing scientific facts creatively and then their creative ideas impel them to dig deeper into the science behind their stories, poems, drawings, sketches, and dramatizations. There have been some truly interesting results. I had a student who created a collage comparing the tree's roots to people's roots; another child who wrote a poem about the feelings deep inside the tree when winter comes and the birds leave her branches to fly south; another child who created a series of diagrams about photosynthesis, along with a painting of his favorite tree. This process fosters new visions of the intriguing world of trees, such as the following poem by one of my third-grade students.

> The mighty tree stands over the bushes
> Like a mighty king
> Standing proud and tall
> Swaying with joy in the wind

the bushes quivering
in the presence of this character
its once green leaves turn bright yellow and red
falling one by one on the dark soil
for it is fall now; the leaves raked up
but its green leaves will come again.

The following chart offers a number of examples within each subject area that illustrate how the arts apply to specific learning situations in language arts, social studies, science, and mathematics. To relate this to differentiating, we've created a column of examples for adjusting *process* in a lesson or unit and for adjusting student *products*.

Arts as Process	Arts as Product
LANGUAGE ARTS 1. Paintings used as story starters or as catalysts for poems. 2. Music played to create mood for a speech or presentation; to generate ideas for stories, poems. 3. Dramatic role-playing to understand point of view in stories. 4. Mime of a story or poem as teacher reads it out loud.	**LANGUAGE ARTS** 1. Create paintings/drawings of a story plot; collage of a poem. 2. Invent rap of biography of famous person; create soundtrack for a story. 3. Adapt a popular story to create a chamber theater piece. 4. Choreograph dance to interpret story or poem.
SOCIAL STUDIES 1. Prints of historic period as source of ideas and concepts. 2. Role-playing of different cultural views of an issue; impersonations of a key historical/political figure. 3. Learn dances of another culture or another historical period to gain insight into the people.	**SOCIAL STUDIES** 1. Incorporate ideas from history, politics, and culture into a visual art piece. 2. Compose song, rap, or melody around two key concepts in a historical event. 3. Perform a chamber theater adaptation based on a story about immigrants at Ellis Island.

Arts as Process	Arts as Product
4. Use of music from another culture/time period to explore characteristics of that culture/time period.	4. Create a dance or mime history of an event.

SCIENCE	**SCIENCE**
1. Paintings/prints to explore light, shadow, gravity, and perspective. 2. Music and sound as source for identifying different science phenomena. 3. Movement used to learn actions and rotations of planets in solar system. 4. Documentary of a scientist to generate a discussion of his or her discovery.	1. Create diagram, painting, or drawing that shows two scientific facts about the rainforest. 2. Create a surrealist-type painting about time, space, light, or gravity. 3. Impersonate a scientist and explain what she or he most valued about a discovery. 4. Create a dance or mime project around several science themes (e.g., gravity, time, light).

MATHEMATICS	**MATHEMATICS**
1. Prints/photographs to identify geometric shapes; use of cubism to explore properties of cubes and other shapes. 2. Use of rhythms to explore idea of fractions (whole notes, half notes, etc.). 3. Dramatization of math problems to understand process and find solutions. 4. Use of jumping to work out the results of an addition problem; creation of physical movements to express different operations—addition, subtraction, and so on.	1. Create a geometric painting that expresses facts about properties of geometric shapes. 2. Create a drawing or diagram to show a mathematical operation. 3. Impersonate a number or a mathematical symbol and write or list what is most valuable about it; provide examples. 4. Choreograph a dance or mime piece that expresses at least three key math facts; improvise new mathematical situations by extending the dance or mime piece.

The point in dividing process and product in this way is to illustrate how teachers can best use the arts for differentiating in the classroom. There will be times, for example, when integrating a visual or performing arts idea will be the best way of introducing a unit or of enabling your students to process new content at a deeper level. At other times, you can use the arts to create alternative product ideas, particularly for kinesthetic and visual learners. The following are synopses of how you can begin thinking about the arts in the different subject areas.

LANGUAGE ARTS

Reading. Even advanced students can sometimes become passive readers. The arts sharpen observation and stimulate a more imaginative and analytical way of reading. Examples of activities that have worked well with primary students include the following:

- Students draw, sketch, and paint characters from a story and then look in the text to see what gave them these visual impressions. They explore additional details from the text and compare art with their peers.

- Students talk about the environments described in the text and where they are in relation to each other. How do they picture it in their minds? How many details can they remember? What sounds do they hear?

- Children pick a character from the text and mime it to the class— select a favorite scene or some characteristic they like the most. The same can be done with a scene, where students select pivotal moments in the book and mime it to the class.

- Children choose a conflict, issue, or problem raised by the text and stage a debate, with different students assuming the role of specific characters.

Writing. Primary students need more creative approaches to composition. When used appropriately, the arts present a wide range of sources for writing (e.g., essays, stories, and poetry). Here are some examples:

- Teacher provides visual catalysts (paintings, photography, video, etc.) for students to imagine what happened before and/or after the scenes depicted. If they were detectives, what would they conclude from these images? Why?

- Children compose free-verse poems by using paintings and photography as catalysts. If this painting were music, what would they hear? What would they feel, see, hear, and smell if they were inside the painting?

- Students listen to music and invent a story around it. What does the music suggest to them? Children learn the different parts of a symphony—and how they follow the structure of a story. They sketch ideas for each section and construct a story line.

- Children write a biographical sketch about a famous person based on a text as well as a picture or portrait. They tell their story from a variety of viewpoints: this individual's friend, teacher, mother or father, sister or brother, or the family dog.

- Children create a chamber theater piece out of a short story. Teacher asks them to select the most important scenes. What scenes do they consider most important and why? Some students are narrators and others speak and act the parts of the characters.

SOCIAL STUDIES

Studying history, geography, and other social studies subjects through the arts allows students to consider multiple viewpoints and to gain more vivid impressions of events, processes, and people. Activities such as the following ask children to use their imagination and analytical abilities in new ways:

- Students pretend to be an important person in history or a friend or relative. They (a) write a short essay about an important issue in this person's life, (b) dress and act the part of this person while the class asks questions about his or her life, and (c) create a visual art piece that expresses something important about this person and present it to the class.

- Students act as reporters who travel back in time to cover an important event. They use prints and pictures to imagine what life was like then and write an article about the people they interviewed. They accompany it with sketches or pictures of what they saw.

- Children explore music, dance, dress, or art of another culture. They ask, "How is this different from the music, dance, art, or dress of my culture?" Children explore arts to describe what they think is important in this culture. They write, discuss, and/or act out their ideas.

- Some famous paintings have traveled many miles and seen a great deal of historical change before they finally landed in a museum. Students create a map of the journey of the *Mona Lisa* from King Louis XIV's palace in Versailles, to a hiding place during the French Revolution, to the trunk of a thief who kept it for 3 years and was caught trying to smuggle it into Italy, to its permanent home in the Louvre. They write about this journey from the point of view of the painting.

- Students become cartographers. They create a small-scale illustration of their neighborhoods. Using rulers, a stick (at least 8 inches long), pencil, and examples of other maps, children figure out compass points (north, south, east, west) and choose a scale (e.g., one inch for each block). They create symbols for landmarks, such as homes, bridges, railroads, and churches, and draw and label streets. They also include an explanation of the symbols.

- Children create a mime or creative movement piece about different political systems and/or social class, attitudes, and conventions. In groups, they create a story that includes one or more of the following: a narration of the story, mimed expression, set design and costuming, and sound/music. They follow the activity with writing or discussion.

- Students choose a famous explorer, learn about his or her life (through books, magazines, prints, stories, videos), and write two or three journal entries about his or her travels. They include sketches of maps, drawings, and anything else that will bring this explorer to life.

SCIENCE AND MATHEMATICS

Science and mathematics have immediate ties to the arts. Pop art's Roy Lichtenstein said, "Organized perception is what art is all about" (Piper, 1981, p. 95). Musicians and choreographers use mathematical thinking as they focus on patterns, themes, lines, rhythms, directions, and the flow of movements. Leonardo da Vinci studied perspective and depth in painting, applied mathematics and science to every aspect of his work, explored anatomy, invented machines, and sketched designs for technology far in advance of his time.

Thomas Locker, a contemporary artist, has integrated science and art in a format designed especially for teachers' classrooms. His *Sky Tree Portfolio* (Locker & Christensen, 1995), *Cloud Dance* (2000), and *Water Dance* (1997) contain exquisite paintings of nature with information and activities that promote scientific inquiry. Locker contends that the study of nature as a whole (art) and as parts (science) are both critical to an appreciation and understanding of the natural world. His books demonstrate how each field prompts the wondering child to question and explore. For example, observing the qualities of clouds may lead him to ask, "Why do they appear white in the day, but reddish or even purple later in the day?" Or, a study of the science of "folded mountains" may stimulate questions such as the following: Where in this painting can I see signs of colliding plates in the "folded mountains"? How has the artist brought this unseen drama to life?

Science

- Children create a troposphere on one wall in the classroom, with altitudes labeled. They identify types of clouds they see outside and create art representations that can be attached and identified on the troposphere.

- Students interested in movement create a dance or mime piece about the properties of gravity, flight, momentum, energy, and other scientific phenomena.

- Children listen to weather reports and pay attention to what is said about clouds. They write an imaginary forecast focusing on the movement of clouds (light clouds, storm clouds, etc.) and what this means for people.

- Children explore creation stories from different cultures that relate to water. They mime, dance, or act them out for the rest of the class.

- Students explore what makes volcanoes explode. They write an autobiography as a volcano, describing its life before and after an explosion. Alternatively, they choreograph the process.

- Students spend time listening to the natural world and observing it in detail. They describe what they saw, felt, heard, and touched and choose an artistic medium for expressing the science dimension of this work. Examples: free verse poem, painting, musical composition.

Mathematics

- Students identify shapes and patterns, as well as measure lines in paintings, prints, and photographs. They draw a picture using only geometric shapes but use them in any way they choose.

- Students copy a painting and change the proportion of things (e.g., make the house smaller than a tree, the bird larger than the child, etc.). They observe how surrealist paintings play with the concept of proportions.

- Students follow straight lines, curves, and circles; they choose a shape or collection of shapes to dance in—circles, rectangles, triangles, and so on.

- Students examine perspective in painting. How did the artist make the tree appear close by? How did she create the illusion of distance? Children explore the following questions: Why do things far away appear small? Are they really small?

- Students learn about whole notes, half notes, and quarter notes. They tap the beats with their feet and clap their hands, and they identify notes in a range of music. Students make links between this and fractions (part of a whole).

- In groups, students act out math problems and create solutions. They extend the dramatizations to create new mathematical situations.

- Children practice writing numbers by creating the correct shapes with each other's bodies. Each group creates a number while the other students guess what it is. More advanced children do double- or triple-digit numbers—practicing the move from one number to the next smoothly.

The activities outlined here illustrate ways that primary students can create meaningful links with the curriculum. The arts can accommodate significant differences in culture, learning styles, ability, and knowledge without requiring significant adjustments.

ARTISTIC TALENT

This chapter would not be complete without including a brief section on artistic ability in young students. Many teachers question their capacity to use the arts in the regular classroom. They say the following:

> "I have no training in the arts, so how can I use them effectively in the classroom?"

> "These kids are so young. Do they really need exposure to the arts at this time?"

> "I would feel nervous guiding a child in any art form. What if I do more damage than good?"

You don't have to be an artist to encourage artistic ability in young children. Nor should you minimize your creative potential simply because you haven't spent years training in specific art forms. Children with creative and artistic talent are among the least understood students, and the primary grades can make all the difference in their future growth and success. The suggestions that follow will give the "different drummers" in your class what they need to begin exploring their special talents.

Resources. When opportunities arise, give artistic children resources to support their interest. This might include simple instructional books, examples of paintings, CDs of music, photographs of choreographed dances, videos, biographies of artists, and other materials. Some of this you may already have; other sources you could get at your school or local library or, in the case of visual art, at a museum bookstore.

Whenever possible, try to arrange for an artist to visit your school or classroom. In Chicago, arts groups do residencies in the city schools, and there is often funding set aside for this purpose, particularly if the whole school benefits. Opportunities to interact with artists and participate in special workshops give young children a deeper understanding of a particular art field and, for many young children, offer a much-needed vision for their future. Other resources could involve field trips to museums, special exhibitions in your community, or theater, music, dance, and mime performances. How much you can do obviously depends on what sort of funding exists for cultural events or workshops in your district.

Artistic outlets. Children with special talents in the arts obviously need time to pursue their interests. You can support this through individual arrangements with the child. It is not unusual for teachers to make agreements with students about extra time in the art room (or music room, or resource room with a special mentor) after they've completed assignments. In addition, you can supply art materials (sketch paper, paints, magic markers, crayons, clay, costumes, props, etc.) and incorporate art activities into the curriculum wherever it serves learning goals. These experiences will give talented students more opportunities to extend their learning through a creative medium.

Artistically inclined children also need opportunities to display their work or perform. The practice of exhibiting and performing gives young artists valuable experience and training. These activities need not be confined to the school. Children can submit entries to local banks, coffee shops, libraries, or airports. They can also mount theatrical and dance performances for community stages during fairs, special events, or as part of a fund-raising effort for the school. Obviously, some activities require more experience in the arts than others. But it is always possible to find helpers within your own network and in the larger parent community. Thespians, cartoonists, musicians, and many others have a way of appearing when you put the word out.

As soon as you notice a special artistic ability in a student, contact the parents. Don't assume they know about it. If they are at a loss as to what options exist for training or education, or if they have no financial resources to support their child's ability, help them investigate resources in the community. Not only are there community centers that occasionally offer arts classes at reasonable prices, but studios frequently have scholarship funds set aside for families who need support. The authors of this book know a number of cases where this kind of early intervention has made a world of difference to young children with artistic talent.

LOOKING AHEAD

As the language arts chapter will show, the arts are indispensable for developing skill and understanding in young learners. The versatility inherent in both performing and visual arts allows you to incorporate them in any part of your unit, depending on the demands of the material to be taught and the needs of your students. Used in an organized way and tied to specific learning goals (rather than just tossed in as enrichment), the arts are practically unsurpassed in their ability to stimulate cognitive growth and strengthen skills in a range of learning situations.

5 Differentiated Instruction Applied to Language Arts

The Center for Gifted, National-Louis University, Evanston, Illinois

The reader writes the story.

—*Annie Proulx*
(upon receiving the Pulitzer Prize for fiction)

Young children often develop a fascination for language long before they begin kindergarten. Parents are first to notice this awakening. Without any adult prodding, their children hungrily absorb words and sounds from anything their environment offers them—picture books, cereal labels, songs, raps, street signs, posters, and murals. A child may take charge of the grocery list and ask a parent how to spell things, sing along with the jingles from four or five commercials, memorize rhymes, and reproduce the letters from a poster on the wall of the grocery store. In response, many parents read with their children, take them to the neighborhood library, teach them songs and rhymes, and look for any sources they can find to nurture their growing interest and curiosity.

However, not all preschoolers have an ideal environment for this awakening to take place. They may be in a home where both parents work long days and have little time or energy to read to their children or support their first steps into the world of letters. Or they may live in a television-dominated house where everyone slumps down on a couch at night and watches several shows before going to bed. Growing up in a place where electronics permeate the atmosphere (and this is not uncommon in all sectors of American society), these young children have little opportunity to develop a serious interest in books or reading.

There are still other American homes where young children's first contact with text is another language, another writing system (e.g., Chinese characters, Arabic script), or another dialect. These students have special difficulties to overcome but also unique strengths to bring to their study of language arts. Navigating two linguistic worlds has forced them to develop skill in constructing and translating meanings. Among young students from non-Western cultures, the process of finding ways to express equivalent concepts in two languages is especially difficult. For example, a radio show in Uganda called *Wokulira* (in Luganda) has no equivalent in English. When the second author of this book asked a young student about it, he said, "It means, 'by the time you've grown up, you've seen amazing things.'" Young children in Kampala, many of whom are bilingual, negotiate these kinds of meanings every day and develop a versatility and mastery in language, despite the challenges they may have in some areas of English.

Teachers in primary school charged with the responsibility of laying the foundation for their students' lifelong pursuit of reading and writing might ask themselves:

- How can I harness the strengths my students have in language?

- How can I build on what these children bring to my class—in the area of knowledge, skill, and experience in language?

- How can I accommodate children with striking differences in ability, culture, language, and learning style?

- What structure can I create to ensure that all my students learn the fundamental concepts and skills they need while still allowing freedom and variety in *how* they get there and *what* they produce?

- How can I create adjustments in language arts content, process, and products without losing the direction and continuity of instruction?

THE BIG PICTURE: LANGUAGE ARTS GOALS

Children's early exposure to the written word influences not only their growth in literacy but also their attitudes about themselves as readers and writers. When Annie Proulx said that the "reader writes the story," she was referring to the way readers invent, imagine, and make sense of a written story while they read. The reading process is something like a journey. A child who begins to read draws on his own resources—his experiences in life; his experiences with books, signs, labels, and graffiti art; and his experiences in language (or languages and dialects). He plies the new waters of this text with all that he has and gains new vistas from his journey, which he then takes back with him into the world of speaking and also of writing. Speaking, reading, and writing are a complex, interactive process of creating meaning. Even before children begin reading, many of them are already on the journey:

> James has several favorite stories. He goes through each book and tells the story, using the pictures as cues.

> Mercedes makes little "books" by folding a few pieces of paper together and having her mother staple them in the middle. She draws sketches on one side and dictates a short narrative about the pictures, which her mother writes down on the other side.

> Tanya acts out some of her grandmother's tales while she's telling them and then draws pictures about it.

When differentiating the language arts curriculum, the first step is always to become familiar with the experiences and knowledge your students are bringing to the subject (see Chapters 1 and 2). What kind of background in language (stories—written or oral, jokes, rhymes, rap, graffiti, songs, languages, dialects, etc.) do your students have? This knowledge will aid you in the second step, which is identifying the most essential concepts, skills, and understandings of language arts. Despite differences in background, ability, and experience, all students need certain skills and understandings to read and write well. By way of illustrating the importance of this step, here is a story from a mother of a child who struggled to read:

> Timothy always enjoyed reading and began his first book before kindergarten. But as time went on, he slowed down. By third grade, Timothy was beginning to avoid reading assignments. The reading specialist, his teacher, and I met together and realized that Timothy lacked strategy in his reading. He thought he had to remember *every detail* and so he'd go over and over the same passages. Because he learned to read early, the teacher thought he didn't need the instruction that other students had. Consequently, he never really learned how to distinguish the important from less important points. Targeting this as the core of the problem and giving him special instruction has made all the difference.

Even confident readers may form habits that limit their comprehension and insight. You may have a child who whizzes through a text without considering the meaning in any depth at all. Or you may have a student who, because of cultural difference or his own idiosyncrasies, pursues questions or issues that have only a peripheral relationship with the text. Or you may have a group of students who read passively, never interacting with the text in a way that helps them understand, question, clarify, or even think about what they're reading.

Reading is a highly active, constructive process. Consider the strategies children use when they read (Harvey & Goudvis, 2000). They

- make connections between what they know and new information,
- ask questions of themselves and the texts,
- visualize and draw inferences during and after reading,
- distinguish important from less important ideas in texts,
- synthesize information and ideas from different texts.

These are crucial reading strategies that obviously you want all students to gain whether you are teaching word recognition in kindergarten or interpretation of a story in third grade. Creating connections between the children and the text; asking questions and encouraging them to ask questions; giving them opportunities to engage all the senses (see, hear, feel, do) while learning stories, words, and sounds; and creating and inventing within this process give students the preparation they need to become thinking readers. They will be able to do the job of readers, which is to "write the story"—construct the meaning, analyze the motives of characters, and interpret the story.

Writing is intimately connected to the reading process. More than the skills of grammar, composition, usage, and spelling, the art of writing involves

- thinking on paper;
- organizing thoughts into ideas;
- asking questions of one's self and of the ideas written down;
- creating sequences for ideas in the form of sentences and paragraphs;
- applying the structure of stories, essays, and poems that one has learned from reading to what one is writing;
- testing out what one has learned about usage and about literary devices through different speaking, writing, and arts activities;

- synthesizing ideas from different texts and expressing them through writing.

You may have developed your own list of priorities for the language arts curriculum. Undoubtedly, different pressures come to bear on any decision you make about what is essential—for example, state standards, the curriculum priorities identified by the school board and district, the unique demographics and learning needs of your community, and the grade level. Many classroom teachers feel that as long as they can incorporate topics from state goals and standards (to the extent that these are reasonable and achievable), they will be meeting everyone's expectations for student learning.

But curriculum standards can be a burden to some teachers, as the following examples illustrate:

> I refer to the standards regularly, but they're a little overwhelming. Who can do all that in one year?
>
> —*Second-grade teacher*

> The problem with standards is that they don't adjust to differences in circumstances. At least one third of my kids are from other countries, and then there are others who're definitely above grade level and so on.
>
> —*Third-grade teacher*

> Curriculum standards may be needed to create continuity throughout the state, but they can be confining. It's hard not to know how we're supposed to follow them. Should they guide our own curriculum plans? Or are they just a reference we should check once in a while?
>
> —*First-grade teacher*

A useful way to think about curriculum standards is as guideposts to include in your journey, but not as ends in themselves (see sample of standards at the end of this chapter). A certain number of standards focus on specific skills and knowledge and therefore may not apply to all your kids' learning needs. In this case, you can still adjust them to the experience and ability of individual students. As future examples in this chapter will show, you can use the standards in a couple of ways:

1. as a way of keeping track of important content you might have overlooked,

2. as a guide to some of your own decisions about what concepts and skills you feel will most advance your students' understanding in the curriculum.

THE FIVE-STEP PLAN

As described in the introduction, the word *curriculum* means "to run" in Latin—hence the reason this book uses the idea of a journey as a metaphor and structure for differentiating. The sequence begins with what the students themselves bring to a subject or planned lesson (abilities, difficulties, culture, learning styles, etc.), then focuses on the destination—where they should be in terms of understanding and skill by the end of a lesson or unit—and on evidence of student understanding (e.g., behaviors, comments, assignments).

Wiggins and McTighe (1998, p. 9) call this a "backward design process" because it literally plans from the end and works backwards. It asks first, "Where do I want this unit or lesson to leave my students in terms of knowledge, skill, and understanding?" If your unit is a journey, you may decide, for example, that the whole class will travel from Town A to Town B. This is essential content. Depending on need, ability, and interest, students may

- take the most direct route;
- travel circuitously, stopping periodically at key sites;
- ask for extra maps or a compass to stop from driving off course;
- count the miles along the way;
- stop for a while to paint the view.

During the journey, you may need to stop the travelers to take stock of their progress (assessment) and make some changes to their itinerary (adjust instruction) or gather new supplies (find new sources). When they reach Town B, all the students will have similar knowledge and understanding based on their trip, but because the process differed, they will have seen, discovered, and acquired ideas and understandings unique to their own journey.

In this and the next three chapters, we will use the metaphor of a journey to differentiate the curriculum. Here is a review of the five-step process:

FIVE-STEP PROCESS

Step 1: Know the travelers (children)

- Are they prepared for the journey? What skills and abilities do they have?

- What differences in cultural background, life experience, and home life influence their ability to embark on this journey (i.e., learn)?

Step 2: Determine the destination (learning goal)

- Where do you want the children to be at the end of this journey (i.e., what do you want the students to understand or to be able to do)?

- What learning standards and curriculum goals will this journey address?

Step 3: Identify proof or evidence that they have reached the destination (i.e., understand what has been taught)

- What behaviors and comments would tell you that the students understand?

- What products, performances, constructions, and experiments would express understanding of the concepts, skills, and information taught?

Step 4: Plan the journey

- How should the journey begin (how should the subject be introduced)?

- What teaching strategies should be used?

- What learning activities?

- What resources involved?

- How will the students be grouped?

Step 5: Reassess and adjust according to new needs and changes

- What are the criteria for knowing that the children have reached the destination (understood the concepts and processes involved)?

- What rubrics can be designed to give you the information you need to know if the child is on track or if he or she needs further adjustment?

This structure gives you the assurance that, even though Justin is making a model of the Chinese longhorn beetle prior to writing his report and Shannon wants to do some architectural sketches in her report on America's first skyscrapers, they will both have moved toward some core knowledge and skill. Once you've identified essential learning in a subject, you can choose "destinations" that benefit all students but adjust the "itinerary" and the complexity of the "course" according to different learning styles and abilities. One child may write a detailed biography and another student a fairly simple one, but they're both on the same journey: choosing a subject, asking questions, researching, outlining and designing, and writing.

Chapters 1 and 2 offer practical information and examples that illustrate the importance of the first step of the five-step process (i.e., "Know the travelers [learners]"). The following pages describe each of the remaining steps in detail, focusing on language arts and providing examples from elementary classrooms.

CHOOSE THE LEARNING "DESTINATION" (STEP 2)

Determining the learning "destination" is the second step of the five-step process. As mentioned in Chapter 1, selecting "essential" topics to teach should involve the following criteria (Wiggins & McTighe, 1998, pp. 10–11):

- To what extent does the idea, topic, or process represent a "big idea" having enduring value beyond the classroom? In language arts, this might be a unit on distinguishing what's most important in reading—the main idea.

- To what extent does the idea, topic, or process reside at the heart of the discipline? A unit on composing an essay of several paragraphs resides at the heart of the discipline in that students have to express their ideas on paper and communicate meaning.

- To what extent does the idea, topic, or process require uncoverage? This question is important because it involves planning ahead for common difficulties in a subject. For example, knowing that young students need extra help understanding point of view when writing stories, you can address this at the start.

- To what extent does the idea, topic, or process offer potential for engaging students?

In this phase of your planning, try as much as possible to engage the imagination. Here are some examples:

- Have them discover that words can create pictures, feelings, and smells through a unit on poetry.

- Allow them to invent stories from anything—tales from their family or cultural traditions, a scene in a painting, a cartoon, a conversation, an old family photograph, or a favorite animal in their home.

- Show them what point of view is. Provide experiences where they can reimagine historic events as someone in another time.

- Expose them to the idea of interpretation and give them experience expressing their own vision of a character, a place, or a happening.

You can easily create variations for whatever destination you've chosen.

> Establishing in my mind what I want all students to understand by the end of a unit or lesson simplifies differentiated instruction. Having a sense of what "big idea" or large understanding I'm aiming for is a useful starting point for creating adjustments. Just last week, the kids were all working on book reports, but the larger goal was that they all understand how to find out about and report on a topic. The process we set up required that they (1) choose one or two big ideas, (2) create a structure (outline, sketch, or any other aid that helps them), (3) include one or two examples that stood out to them, and (4) tell what they liked (or didn't like,

as the case may be) and why. From here, differentiating is just a few simple adjustments. Advanced readers tackle more challenging books or compare two books. Kinetic learners (I have about five or six who are strongly oriented that way) construct models, designs, etc. as part of their process. I also have a group of talkative "interpersonal" learners who brainstorm together on how they can get the best information about their topic.

—Second-grade teacher

Choose a destination (concept, skill, idea) that is essential enough and large enough to encompass all learners regardless of their differences. If the focus of a lesson is a specific fact, skill, or calculation, there will always be children who are repeating what they already know and others who have trouble mastering it. On the other hand, if you create a larger goal, you can then adjust up (more advanced), down (less advanced), or sideways (use creative variations; adapt to different learning styles).

Even when teaching the mechanics of grammar, usage, and spelling, try as much as possible to do it in the context of a story, a poem, a rhyme, a song, or some other source. Children can look for verbs in a story, extract verses from a song and study the nouns, act out prepositions, and tap punctuation on the floor or on their desks. You can adjust the level of difficulty by having kids work on different kinds of words, different grammatical constructions, and different source material depending on their learning styles. Skills are not ends in themselves, and young children need to master them in meaningful contexts.

IDENTIFY EVIDENCE OF UNDERSTANDING (STEP 3)

This is the third step. How will you know that your students have understood the concepts, gained the skills, and synthesized the knowledge you intended? This step simplifies the planning process by immediately focusing on specific behaviors and/or products that will demonstrate understanding. This is not always a straightforward process in language arts, where a student may experience changes on a subtle level: a new insight about story structure, a feel for metaphoric language, or a greater imagination in exploring poems, fiction, nonfiction, and theater. But it's possible to identify precisely what a student who has achieved understanding should be able to do (explain, write, construct, apply, etc.). Here are some examples:

- *Destination*: Students will learn how to make predictions while reading (or listening to) a text.

  > *Evidence:* The children can make predictions about the outcome of a story on the basis of what the characters are apt to do, the action that has happened so far, and what happens in other books like it. They can show this through drawings (if they are kindergarteners), composing the story themselves, discussions, and debates.

- *Destination*: Students will understand what conflict is in a story.

  > *Evidence:* The children can explain what the conflict is in a story and can express this through mime, drama, and/or illustrations. They can write fractured fairy tales, focusing on the conflict or problem in the original and what new one they can put in its place.

- *Destination:* The students will understand what metaphors and similes are and how to use them.

  > *Evidence:* From a list of examples, the children can identify metaphors and similes and explain how they know them. They can find examples in poems they read. They can create their own in free-verse poems.

Obviously, you can adjust these according to individual levels of experience, mastery, and skill. For advanced students who have written poems using metaphors and/or similes, you can introduce them to more advanced poetry or to new poetic forms they've never read before. For children with less experience, part of the "evidence" of understanding might be having them choose a visual image from a painting or photograph (the hair of an old man, the large fir tree, the pointed steeple in the distance) and compare it to something else.

PLAN THE JOURNEY (STEP 4)

The fourth step is planning the actual journey, and as with most journeys, the process of getting there often confers gifts we didn't anticipate. As students apply themselves, practice skills, test ideas, experiment, think, and create, the experience works on them and their teachers in unexpected ways.

If you have a map and know where you're going, you can always find alternative routes. What I find with my class is that we all start off together—at a sort of launching point. But then things come up. A couple of children already know a couple of steps, so they skip those. Others struggle along because their learning styles are different, and so together we figure out another way for them to process the new concepts. Other kids have other issues, and so on. As we get nearer our goal, unexpected discoveries and new ideas start to emerge because the kids are working at the pace best for them, and they can process information in their way. There's always something interesting that happens along the way—some kid breaks through a limitation or the students give me some new insight about them or about learning.

—Kindergarten teacher

Differentiated instruction can make this kind of learning happen because it responds to the readiness of students for the subject at hand and gives them the activities, resources, and support they need to build on their knowledge and understanding.

Introduce a New Unit to Preassess

As you prepare your unit, use the source materials you've gathered to create a strong catalyst for introducing your subject. Make sure the sources are appropriate for your students (bearing in mind their special needs, abilities, experiences, and interests) and help you target essential learning in your unit or lesson. Focus on how you will integrate higher level thinking and engage the imagination from the moment the class begins. Ask yourself: "To what extent will I be able to assess my students' level of knowledge and understanding?" For young children, activities that enable them to imagine, construct, experiment with hands-on materials, and create visual art have proved most effective. Here is an example:

In preparation for a unit on folktales, I had a number of tales from different cultures, prints of characters and scenes from well-known folktales, videotapes, and audiotaped music. I had the class shut their eyes and imagine that they live far, far away in a small village on the side of the mountain with no computers, videogames, or movies. I described the kind of village they lived in and how they lived—the struggles they had and the things they loved. I also described some of the people—especially the unusual ones—who lived there. Then I began asking questions: What stories do you think came from that village? How do you think they were created? By one person? By different people? Why do you think this? If you lived there, what kinds of stories might you tell? I then had the children think about two questions: What characters live there? What happened there? The children sketched out some imaginary characters they "saw" in this village and thought about what happened to them. I had students share their thoughts and sketches. After the sharing, I felt that the ground was prepared for us to explore what a folktale is and how it differs from other stories they might encounter.

—First-grade teacher

This kind of beginning immediately engages children's interest, whatever their knowledge or ability. In a direct and imaginative way, it helps them think about the connection between the "folk" and their tales and conceptualize the folktale genre in comparison to other genres. As an inductive reasoning strategy, it provides opportunities for intuitive insight into the world of folktales that will reinforce subsequent lessons. A teacher could also use other sources he or she has at hand (visual, aural) to inspire even more imaginative responses. In this way, advanced students already familiar with the content will have a variety of ways of looking at folktales, and children with little literary experience will have a better chance of grasping the main idea. This activity will also be something you can refer to again and again throughout the unit to underscore specific points.

From the students' responses, you can also get a handle on what students should move on to the next phase of the unit, which ones need to reinforce points just learned, and which ones need more advanced work. For many teachers, an introductory assignment such as this serves as a preassessment where they can identify specific areas of strength and weakness. Because the assignment is open-ended and integrates more than one medium, children can exhibit strengths that would be invisible in a pencil-and-paper task.

There is a wide range of choices for preassessments. The previously described activity by a first-grade teacher is obviously a more lengthy one, but this is sometimes necessary to assess areas of mastery and need. Other possibilities could include simple pretests or a short task that requires students to show what they know about a particular subject. Some teachers do this before creating an introductory activity, and others use the introduction as an assessment of student readiness.

Sequence Teaching Strategies and Learning Activities

In differentiating, it helps to create a sequence of what you will do and what the students will do during an activity. This is something you can always change along the way, but it will provide a useful map of the terrain the children have to traverse to reach the "destination." With the abilities and learning needs of your students in mind, consider what new concepts and skills you will introduce and the thinking process involved.

- Are you in a kindergarten class where children are looking for patterns and relationships in words?

- Are you having your second-grade class make predictions about the future development of a story?

- Are you preparing third-grade students to compose their own free-verse poems?

Think about the different elements in your students—their culture, life experiences, and passions. What will most invite them to the "table" you've provided? What will enable them to understand these concepts and use the strengths they have to advance their knowledge and skill in this area? Lecture and direct instruction have their place in communicating new information effectively. But in language arts, strategies such as questioning, role-playing, guided imagery, and inquiry-based instruction can often go farther in nurturing the growth of reading and writing ability. Below is a series of examples. They are intended as ideas to help you get started structuring your units in such a way that you can differentiate more effectively.

- *Destination:* Children will understand what point of view means and its role in fiction.

  Standard: Understand how literary elements and techniques are used to convey meaning.

  Evidence of understanding: Can describe what different characters feel. Can write about or draw a character's point of view from a story.

Teaching strategy: Questioning and guided discussion. For example, you could have students choose a character they want to be. Ask, "What do you like about being this character? What kind of environment do you live in? What kinds of other animals/people do you see or know? What do you feel about the other characters? About the situation in the story?" Then have the children switch to a new character in the story. As the children respond to the questions, you could write down their thoughts or create a sketch on the board.

Learning activity: From the notes on the board (or notes the children have written themselves), have children further explore the story based on their character's point of view. Provide related posters as well as material related to the characters (e.g., if a child has chosen to be the wolf in a fairy tale, have photographs and magazines of real wolves) so that students can draw on more than one source to develop their ideas. The children could then compose two paragraphs (monologue) or a poem about themselves as this character and what they think about the story. Is it fair? What would they prefer to have happen? They can accompany this with drawings or dramatizations.

Resources: Visual materials (paintings, drawings, sketches from stories), posters, books.

Grouping: Children work individually.

Adjustments: Vary complexity level of texts according to ability; allow children with different learning styles to do preliminary activity to help them process their ideas (e.g., painting, dramatizing, composing a song for their character).

• *Destination:* Children will understand the big idea in a text.

Standard: Apply reading strategies to improve understanding and fluency.

Evidence of understanding: Students can say what the difference is between a big idea and a small one. They can draw what they feel is most important from a text. They can identify the "big idea" of a painting and a smaller part (e.g., "The big part of the painting is the whole farm; a little part of the farm is the barn").

Teaching strategy: Questioning; guided inquiry; direct instruction. Present pictures that have a lot of different things going on in them and ask, "What things do you see inside this picture? What do you see along the edges of the picture? If you had to choose one thing that this picture—the whole picture—is about, what would that be?" Through direct instruction, make a link between seeing the big idea in a painting and the big idea in a text. Read a short paragraph and show pictures.

Learning activity: Students provide a rationale for what the big ideas are for them. They draw their ideas and discuss their choices.

Resources: Paintings, photographs, prints, books, magazines.

Grouping: Interest groups.

Adjustments: Tiered groups (e.g., Group A uses pictures to write down big/small ideas represented in pictures; Group B reads paragraphs describing a person, place, or situation and discusses big/small ideas; Group C reads articles or short stories and identifies big ideas).

- *Destination:* Children will understand that stories usually have some kind of conflict or challenge that the characters have to resolve.

  Standards: (a) Apply reading strategies to improve understanding and fluency. (b) Read and interpret a variety of literary works.

  Evidence of understanding: Children identify the most important characters in a story and the main conflict or problem in it. They make changes to a character in an existing story and create a different kind of problem or conflict.

  Teaching strategy: Teacher reads a fairy tale and then a fractured fairy tale (e.g., *Little Red Riding Hood*) and asks: "How is the main character different in the fractured fairy tale? What is the main problem in the story? What does Little Red Riding Hood want to do? What does the big bad wolf want to do? What problem does Little Red Riding Hood have in the woods?"

  Learning activity: Children invent a fractured fairy tale of their own. They create a major change in one or two characters to weave a new story. They brainstorm ideas and explore: "Does my story have a problem or conflict as in the original fairy tale? How can I create more suspense? How do the changes in character affect the story line?" (Examples: Little Red Riding Hood as a tough girl, completely unafraid of the wolf and able to save her grandmother; a Cinderella story from the point of view of the stepmother, who believes Cinderella has made up stories about her; the three little pigs as enormous pigs.) Kindergarteners or first graders can also attempt this but by telling and drawing rather than writing.

Resources: Choice of four well-known fairy tales, including similar versions in other cultures (e.g., Ed Young's *Lon Po Po,* a Chinese rendition of the Red Riding Hood story); examples of fractured fairy tales; posters; art materials.

Grouping: Interest groups (according to the fairy tale they prefer) for brainstorming and sharing stories.

Adjustments: Create cluster group for advanced writers to share ideas on their stories. Provide a list of guiding questions for those who are struggling (e.g., What is the new wolf like in *The Three Little Pigs?* Or, what are the pigs like? What new problem does the wolf have to face?).

- *Destination:* Children will understand what such poetic elements as metaphor, simile, imagery, and rhythm are and their role in poetry.

  Standards: (a) Understand how literary elements and techniques are used to convey meaning. (b) Communicate ideas in writing to accomplish a variety of purposes.

  Evidence of understanding: Children can write free-verse poems using these elements. They can identify and explain each element in a series of poems.

  Teaching strategy: Whole-group instruction and inquiry. You can take the class through the process of writing a free-verse poem. Present a poster or picture on any topic, such as nature. Encourage the students to think about the atmosphere of the picture—the color, the feeling they get, and what certain images mean to them. Ask questions such as the following: If you were to think of the people (or animals) in this picture as colors, what colors would they be? If you were to think of them as music or sound, what would you hear? If they had texture or temperature (such as cold, smooth, warm, liquid, etc.), what might they be? The same process can be done with music. Asks for words, phrases, or parts of sentences to put on the board. Individual children contribute them, each building on the previous word, phrase, or part of a sentence, each suggesting some new aspect of the picture that no one else has seen. As the students offer their ideas, you write them down on the board so everyone can see each line and build on them. Once the students have shared their ideas, read the whole poem with respect and appreciation and then talk about the images conveyed.

Learning activity: Students compose their own poems. You can provide a wide range of catalysts (e.g., posters, pictures, paintings, films, musical recordings, books, games, puzzles, etc.) and guide students in deciding what they would like to use. Ask questions about visual sources:

- Notice the picture of X (person or animal); what is he or she staring at? What exists outside the lines of the painting? What does the expression on the person's/animal's face tell you? What do you imagine has just happened before this picture was taken?

- Pick a color, shape, or something that you like the most about this painting, print, photograph, or film. Write whatever words or phrases that come to you.

- Listen to this music or sound recording while you observe a painting. What does the music or sound tell you about this scene? Close your eyes and imagine movements around you, the touch of them against your skin and face, the smells.

- Look at this environment. Imagine living there yourself. What sounds do you think you'd hear? Walk around in the painting/print and imagine what you would see, who you would talk to, and what you might smell as you passed the little shops.

Resources: Visual sources (paintings, prints, books, films); different musical recordings.

Grouping: Interest groups; cluster groups for more experienced students.

Adjustments: Tiered groups based on assessment: Group A for students who write a poem as though it were a paragraph;

Group B for students new to metaphor, simile, and other literary devices; and Group C for children who are comfortable with poetic language and eager to share and experiment.

- *Destination:* Children will understand what biographies are and how biographers gather information.

    Standards: (a) Locate, organize, and use information from various sources to answer questions, solve problems, and communicate ideas. (b) Apply acquired information, concepts, and ideas to communicate in a variety of formats.

    Evidence of understanding: Children can find examples of nonfiction at school and at home (books, newspapers, magazines). They can search sources to check facts and discover what is true and what is not. They can search for information on a real person and write about it.

    Teaching strategy: Questioning; guided inquiry. Teacher has students interview each other. The class draws up a series of questions to get started (e.g., Where were you born? How many kids are in your family? Did you always live where you live now? Do you have any animals? What was the most exciting thing that happened to you?).

    Learning activity: Children write portraits of each other based on interviews. They share their "biographies" with each other and ask if there's anything that should be added or changed. They include photographs or drawings of each other. From here, the class can move on to create a portrait (using text and art) of a famous person. Provide a wide variety of examples, drawing on different areas of accomplishment (arts, technology, literature, human rights, environmental science, etc.) and different cultures. The children can choose sources from articles, books, videos, artwork, prints of the person, photographs of the person's work, and so on. Guide the students on creating an outline of most important points about a person and have them write a short biography.

    Resources: Books, magazines, short films, pictures, drawings.

    Grouping: Pairs.

Adjustments: Accommodate different learning styles by using visual materials to sketch, draw, and make charts and create opportunities for them to dramatize or impersonate the individual they've studied. Add a creative component by having students explore point of view and write their biographies as though they are a friend, a family member, and so forth.

● *Destination:* Children will understand how the main elements of story—setting, characters, plot, dialogue—work together.

Standards: (a) Understand how literary elements and techniques are used to convey meaning. (b) Read and interpret a variety of literary works. (c) Speak effectively using language appropriate to the situation and audience.

Evidence of understanding: Students can identify the elements of fiction in a story. They can interpret these elements through a chamber theater activity.

Teaching strategy: Direct instruction, guided questioning. Go over the different elements of story (setting, characters, plot, dialogue). Next, choose specific scenes from a story for the children to focus on. Ask questions, such as the following: Where are we in this scene? What time of day/year? What happens? What is most important about this scene? Who are the main characters? If we were to act this story out, would we include this scene? Why? Encourage the children to write down their ideas on how they would dramatize this story. What are the most important moments to them?

Learning activity: It's important that everyone have some special role to play in a chamber theater production: actors, narrators, set designers and artists, sound technicians, and scriptwriters. If one book is chosen for an entire class to dramatize, then each scene should have a different narrator. Some students may have a particular interest in creating a soundtrack or in designing a backdrop for their scenes. Children who have no interest in performing should be able to contribute in one of these ways. Staging: Provide each group with instructions to help them stage the scene they've chosen (example:

(1). Narrator says everything except the dialogue. (2). The characters say the dialogue. (3). Children can play other events such as weather or sound. Tie each step of the activity to essential learning about story—setting, characters, dialogue, and plot.

Resources: Videotape, books, stories, costumes, props, art materials.

Grouping: Groups according to interest in specific scenes.

Adjustments: Chamber theater allows children with different learning styles to capitalize on their strengths. You do not have to stick rigidly to narration and dialogue. Some students might prefer to convey the scene through mime and music. Children with particular sensitivities should be able to explore this. You might have a student who can learn the most in this process by creating a soundtrack for the scene that his group is "interpreting."

ASSESS AND ADAPT INSTRUCTION (STEP 5)

This is the critical fifth step in the five-step process. At certain points in the "journey," you will need to take stock of your students' progress (see Chapter 2 for detailed information on assessment). You will need to consider the following:

- Are all my students achieving what I anticipated?

- Do they fully understand the assignment?

- Do they have the means (appropriate activities and materials) to engage in the material?

- Does my lesson or unit challenge students who are ready for more complex tasks as well as support those who may need more time learning a concept or practicing a skill?

Consider what changes you can make to increase your students' understanding—what activities they can do to prepare for future learning and what other ways of working will enable them to demonstrate mastery. In language arts, this would mean, for example, giving some children opportunities to interpret texts, to synthesize ideas from more than one text, and to imagine other possibilities within a text. For less confident or very young students, you might need to simplify or give them smaller steps. They could act out a story narrated by the teacher, anticipate a story's plot by drawing it, write a paragraph rather than an essay and include drawings, or dictate stories rather than write them.

Here's an example of how one teacher assessed her students:

> My class was composing stories. I had used a series of prints pinned up in the front of the class. One group of prints was for the setting; another for the characters; then three other groups for the beginning, the climax, and the end of the story. The kids chose the prints they wanted and created a story of their own. The results showed significant differences between students in terms of grammar, usage, vocabulary, and imagination. Some students showed exceptional imagination but had problems in specific skill areas. Other students had a firm grasp on composition but had too many characters to keep track of. Others struggled both with grammar and basic story composition. The next day, I returned their papers and assigned them a color corresponding to different work areas. Some students practiced skills by checking each other's and, in some cases, reviewing specific grammar rules on work sheets. Others who had problems with the original assignment used prints of their choice and practiced writing simple sentences that describe what happened before and after the picture. Still other students read a short story and wrote down who they thought the main characters were and their reasons why. I had work cards for each of these groups that listed, in clear language, what each child had to produce by the end of the session and the materials they could use.
>
> —*Third-grade teacher*

Most teachers evaluate student progress in this way—by observing the children in different tasks and identifying where they need adjustment. An important extension to this process is giving students opportunities to assess their own work, beginning with their strengths. Examples might include the following:

- reviewing their portfolio to see where they've progressed,
- assessing improvements in an assignment they edited,
- evaluating the ideas they explored in an independent study.

As Chapter 2 brings out, the early years of schooling are pivotal ones in terms of the children's understanding of themselves as learners. It is critical that young students have experiences reviewing and evaluating their achievement in different learning contexts. What stops some teachers from having students assess themselves is the lack of any clear goal or focus. On what basis do the children evaluate themselves? What is the intended outcome? Here's an example of how one teacher encourages a wholesome kind of self-assessment in his students:

> I often write down the important elements of an assignment on the board so that the kids can keep referring to them. Sometimes, I have "criteria cards" for certain assignments, which I keep in my drawer and place in several work areas so the kids can check them. This helps the students a lot when it comes to assessing their own or their peers' work. If I just ask a child what she likes about something she did, I get a lot of hemming and hawing. But criteria lists give the kids a focus and help them evaluate specific strengths and weaknesses. I had a child who was painfully shy, but the criteria list enabled him to tell me what he liked about his work, where he thought he did well, and where he needed more help.
>
> —*Second-grade teacher*

When children have a firm grasp on the criteria by which their work will be judged and gain practice in evaluating their strengths and weaknesses, assessment becomes less frightening and less mysterious. Repeated experiences such as this can have lifelong consequences— diminishing the perfectionism and self-belittlement that can cripple a child's growth and development at an early age.

In addition to the kind of qualitative assessment just considered, you may occasionally find rating scales or rubrics helpful in targeting areas of specific need. On the following page is an example of a rating scale and a rubric (see Chapter 2 for more information).

RATING SCALE

Name: _____

Assignment: Write a fractured fairy tale by changing a character.

Learning objectives:

• To understand how character affects plot.

• To learn how important characters are to the suspense and conflict of a story.

Criteria: **Rating Scale (1–3):**

• The changed character is vividly described. _____

• The changes to the plot are based on the character. _____

• The new story works as a story. _____

Comments: _____

_____

RUBRIC ON BIOGRAPHICAL EXHIBIT			
Criteria	**Come for help.**	**You're on the right track.**	**Excellent work. Keep going!**
Notes on three events: • **Times** • **Places** • **People involved**	No notes present.	Notes include two events; notes omit times, places, or people involved.	Notes include vivid detail on three events; all key points covered.

Criteria	Come for help.	You're on the right track.	Excellent work. Keep going!
"Memory collection": • **Meaningful objects that remind you of this person (gifts, objects owned by person, etc.)** • **Photographs or sketches that remind you of special experience**	The collection doesn't have anything that belonged to the person.	The collection has one of the two categories but not both.	The collection was thoughtfully compiled and is complete.
Three scenes (painted, sketched, or depicted through collage) of important events in this person's life	No more than one scene is present, or scenes are sketchy, hastily done.	Two scenes are completed; scenes have detail and imagination.	Scenes are detailed and expressive. All three are complete.
Writing under each sketch: • **Composition quality** • **When events happened** • **What happened** • **Who else was part of the experience**	Writing is full of incomplete sentences. Includes only one of three elements (when, what, who).	Writing is clear but has minor grammatical errors. Includes two of the three elements.	Writing is excellent—clear, vivid, and complete on all points.

Both the rating scale and rubric provide an opportunity for you and the child to sit down and go over the most important elements of an assignment and what changes she might need. Be sure to begin, as always, with what the students are doing well. A rubric is particularly helpful in making assessment more transparent to the student and helping her see where her work falls within different areas of an assignment. A child may be at a fairly advanced level in some areas and a more beginning level in others. Unlike traditional assignments where a student could receive a low mark based on one criterion (e.g., composition), a rubric has a number of criteria. By increasing the number of areas where a child may show her strengths, you are giving her a more solid foundation to build on.

In a differentiated classroom, assessment should always increase students' understanding of their own needs as learners and help you make appropriate adjustments as the class progresses through the curriculum. As explained more thoroughly in Chapter 2, assessment is the steering wheel that enables you to navigate your students through the many options and opportunities that a differentiated curriculum provides.

LOOKING AHEAD

The next chapter applies the five-step process to social studies. It draws on the skills and learning that students gain from language arts and examines what young children need to support their earliest lessons in history, geography, and other related subjects.

SAMPLE OF STATE GOALS AND STANDARDS (ILLINOIS)

Goal 1: Read with understanding and fluency

Standards:

- **Apply word analysis and vocabulary skills to comprehend selections.** (Early elementary: Apply word analysis skills to recognize new words. Comprehend unfamiliar words using context clues and prior knowledge; verify meanings with resource materials.)

- **Apply reading strategies to improve understanding and fluency.** (Early elementary: Establish purposes for reading, make predictions, connect important ideas, and link text to previous experiences and knowledge. Identify genres [forms and purposes] of fiction, nonfiction, poetry, and electronic literary forms. Continuously check and clarify for understanding. Read age-appropriate material aloud with fluency and accuracy.)

- **Comprehend a broad range of reading materials.** (Early elementary: Use information to form questions and verify predictions. Identify important themes and topics. Make comparisons across
reading selections. Summarize content of reading material using text organization. Identify how authors and illustrators express their ideas in text and graphics. Use information presented in simple tables, maps, and charts to form an interpretation.)

Goal 2: Read and understand literature representative of various societies, eras, and ideas

Standards:

- **Understand how literary elements and techniques are used to convey meaning.** (Early elementary: Identify the literary elements of theme, setting, plot, and character within literary works. Classify literary works as fiction or nonfiction. Describe differences between prose and poetry.)

- **Read and interpret a variety of literary works.** (Early elementary: Respond to literary materials by connecting them to their own experience and communicate those responses to others. Identify common themes in literature from a variety of eras. Relate character, setting, and plot to real-life situations.)

Goal 3: Write to communicate for a variety of purposes

Standards:

- **Use correct grammar, spelling, punctuation, capitalization, and structure.** (Early elementary: Construct complete sentences that demonstrate subject-verb agreement; appropriate capitalization and punctuation; correct spelling of appropriate, high-frequency words; and appropriate use of the eight parts of speech.)

- **Compose well-organized and coherent writing for specific purposes and audiences.** (Early elementary: Use prewriting strategies to generate and organize ideas. Demonstrate focus, organization, elaboration, and integration in written compositions.)

- **Communicate ideas in writing to accomplish a variety of purposes.** (Early elementary: Write for a variety of purposes, including description, information, explanation, persuasion, and narration. Create media compositions or productions that convey meaning visually for a variety of purposes.)

Goal 4: Listen and speak effectively in a variety of situations

Standards:

- Listen effectively in formal and informal situations. (Early elementary: Listen attentively by facing the speaker, making eye contact, and paraphrasing what is said. Ask questions and respond to questions from the teacher and from group members to improve comprehension. Follow oral instructions accurately. Use visually oriented and auditorily based media.)

- Speak effectively using language appropriate to the situation and audience. (Early elementary: Present brief oral reports, using language and vocabulary appropriate to the message and audience. Participate in discussions around a common topic.)

Goal 5: Use the language arts to acquire, assess, and communicate information

Standards:

- **Locate, organize, and use information from various sources to answer questions, solve problems, and communicate ideas.** (Early elementary: Identify questions and gather information. Locate information using a variety of resources.)

- **Analyze and evaluate information acquired from various sources.** (Early elementary: Select and organize information from various sources for a specific purpose. Cite sources used.)

- **Apply acquired information, concepts, and ideas to communicate in a variety of formats.** (Early elementary: Write letters, reports, and stories based on acquired information. Use print, nonprint, human, and technological resources to acquire and use information.)

6 Differentiated Instruction Applied to Social Studies

Quest Academy, Palatine, Illinois

*To excel the past we must not allow ourselves to
lose contact with it; on the contrary, we must feel it
under our feet because we raised ourselves upon it.*
—*Jose Ortega y Gasset*

For most young children, the world is their home and neighborhood street. If their families move from one town to another, or if they travel in the summers, they begin to see a larger horizon of places with different terrains, towns, and people. But even here their concept of geography depends on concrete experiences. A 5-year-old once moved to England with her family, crossing the Atlantic by ship. Pulling into Liverpool, she burst into tears, and when her parents asked what was wrong, she cried, "Where's the beach?" All across the ocean, she had been anticipating sandy beaches, based, no doubt, on the assumption that if England is an island, then it must be beach.

Similarly, young children understand past time as they experience it. They can tell you about "when I was little," and some can explain what happened "before I was born," but you cannot expect them to conceptualize an event "200 years ago." To make both history and geography meaningful to young children, therefore, we need to give them ways to touch, feel, sense, and imagine other times and places. Through direct learning experiences, a time when only Native Americans and animals crossed the plains of North America or a place as far as Mount Kilimanjaro in East Africa can become something they can "feel under [their] feet."

THE BIG PICTURE: SOCIAL STUDIES

In many ways, the social studies are explorations in time and space. Children use many of the same skills and proficiencies as in language arts (reading and writing) and develop thinking through imagining, visualizing, intuitive sensing, measuring, feeling, speaking, constructing, and moving. They study and design maps; explore other cultures and societies through food, song, dance, clothing, architecture, and stories; and dramatize events in government and law.

Because young children process information and concepts in concrete ways, you need to design social studies experiences that enable them to internalize new concepts. Here is an example:

> We were learning our directions: north, south, east, west. The children understood that the sun rises in the east and sets in the west. We also live near Lake Michigan, which is always east of us, and this was another way we could tell where we were. I had put a blue sign saying "east" on the side of our classroom facing the lake and, from there, let the children tell me where to put the other signs. We named towns and places we knew in our area of Illinois and where we thought they were—near the lake or far? Toward the end of this process, one of my Mexican students blurted out, "My grandma calls where we live El Norte!"
>
> She had suddenly understood why her grandmother, who lived in Mexico, always called the United States "El Norte," and this led the class to think about spatial relationships. Another child who moved from Canada said that Canadians could call America "the south" if they wanted to. For a whole week, we explored these concepts, and when we began working with globes, these kindergarteners understood that where a particular place is depends on where *they* are. We made an enormous map of North, Central, and South America with major rivers and lakes colored in with blue.

The kids enjoyed standing in different places and saying where they were in relation to other kids, while others looked on maps and tried to figure out the names of the places.

—*Kindergarten teacher*

Developing hands-on experiences that help young children discover and conceptualize essential content is indispensable. You can approach this challenge through four fundamental questions that encompass not only history and geography but also other related fields—economics, government, culture, anthropology, and archeology. The four questions are as follows:

1. Where in the world am I? (land/ocean; north/south/east/west; continent; country; state; town; government; culture; economics)

2. What is beyond my street, town, state, country? (other lands; oceans; cultures; histories; governments)

3. What was here a long, long time ago? What was my town? Who lived here? (early settlers; Native Americans; environmental surroundings; economics; government)

4. What was in other places a long, long time ago? (governments; economies; histories; peoples; cultures)

These questions begin with the child's level of experience. The first and second questions are more oriented to geography, where students begin conceptualizing themselves in the world and understanding where they are in relation to other lands and oceans. They focus on physical space and expand into other areas, such as government and culture. Children can

- visualize spatial relations;
- measure distances;
- compare and contrast;
- trace and improvise with shapes (states, towns, bodies of water);
- move along directional lines;
- estimate sizes, distances, shapes.

The third and fourth questions focus more on history, both in their own place and in places outside their country, continent, and town. They include related subjects such as culture, anthropology, economics, politics, and sociology. To "feel [the past] under [their] feet," young students can

- imagine themselves as living in another time;
- role-play different scenarios in history;

- interpret events or ideas through mime, dance, dramatizations, and paintings;

- pose questions about the past;

- search and gather information from a range of media and materials;

- synthesize ideas from different sources.

Using the questions, your list of state standards (see sample standards at the end of Chapters 5–8), and your knowledge of your students' needs, you can identify the most important concepts, proficiencies, and skills that you want them to master. As in the language arts chapter, you can use the standards as a map of the territory to be explored—the essential content all students should gain in their "travels." Looking ahead to the next few months, for example, a teacher might realize that the units he's planned fall under several categories or broader ones:

1. chronological and spatial thinking,

2. cause-and-effect relationships (e.g., in history, environment, politics, economics),

3. research process (gathering information, analyzing and evaluating evidence),

4. interpretation and point of view.

These are only four possible categories. When you identify the essential content of a subject, you can anchor the learning activities in one of these categories. This will simplify the process of creating adjustments for children who need it.

> Before I started my first-grade unit on Mexico, I knew that I wanted all my kids to master the process of posing a question, finding sources, and presenting their findings. Because many of my students are Mexican, they were able to come up with questions they wanted to explore (e.g., "How do people live in my mother's village? What do they wear? Who are the famous singers and actors? Who's in charge of the towns?"). They interviewed their families, read, looked at photos and prints, explored maps, sketched, and wrote their ideas. Because of the range of ability in my room, I created tiered groups with increasing demand in terms of skill (reading and writing) and level of thinking.
>
> —*Third-grade teacher*

Standards can sometimes aid in defining priorities for a process such as the above. However, for many teachers, standards feel like an endless "to-do" list that they have little hope of completing. In addition, because social studies as a general subject includes four or more disciplines, it presents educators with vastly more territory than other subject areas. Rather than try to "cover" this territory, many teachers prefer to make choices about what areas they will explore deeply. The best way to do this is to identify (a) what you believe are the most important concepts and skills young children should gain from social studies and (b) what areas of study will get them there.

Chapters 1 and 2 cover this step in detail. See added text on pages 126–128 in Chapter 5.

CHOOSE THE LEARNING "DESTINATION" (STEP 2)

As explained in the last chapter, choosing your learning "destination" must follow a thorough review of who your students are and what unique knowledge, skills, needs, and interests they bring to your learning table (see Chapters 1 and 2). Then, as before, consider the following points (Wiggins & McTighe, 1998, pp. 10–11):

- *The "big idea" of enduring understanding.* In social studies, this might be that the geography of a place (north, south, east, west; mountains, plains, desert, etc.) affects how people live.

- *The idea, topic, or process that resides at the heart of the discipline.* An example might be a unit where children imagine being someone from a different place or time and write or sketch their "experiences." Point of view is essential to understanding culture and history.

- *The idea, topic, or process requires uncoverage.* An example of this might be synthesizing information from different sources (books, prints, talks with people) and identifying what's most important. To do this, children need to learn how to ask questions, search for answers, and pick out the most important points.

- *The idea, topic, or process engages students.* An example might be to write historical fiction, design a historical village, or design a map based on their particular interest—animal life, trees, famous people, and so on.

Most teachers of young students integrate the different areas of social studies within specific topics. You may have sessions where children practice their map skills or focus on historical events, but many of your units most likely combine the disciplines of history, geography, economics, politics, sociology, and culture. A kindergarten teacher, for example, may combine lessons on the seven major continents with climate, clothing, and culture. Young children trace the shapes of continents; examine where the bodies of water, forests, mountains, and plains are; explore pictures of people and animals; sample foods; wear the clothing; and touch objects from a particular area (utensils, pottery, crafts, jewelry).

Integrating the subject areas of social studies gives young children choices in how they process the information and concepts. Geography, history, economics, political science, and other disciplines demand different strengths—visual thinking, imagining, reasoning, intuiting, analyzing, and synthesizing. In various ways, all of these disciplines focus on one thing: the world around the young child—the world of land, sea, mountain, and desert; of places and peoples in times gone by; of the endless exchange of goods and services; and of law and government. From babyhood through the toddler years, the young child's universe has revolved around home and family. The early elementary years give them their first forays into the world beyond. Below is an example of how one teacher engaged her students in geography:

> I had created an enormous blank map of the United States, pushed back the desks, and set it on the floor. The point of the map was to give my students a tangible way to conceptualize, feel, experience the scope and variety of the United States. Through the map we reviewed directions (north, south, east, west), and the children could crawl right onto the map to find our state (Illinois) and where we were in relation to other states and focus on the different terrains and climates. One group was in charge of water—the major rivers, the lakes, etc. Another group did mountains. Another deserts. Another the plains. They consulted other maps. They measured. They drew the water, mountains, deserts, plains. Some kids created symbols for certain animals, so we could tell where the wolves were, where you could find bald eagles, where the salmon run. They listened to weather reports at home and made cutout images of snow, wind, and rain and stuck them on the map with little bits of tape. What I noticed was how constantly the children touched the map, feeling the different places, delighting in every new detail added that made it more real, telling everyone who would listen where they lived or where they had

gone to visit someone. Children kept adding things to it. A couple of children wrote poems, and I hung them along the edge. Others wanted to mark other towns or places where their families came from. This map became a reference for everything we did in social studies.

—Second-grade teacher

Finding a catalyst such as this enables you to tie history, political science, economics, culture, and sociology to specific places that the children can see, trace, feel, and imagine. Because of the range of processes involved (e.g., visual thinking, measuring, reasoning), this interactive map can reach young students with different learning styles and needs.

IDENTIFY EVIDENCE OF UNDERSTANDING (STEP 3)

As with language arts, you need to think carefully about how you will know that the children actually understand the concepts and skills you teach. In social studies, evidence of understanding can take a number of forms, but in each case, it needs to demonstrate that a child has internalized whatever concept or skill you plan to teach. Young children can perform a series of tasks without necessarily understanding the concept well enough to apply it to other contexts. For example, a first grader might be able to tell you that Maine is in the east and California is in the west (because that is what he learned in class), but he may not be able to tell you which states are east and west of Illinois when he looks at a map.

If you intend children to understand directions on a map and where they live in relation to other places, bodies of water, and mountains, deserts, and so forth, you could design activities where they can

- explore directions based on geographical features (e.g., in Chicago, Lake Michigan is always east; in Oregon, the Pacific Ocean is always west);
- show the directions on a map and combine directions (e.g., north and east vs. north and west; south and east vs. south and west);
- use a compass to determine directions in the classroom and walk north, south, east, and west when asked;
- describe how to get from one town to the next in terms of directions (e.g., "you drive on Highway 90 east to get to Massachusetts from Chicago").

Consider many different ways that children can demonstrate understanding (drawing, diagramming, moving, explaining). Cognitive growth
can be uneven in young students. There are children eager to read (or
already reading) by the time they enter kindergarten; others become
active readers in third or even fourth grade. It's not uncommon to see a
young child struggle to acquire a particular skill or concept (such as map
reading) and then suddenly master it. During this extraordinary time of
learning and growing (K–3), you can provide a variety of ways for children to engage in new material, not pushing too hard in any area where
a child needs more time to mature.

PLAN THE JOURNEY (STEP 4)

As explained in the previous chapter, creating a catalyst that enables children to engage their whole selves in a process is indispensable. You can
use maps through the ages, artwork, costumes, building materials, stories, myths, cartoons, prints of animals, performing arts traditions from
other cultures, pictures of homes around the United States or the world,
and historical fiction. A teacher found that using the concept of the story
was a good catalyst for social studies:

> Young children love learning through stories, and I think we
> can capitalize on this more than we do. In a series of units, I
> had my third-grade class explore various bodies of water in
> the United States. What I wanted them all to understand was
> that each body of water was created in its own way and that
> people depend on it for different things (e.g., food, drinking
> water, and transportation). I read them Thomas Locker's
> Water Dance and explained that every river, stream, lake,
> and pond has a story. We spent a great deal of time on Lake
> Michigan since we're in the Chicago area. Some kids drew
> sketches of how the lake began as a glacier; others wrote sto-
> ries about Native American populations near the shore; oth-
> ers created maps of early settlements in the Chicago area.
> Children expressed their ideas in a variety of ways—a
> mime/dance piece about the lake's changes through time;
> autobiographies from the point of view of the lake; poetry
> about some aspect of the changes that the lake has seen; art-
> work, essays, and stories.

—Third-grade teacher

Introduce a New Unit to Preassess

As you begin a new unit in social studies, think about the students who may have already mastered a portion of the content. Consider also those whose verbal/writing skills have not caught up with their growth in other areas and who therefore need other ways to process new concepts or practice new skills. To engage the children in such a way that everyone can learn the same content at a level and in a way appropriate for them, you obviously need a clear understanding of their experiences, abilities, and problem areas. Sometimes, preassessment can be done simply, as follows:

- a map test to gauge children's map skills or knowledge of specific geographic information;
- a paragraph answering the question, "Tell me everything you know about . . .";
- explain (in writing or out loud) what a "custom" is and provide an example in another culture and in America.

Other units ask much more of students in terms of higher level thinking and skill development. When you need to know the level at which young students can work on a project, try doing an introductory activity where you can observe the children firsthand. The following teacher illustrates this:

> We were spending the week exploring how our area looked many, many years ago. I wanted the children to understand that environments change over time. As an introduction, I had prints of what our area once looked like and read a story about the little rural house that became dwarfed by the city that grew up around it (*The Little House*, by Virginia Lee Burton). I had them close their eyes and imagine living in this other time. I asked, "If you were a tree that lived for many years, what would you say about the changes in your world?" The children sketched their ideas and told stories. Some of the children could already write enough to get their ideas out; others could not; others were able to tell their story while miming it at the same time. Still others had grandparents who remembered specific things, such as, "Over there where the new mall is, there was once an apple orchard where they used to go and pick apples."
>
> —*Kindergarten teacher*

From the students' responses, you can gauge their level of understanding and the skills they have. Because social studies often involves more than knowing specific facts or mastering certain skills, an introductory process like this will help you plan appropriate instruction. Not only will you see which students need what, but you'll be able to assess the range of ability and skill in this subject and also the areas that need "uncoverage." For example, some children may understand that in the place where a supermarket now stands, cows once grazed a long time ago. But they may not understand that the land all around them was different—dotted with farms and covered by forest. To internalize the concept of the past, children may need to explore historic sites and the material culture of the time—horses and buggies, building styles from older times, clothing, and technology. Picture books such as Aliki's *Corn Is Maize: The Gift of the Indians* can open up this sort of investigation for young children.

Sequence Teaching Strategies and Learning Activities

The following are examples of how you can structure your units, beginning with what you want the students to understand. As you rethink your own curriculum, turn the goals that you have into a statement that says *where you want your children to be* as a result of these units. Explore ways that will accommodate the great need of young children for a full, sensory experience—touching, feeling, moving, hearing, speaking, imagining. When you read a story, have several children mime the action, rotating them so that everyone has a chance. Draw sketches on an easel to give them a picture of someone in history or in another environment (you don't have to be an artist; most kids are enthralled to see their teacher sketch things out as they talk). Ask the students for details to add to the picture.

- *Destination:* Children will understand that Africa is a continent of many countries, peoples, features, and climates.

    Standard: Locate, describe, and explain places, regions, and features on the Earth.

    Evidence: Children can explain the difference between a country and a continent. They can name countries in Africa and show where they are. They can draw many features on a map of the African continent such as desert, forest, and rivers, as well as some of the major groups of people, plant life, and animals.

Teaching strategy: Inquiry; guided imagery and questioning. Example: Guide the children on an imaginary trip to Africa. To review map-reading skills, have a map of the world and ask, "Where are we on the North American continent?" When the children figure out where their state is, have them imagine that they're going to travel from where they live to the East Coast of the United States and then across the Atlantic Ocean to Africa. Ask, "Which side of Africa will we land—west or east? What kind of climate, land, people, plant, and animal life will we find?" Provide different sources to feed the children's imagination. Create an itinerary for their exploration of the continent (e.g., west to east; then follow the Nile from its sources in Uganda and Ethiopia to Egypt and then back down, across Lake Victoria to end eventually in South Africa). You can divide the class into groups to focus on specific areas of the continent (north, south, etc.) and the people, animals, geographical features, climate, and so on.

Learning activity: Children work on their own blank maps of the African continent. They fill in country names where they "travel." They examine different maps of the continent—geological, climate, cultural, and ethnic—and add details that interest them. They write journal entries (and create sketches) of their experiences journeying by car, train, foot, boat, and so forth, including details about the people they met, the food they ate, the music, animal sightings, and so on. They design symbols for a legend and place those symbols in the right areas of the map.

Resources: Maps; globes; compasses; magazines; photography of the different places, peoples, and animals in North, South, East, West, and Central Africa; art supplies; writing materials. Ask the students if they have anything from Africa they would like to share—baskets, tapes, instruments, videos, and so forth.

Grouping: Voluntary interest groups; pairs; independent.

Adjustments: Independent study for advanced students (explore other aspects of the continent such as musical traditions, stories, environmental issues). Children who need more practice with map reading can spend more time on directions and the different geological features. You can use a simple story to aid them (e.g., Tomie dePaola's *Bill and Pete Go Down the Nile*).

- *Destination*: Children will understand that the Native Americans were the first Americans and that they include many different ethnic groups with their own culture, language, and connection to the land.

  Standard: Apply the skills of historical analysis and interpretation.

  Evidence: The children can identify the Native American ethnic groups who lived in their state long ago and give examples of Native American words for places near them. They can sketch the kind of homes the people built to survive in the environment and explain how their clothing and food sources related to their environment. They can show on a map what Native American groups live in their state today.

  Teaching strategy: Inquiry; guided questioning. You can use a variety of sources (see bibliographic sections at the end of this book) to engage students' imagination about the Native Americans who lived before the White man came to the continent. Read stories, show videos, and have crafts for them to touch and observe. Some teachers also ask if any students in the class have Native American heritage. If some do, you can invite them to share what they know and possibly use them as a resource. Focus on your state in the introductory part of your unit or lesson. After the children have had time to respond to the catalysts you've provided (stories, paintings, photographs, etc.), ask them to focus on the kind of place their state was long ago. Was it mostly forest, plains, mountains, or desert? Where are the rivers, lakes, and sea? Ask the children to predict (based on their knowledge of climate and terrain) how Native Americans must have lived in the past, what sorts of materials they would have used for clothing and shelter, and how they provided food for themselves.

  Learning activity: Children choose a Native American place name and create a past-to-present display of the people who lived there. For example, those who live in Chicago might begin with the original Native American name—"Chicagou"—a name conferred by the Potawatomi Nation. It means "stinky onion" in honor of the many stinky onions they found there. The students could create an art piece about the "stinky onion" and write short essays, biographies, or historical fiction about the Potawatomi Nation—their early life by the Great Lakes and their life today. Through materials you provide and any human resources available to you (e.g., someone from a particular nation), they can explore architecture, culture, tales, ceremonies, and philosophy and compose a poem for their display. They can design a collage of images and text that integrates historic events with Potawatomi names, traditions, stories, and material culture.

Resources: Prints and pictures of Native Americans in your state, magazines, books (historical books, tales, sayings), materials from a Native American nation (check the Internet for Web sites designed by nations that sell materials for schools), art sources, maps.

Grouping: Learning-style groups. Some students could express their understanding through writing (poems, stories, essays); others can create maps with diagrams and sketches telling the story; others can construct dwellings and so forth.

Adjustments: Many options are possible here. Advanced readers can explore related topics in depth, as well as compose biographies and stories; other students can construct a model village; others can create comparative maps of the areas in your state where Native Americans lived long ago and where they live today.

- *Destination:* Children will understand what representative government is and how it differs from other forms of government.

    Standard: Understand and explain basic principles of the U.S. government.

    Evidence: Children can define the word *represent* in their own words. They can vote for some students (each one with a group) who will "represent" the interests of the class within certain categories (class behavior between students, curriculum topics to be included, etc.). They can compare representative government with dictatorial forms of government.

    Teaching strategy: Direct instruction; simulations and role-playing; guided discussion. You can begin by introducing the concepts of representative rule versus a situation where the ruled have no say in what happens. Begin with a simulation. Example: Have children imagine that you've just created a whole new set of classroom rules that the children must obey. They could include: absolute obedience to anything you say; refraining from all speech, even to ask questions; no laughter; no moving around in their seats; and especially no whispering to each other about how bad the class is. You can write these laws down for the children to see, saying, "These are now laws because I created them and I'm in charge. If you break any of these laws, you will be sent to jail (in the corner) until I decide to let you out." Start ordering the children around, giving them random assignments such as moving the trash can to another place in the room, rearranging books, hopping in a certain way, and so forth. Send the children to "jail" at the slightest infraction (you can construct a "jail" from cardboard) and have several children be the police who arrest students and take them there. Obviously, you need to do this sensitively so as to avoid scaring the students. Most young children fall naturally into simulation, because it reminds them of their own play. After the simulation, ask, "How do you feel about this situation? Why don't you like it? Is this a fair system? Why or why not? How could it be different? How would you make sure that the kids in the class can be part of the rules?" Guide the discussion in such a way that students stay focused on the concept of representation.

Learning activity: Divide students into groups and assign a "representative" for each. Give each group a list of areas of classroom life that they can debate and propose rules for (e.g., who talks when; the sharing of supplies that everyone likes to use; what new topics could be included in the curriculum; what favorite activities they would like to do, etc.). They tell the reasons why and the spokesperson writes them down. Each group has a spokesperson who states what the group wants—thus "representing" them. The whole class discusses and votes on each "law." You can make links between this and our own Congress, although the legislative process is far more complex in government. Explain that you have "veto power" and what that is. You can then veto some of the laws passed by the class and offer a compromise. This activity can lead to a number of extensions. The children can write short essays on what they liked about the representative government exercise versus the dictatorial one. They can create a story about belonging to a country where they had no representation and how they felt coming to the United States.

Resources: Posters and markers for writing laws, art materials, stories about immigrants to America escaping dictatorship.

Grouping: Voluntary groups; independent work.

Adjustments: After the initial group activity on law, children can work at tables according to specific needs. Some may wish to read about former political prisoners who have helped change government for their people (e.g., Mandela). Others could interview people in their family who came from less democratic countries and ask why they came to the United States and how it was different. Still others could create a diagram of the U.S. government and a map of the legislative process.

- *Destination:* Children will understand what "currency" is and how it evolved from simple trade.

   Standard: Understand the development of economic systems.

   Evidence: Children can describe from personal experience what trade is (e.g., "I traded my stuffed koala bear for a Madeline doll"). They can name precoinage currencies used in other cultures and create their own currency. They can engage in discussions about the "value" of assorted objects in terms of this currency.

   Teaching strategy: Inquiry; guided simulations; questioning. Provide a wide range of objects that the children can "trade." Explain what *bartering* is in a trade situation like this. Give the students clear directions about who they are, where they live, what they need to trade, what they need to "buy," and ideas on how to barter. (Some of them may need food for their families and have baskets or clothing to sell; others need shoes and have shawls to trade, etc.) You can improvise a marketplace where the children can barter. Focus their thoughts on how they decide the value of the things they want to trade. After the activity, children write about their day at the marketplace and draw pictures of the scene. Ask, "What items did you need when you were trading? What did you have that others needed or wanted? How did you barter? What was difficult about this? What did you like about it?"

Learning activity: Expose the children to books and pictures on precoinage currencies. Examples could include *cowry shells*, used from ancient times (4000 B.C.) in the African continent and throughout the world. Another example is the *manilas*, which entered West African economies in the 15th century. Made of copper or brass, they were shaped like bracelets, and different sizes had different values. Have the students create a currency of their own from commonplace objects (rocks, metal objects, different-sized paper clips). With guidance, they can work out, for example, how many paper clips equal the value of a rock, as well as which objects will buy specific foods, clothes, and other things they need. They can jot these down as approximate amounts. Explain that they can still barter as before, but this time, they will use these objects as a "currency." Again, provide scenarios that identify who they are, what they need, and so forth. Have the children make entries in their journals about what they sold and bought, what the exchange of currency was, and how they know whether they made a good or fair trade. You can reinforce the concepts learned through a number of writing activities comparing the two experiences, drawing the currencies and their value in the marketplace and so on.

Resources: Cards with directions for the simulations, costumes, examples of cowry shells, a variety of objects for child-created "currencies," journals, art materials.

Grouping: Groups and roles assigned according to ability and knowledge.

Adjustments: Advanced students can work in a cluster to create more sophisticated currency. Children who need more practice can continue to trade and make notes on the results.

- *Destination:* Children will understand the relationship between geographic location and a people's way of life (culture, clothing, arts).

    Standard: Understand relationships between geographic factors and society.

    Evidence: Children can give examples of environments that determine the kinds of homes people make, clothing they wear, food they eat, and stories they tell. They can sketch examples of homes made from local materials (e.g., igloos, log cabins) and give examples of cultural traditions that draw from environmental features (e.g., dances that imitate the movements of animals).

    Teaching strategy: Direct instruction; inquiry-based instruction; questioning. Choose a number of different places and climates (e.g., Alaska, Sahara, Peruvian rainforest, the mountains of Nepal). Read a story about a particular environment (e.g., *Bringing the Rain to Kapiti Plain: A Nandi Tale,* Dial, 1981) and other stories. Pose questions, such as, "How do nomadic people who travel through desert areas live? How do they create shelter? Where do they find food? What sort of clothing do they have? What do you see in the culture of the people (songs, dances, stories, ceremonies, etc.) that comes from the environment?" Similar projects could focus on other environments—polar, rainforest, coastal, and so on. Ask, "If you lived in a world of snow, what kind of house would you build? What would you wear? What would you eat?" Through stories, videos, photographs, magazines, and other materials, guide students in exploring how different people adapt to their environments. Help them find these places on the map, trace the shapes of countries or areas on art paper, and create sketches of the people who live there, the designs of their homes, and the local materials they use for clothing (e.g., bark cloth in Uganda), local pigments for color, seeds and stones for jewelry, and so on.

    Learning activity: Children undertake different projects depending on strengths, needs, and interests. With a focus on the relationships between place, climate, and society, they construct small igloos with sugar cubes (or other structure), sketch clothing used by particular peoples, explore legends (such as Pat Mora's retelling of the Mayan legend in *The Night the Moon Fell/La Noche Que Se Cayó La Luna*), and create their own legends through art, song, stories, and poems. The children can craft masks and dramatize local tales, songs, and sayings. They can write journal entries of their imaginary travels with details on the food they ate, where they slept, who they visited, and what they saw. They can identify local flora and fauna in their entries and sketch maps of where they went.

Resources: Books, pictures, *National Geographic* and other magazines, art supplies, construction materials, videos, tapes of sounds in different environments.

Grouping: Interest groups based on their strengths and experiences (e.g., a group constructing or designing homes; a group sketching a map with their own legend indicating the kinds of houses and foods and clothes that exist there; a group exploring mythologies, cultural practices, and stories from different areas).

Adjustments: Cluster group for advanced students who are ready for a more involved project (e.g., a dramatization of a day in the life of a village, the staging of a myth involving the local environment, the creation of their own myths based on the elements or features of a place).

- *Destination:* Childen will understand that the U.S. government and laws protect the freedom of speech.

  Standard: Understand the development of U.S. political ideas and traditions.

  Evidence: Children can explain in their own words what *freedom of speech* means. They can give examples of it.

  Teaching strategy: Inquiry; guided questioning. As an introduction, you can guide students to review their own experiences—at school, in the playground, or at home—when they saw something they didn't feel was right. Brainstorm what these "wrongs" might include: cruelty to animals, teasing other kids, a mean remark, a dangerous trick or prank, and so forth. Encourage them to share their experiences. Ask, "Did you feel free to speak up? Why or why not? What happened? What were you afraid of that stopped you from speaking? Or, what made you decide to speak no matter what?" Most young children have had many experiences where they spoke up about a perceived injustice (especially if they feel they were the target!). Have the children write down (a) what the "injustice" was, (b) what they said, and (c) what happened. As they share their stories, write down the issue at stake (personal property, harm to one's person, kindness, sharing, etc.).

Learning activity: Make a link between the children's experiences and the issues U.S. citizens stand for in demonstrations and rallies (e.g., equal treatment of all people—in pay, access to housing, special services, etc.). Explain the lack of freedom in many other countries where speaking out can get people arrested. Students can explore the lives of brave voices for justice (e.g., Nelson Mandela and the Dalai Lama) who took great risks to speak out against wrongs in their countries. They can examine the hardships of such leaders as Martin Luther King Jr., who acted on his right of free speech to organize rallies and demonstrations. They can write biographies, biographical poems, songs, or raps about individuals who have struggled for the right of free speech.

Resources: Magazines and newspapers, videos, materials on people persecuted for being outspoken, biographies, photographs, prints, art materials.

Grouping: Tiered groups; interest groups.

Adjustments: Children can grasp "freedom of speech" at different levels. Young children have a keen sense of justice, and many of them will be able to relate to scenarios that involve speaking out against, for example, a schoolyard bully picking on kids or someone trying to sneak more snacks for himself. Some young students can make the conceptual leap to larger, national situations, and some cannot so easily. Provide different ways and materials for children to grapple with the concept of "freedom of speech" in the larger world context. They can write letters to "prisoners of conscience" or can create a collage that includes examples of free speech (headlines critical of government policies, signs of protest, quotes from famous speeches, etc.).

ASSESS AND ADAPT INSTRUCTION (STEP 5)

As the last chapter explains, assessment should involve students in evaluating their own work. To facilitate this, you will need to provide clear criteria of the important elements of an assignment. Ideally, the students should know this *while* they are working so that they have every opportunity to demonstrate their understanding and skill within specific areas. When reviewing portfolios, projects, or exercises with the children, keep the following in mind:

- **Start with their strengths.** Ask them what they like about their work (writing/art/map, etc.). You can then add to what they say, noting specific areas where you feel they have done well.

- **Point to the criteria.** Instead of launching into their errors or weak areas, turn to the criteria first. Review these and ask if there are places where they might make changes. Again, you can then add to what the children say and show where they could make improvements. Refer them continually back to their strengths while you do this. Children will be more able to learn from their mistakes if you proceed this way.

- **Clarify areas of need.** Make sure that the children understand where they made their mistakes or what areas of an assignment need strengthening. Keep asking questions to be sure they know what to fix or change.

- **Create a new plan.** Work with the children on a new plan. They can either redo an assignment, move on to a more advanced project (if their work meets all the criteria), or find an alternative way to approach an assignment (due to differences in learning style, for example).

In almost any activity, criteria lists should guide how you assess the students' progress and create adjustments to their assignments. For example, if you're focusing on map-reading skills, you might have three groups of kids, each working at a different level of complexity. One group might have a card with the following criteria listed:

Goal: Understand where north, south, east, and west (northeast, northwest, southeast, southwest, middle) are.

Criteria:

- Can label at least nine states, representing different directions within the borders of the United States

- Can pick four or more states at random out of a box and write down what direction they are in relation to the student's state

Other students may have a more challenging version of this. For example, a group of advanced students may write down directions between two points that would involve choosing the routes and describing the directions to get from Point A to Point B. When you have simple cards like these with the criteria listed, you can easily identify whether a child has really internalized the concept or has a partial understanding. You can also discover other things—which children have special abilities in visual-spatial thinking or who may need to engage the content through other activities such as dramatized storytelling, the construction of models, or creative movement.

This clarifies what's most important in an assignment—both for you and the children—and helps you see the areas where they may need more support or challenge. The importance of this becomes more obvious when students undertake projects that require more qualitative assessments. For example, if children are writing short biographies, staging scenes, or drawing pictures about people at a particular moment in history, you can create a developmental rubric to guide them. Here is an example:

Assignment: Choose a famous person or animal in the past and write a biography that tells why he or she was so important to the people in that time.

> *Example:* The widespread fame of the racehorse Seabiscuit in the 1930s.

Criteria	Come for help.	You're on the right track. Keep going.	Excellent work!
Has background information: • **who** • **where from** • **circumstances of person or animal's beginnings**	Provides little background information	Includes two of the three points (who, where, and circumstances)	Describes all three points in detail

Criteria	Come for help.	You're on the right track. Keep going.	Excellent work!
Explains major difficulties or challenges faced by the person or animal	Includes nothing about what the person or animal had to overcome	Lists challenges, but without any details	Includes description of the challenges in detail
Describes accomplishments of person or animal and how he or she overcame challenges	Lists a couple of achievements	Vividly describes one important accomplishment	Explores a few accomplishments and what these meant to the field in which he or she contributed
Includes outline of the major points you will include in your biography	No outline	Outline includes a few main points	Outline includes, in order, all the major points in the biography
Written in complete sentences and with paragraphs	Incomplete sentences; no paragraphs	Well written in paragraphs, but with sentence fragments	Well written, with no (or few) grammatical errors

With guidance, a third-grade class could use this to guide their process and check their own and each other's work. You can design variations of this for students who need to process information in other ways—sketching, drawing, exploring prints, dramatizing, listening to audiobooks, watching video productions, and so forth. In some cases, writing a biography may be the result of a theater experience, or you may accept a "script" in place of a biography.

> As a teacher in New England, I always like to include a unit on Henry David Thoreau. Many of the kids in my class have been to Walden Pond, and so there is some real-life experience I can draw on in class. I used a criteria card for a 1-week assignment. The children were to go and sit somewhere outside and listen to and observe the nature around them. They made journal entries each week, and I gave them criteria cards that guided them. For example, one of the criteria was for them to think about specific questions. Another one was to write at least one paragraph. Another was to sketch something they saw. Another was to make a list of everything they heard that was natural and everything that was man-made. This helped them and their parents a great deal and gave me guidelines for identifying what specific kids needed and what changes I needed to make as we went along.
>
> *—Second-grade teacher*

When planning further adjustments, you can also use a rating scale for specific students to help you decide what you should change in future class sessions.

NAME: _____

DATE: _____

Project: Students create an imaginary trip across the United States—from east to west. They trace their trip on a map and describe what they did and saw on the way.

Learning objectives:

- To understand how the terrain in the United States changes as you move from east to west

- To develop spatial and visual thinking by exploring maps and the geography of lakes, rivers, mountains, and other features

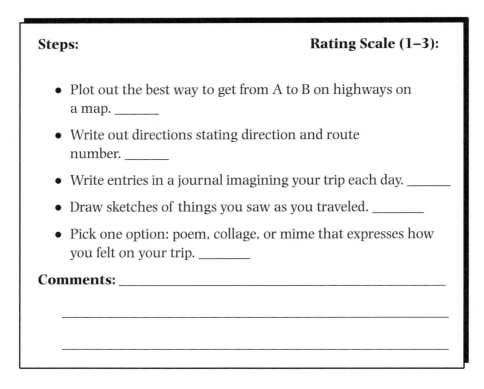

The more you provide different ways for young children to do things, the more they will learn with their strengths—their preferred learning styles. They can draw on their kinetic, visual, aural, and linguistic abilities when the learning environment engages the imagination and provides alternative paths for students with different needs. Through observations, rating scales, rubrics, or other assessments, you can easily add another layer of complexity for advanced students or simplify a process for less skilled or confident children.

LOOKING AHEAD

The next chapter applies the five-step planning process to science. It offers a range of ways to target essential learning goals and at the same time differentiate a lesson or unit in response to the learning needs of your students. The chapter will guide you in creating more flexibility in the curriculum and igniting excitement and interest in the discovery of the wonderful and varied world of science.

SAMPLE OF STATE GOALS AND STANDARDS (ILLINOIS)

Goal 1: Understand political systems, with an emphasis on the United States

Standards:

- **Understand and explain basic principles of the U.S. government.** (Early elementary: Describe the fundamental principles of government, including representative government, government of law, individual rights, and the common good.)

- **Understand the structures and functions of the political systems of Illinois, the United States, and other nations.** (Early elementary: Identify the different levels of government as local, state, and national.)

- **Understand election processes and responsibilities of citizens.** (Early elementary: Identify concepts of responsible citizenship, including respect for the law, patriotism, civility, and working with others.)

- **Understand the roles and influences of individuals and interest groups in the political systems of Illinois, the United States, and other nations**. (Early elementary: Identify the roles of civic leaders.)

- **Understand U.S. foreign policy as it relates to other nations and international issues.** (Early elementary: Identify relationships that the federal government establishes with other nations.)

- **Understand the development of U.S. political ideas and traditions.** (Early elementary: Describe political ideas and traditions important to the development of the United States, including democracy, individual rights, and the concept of freedom.)

Goal 2: Understand economic systems, with an emphasis on the United States

Standards:

- **Understand how different economic systems operate in the exchange, production, distribution, and consumption**

of goods and services. (Early elementary: Identify advantages and disadvantages of different ways to distribute goods and services. Describe how wages/salaries can be earned in exchange for work.)

- **Understand that scarcity necessitates choices by consumers.** (Early elementary: Explain why consumers must make choices.)

- **Understand that scarcity necessitates choices by producers.** (Early elementary: Describe how human, natural, and capital resources are used to produce goods and services. Identify limitations in resources that force producers to make choices about what to produce.)

- **Understand trade as an exchange of goods or services**. (Early elementary: Demonstrate the benefits of simple voluntary exchanges. Know that barter is a type of exchange and that money makes exchange easier.)

- **Understand the impact of government policies and decisions on production and consumption in the economy.** (Early elementary: Identify goods and services provided by government.)

Goal 3: Understand events, trends, individuals, and movements shaping the history of Illinois, the United States, and other nations

Standards:

- **Apply the skills of historical analysis and interpretation.** (Early elementary: Explain the difference between past, present, and future time; place themselves in time. Ask historical questions and seek out answers from historical sources such as myths, biographies, stories, old photographs, artwork, other visual or electronic sources. Describe how people in different times and places viewed the world in different ways.)

- **Understand the development of significant political events.** (Early elementary: Identify key individuals and events in the development of the local community such as founders days, names of parks and streets, etc. Explain why individuals, groups, issues and events are celebrated with local, state, or national holidays or days of recognition. Explain the contributions of individuals and groups who are featured in biographies, legends, folklore, and traditions.)

- **Understand the development of economic systems**. (Early elementary: Describe how Native American people in Illinois engaged in economic activities with other tribes and traders in the region prior to the Black Hawk War. Explain how the economy of the students' local community has changed over time. Identify how people and groups in the past made economic choices to survive and improve their lives. Explain how trade among people brought an exchange of ideas, technology, and language.)

- **Understand Illinois, U.S., and world social history.** (Early elementary: Describe key figures and organizations in the social history of the local community. Identify how customs and traditions from around the world influence the local community.)

- **Understand Illinois, U.S., and world environmental history.** (Early elementary: Describe how the local environment has changed over time. Compare depictions of the natural environment that are found in myths, legends, folklore, and traditions.)

Goal 4: Understand world geography and the effects of geography on society, with an emphasis on the United States

Standards:

- **Locate, describe, and explain places, regions, and features on the Earth.** (Early elementary: Identify physical characteristics of places, both local and global. Identify the characteristics and purposes of geographic representations, including maps, globes, graphs, photographs, software, and digital images, and be able to locate specific places using each.)

- **Analyze and explain characteristics and interactions on the Earth's physical systems.** (Early elementary: Identify components of the Earth's physical systems. Describe physical components of ecosystems.)

- **Understand relationships between geographic factors and society.** (Early elementary: Identify ways people depend on and interact with the physical environment. Identify opportunities and constraints of the physical environment. Explain the difference between renewable and nonrenewable resources.)

- **Understand the historical significance of geography.**
  (Early elementary: Identify changes in the geographic characteristics of a local region.)

Goal 5: Understand social systems, with an emphasis on the United States

Standards:

- **Compare characteristics of culture as reflected in language, literature, the arts, traditions, and institutions.**
  (Early elementary: Identify folklore from different cultures that became part of the heritage of the United States.)

- **Understand the roles and interactions of individuals and groups in society.** (Early elementary: Compare the roles of individuals in group situations. Identify major social institutions in the community.)

- **Understand how social systems form and develop over time.** (Early elementary: Describe how individuals interacted within groups to make choices regarding food, clothing, and shelter.)

7 Differentiated Instruction Applied to Science

The Center for Gifted, National-Louis University, Evanston, Illinois

Science is built of facts the way a house is built of bricks; but an accumulation of facts is no more science than a pile of bricks is a house.
—*Henri Poincaré*

If facts are the seeds that later produce knowledge and wisdom, then the emotions and the impressions of the senses are the fertile soil in which the seeds must grow.
—*Rachel Carson*

Young children have a natural curiosity about science. Often, their questions and observations focus on the natural world—the tree trunks that have a gnarled and strange appearance, the clam that squirts water and disappears in its shell, the mauve color of the clouds at dusk. Parents marvel that young children can absorb so much information while walking along the beach or rambling through the woods. Rachel Carson, who took great delight in introducing her grandson to the wonders of the sea and woods, describes how 4-year-old Roger learned about the world around him:

> When Roger has visited me in Maine and we have
> walked in these woods I have made no conscious effort
> to name plants or animals nor to explain to him, but
> have just expressed my own pleasure in what we see,
> calling his attention to this or that but only as I would
> share discoveries with an older person. Later I have
> been amazed at the way names stick in his mind, for
> when I show color slides of my woods plants it is Roger
> who can identify them. "Oh, that's what Rachel likes—
> that's bunchberry!" Or, "That's Jumer (juniper) but you
> can't eat those green berries—they are for the squir-
> rels." I am sure no amount of drill would have
> implanted the names so firmly as just going through
> the woods in the spirit of two friends on an expedition
> of exciting discovery. (Carson, 1998, p. 23)

Young children such as Roger show what they can learn when moti-
vated by wonder and awe at the natural world they see, feel, and hear
around them. In the "expedition of exciting discovery," they gobble up
information and explore how things work—how crabs survive in the tide
pools, why the crickets come out at night, and which tide is the best for
clam digging. When young children (and even adults) feel the thrill of
new discovery, they can achieve at an extraordinary rate.

THE BIG PICTURE: SCIENCE

In the early grades, science often takes the form of nature study. Ideally, it
extends from experiences the child has had since toddlerhood—observing, touching, listening, sensing, imagining, and visualizing the natural
world. They feel the surface of bark on an oak tree, throw bits of ham in
a tide pool to see what creatures come out, listen to the sounds of rain or
Canadian geese flying overhead, collect rocks, and grow seedlings. Some
of them—if they have parents interested in nature—learn to differentiate
the oak from the maple tree, can identify the song of the white-throated
sparrow, and know where the tree frogs begin their nightly chorus.

Young children explore the natural world to discover what things are
and why they are that way. Without discovery, science lessons have little
chance of holding their interest or stimulating their hunger to understand the physical world around them. The "why" questions that sometimes exhaust parents should be snatched up in the classroom and used
as leads to new discoveries for the child. Whatever learning goal you
establish, include the questions of young children in the unit. What do

they want to know about the solar system? What questions do they have about rocks, volcanoes, and fossils?

> In preparation for a class on clouds, I asked my students to go outside the week before—at least three or four times—and look at the different clouds in the sky. They were to sketch their shapes in their notebooks and describe them in terms of what they reminded them of. Were they thick and puffy like cotton swabs or thin and silky, like you could poke through them with your hand? Are they white, dark, colored in any way? By the time we started our first class on clouds, they were eager to share their findings. As each child shared what he or she found and saw, I wrote what they described in categories, so they could begin to see that they were actually observing types of clouds. Hands started going up, and one after another began asking, "What kinds of clouds are these? Where do they come from? What's my cloud called?" They were so eager to know the names of their clouds, so I divided them into groups with the cloud books and they examined the pictures to see which ones looked like their clouds. We created a troposphere on one wall with altitudes labeled. The students then created art representations of the kinds of clouds they saw outside and attached and identified them on the troposphere. As the week continued and we got into how clouds form, the kids were so involved because of this research they had done in the beginning, and I had them continue to keep a cloud journal and to watch weather reports to see what weathermen said about the movements of clouds. Having the kids record observations before the start of a unit enables them to bring something to the table that is their own.
>
> *—Second-grade teacher*

Science demands some of the skills and processes used in geography, as well as those in visual art. Young children in science can

- observe characteristics (species of birds) and behaviors (migration),
- ask questions (what, why, where, how),
- visualize spatial relations (such as in a solar system),
- measure distances (from the Earth to the Moon, from a mountaintop to the surface),

- study perspective (what would the earth look like from the moon?),
- diagram the formation of things (mountains, clouds, lakes),
- hypothesize about how things work or why things are the way they are,
- gather information (by observing, reading, experimenting, asking, imagining),
- express findings (through a project, an essay, an art piece, a drama).

They can also expand their understanding of science by

- imagining themselves as other living things or phenomena (a mountain, an insect, the moon);
- asking questions of themselves as these living things or phenomena;
- dramatizing a scientific process (the birth of a cloud, the formation of a mountain range, the eruption of a volcano, the orbit of the earth around the sun, etc.);
- interpreting animals, nature, and natural phenomena through mime, dance, dramatizations, and paintings;
- dancing or miming processes involving motion, force, gravity, and flight;
- testing ideas through sketching and constructing models;
- brainstorming creative ways to explore a question or find an answer.

This list is not comprehensive but gives you an idea of the different processes that children should use as they learn new concepts and skills. On the basis of the content you plan to teach for the year, you can create a "process list" for yourself.

Our district harps a lot on standards because our schools have lower-scoring kids when compared to other schools in the state. When I attended a workshop on differentiating, the big issue for me was, How am I going to make sure my kids get to the level my school says they have to get? One idea I got from another teacher was to extract from the standards larger skills and concepts that I can then build units around. For example, in science, we have a standard for early elementary that deals with collecting data and describing observed events. From this and other standards, I got this larger idea of developing observation skills in my kids. In the beginning of my school year, all my units in science had to do with observation of natural phenomena, and differentiating happened within that larger frame.

—Second-grade teacher

Sometimes, because of the pressure on classrooms to meet curriculum standards, children end up experiencing a small fraction of what science actually offers. But if you have a "process list" to refer to periodically, you can ensure that your students are growing in fundamental skill and concept areas of science.

So what are the skills and concepts you want to develop from unit to unit? As you establish the priorities (the big picture) of science, consider the following questions:

- What competencies in science will prepare your students for a lifetime of study and discovery?

- What is science really about for a kindergartener, a first-grader?

- What "big-picture" processes are implied in the standards and curriculum for your grade (see sample list of standards at the end of this chapter)?

For example, a major part of science is observation. Young children need many opportunities to develop their observation skills—to distinguish between species, perceive differences in behavior, and estimate distances. This is something they love to do. If you put them in groups and let them observe a phenomenon, an animal, or a process you're demonstrating, they delight in drawing their own conclusions and sharing them.

My kids LOVE to report on things they've observed in nature. It's so popular and generates so much data for the class to examine and learn from, that I always include it in every class I teach. For instance, we were in a unit on animal behavior. There was one girl who'd never showed any interest in science, and she came to school popping with energy. She couldn't wait to tell what she'd observed. She spent a lot of time observing a group of sparrows picking over crumbs. She noticed that certain birds pecked others away and "hogged all the food." She showed me her notes and a sketch of how the birds were clustered on the ground. Her "data" became significant as the class explored the subject of rank among animal populations, and the term "pecking order" became more meaningful.

—Third-grade teacher

CHOOSE THE LEARNING "DESTINATION" (STEP 2)

Because Chapters 1 and 2 thoroughly explore knowing your students (Step 1), there is no need to repeat it here. You can apply the strategies in that chapter to determine what your students are bringing to specific content in science. Consider experiences they have had in their home communities, special abilities, and learning styles that relate to particular activities.

> Sonya is an inductive thinker. Early in the year, she brought in a box that had about four birds' nests, which she and her dad found in November when the nesting season was long over. As she pointed to each one, she immediately began speculating about how the birds constructed them. One intrigued her especially because it was made of grasses packed together with hard, dried mud. I've noticed that she prefers to cogitate and try to figure things out before checking sources. She gets bored and feels almost "let down" if someone just tells her.

—First-grade teacher

As described in previous chapters, knowing your students will enable you to make appropriate choices for learning "destinations" (Step 2). Select science topics that include the following components (Wiggins & McTighe, 1998, pp. 10–11):

- a "big idea" of enduring understanding;
- an idea, topic, or process that resides at the heart of the discipline;
- an idea, topic, or process that requires uncoverage;
- an idea, topic, or process that engages students;
- an idea that integrates well with other subjects such as language arts, geography, and the arts.

An example of a "destination" that meets these requirements in science might be the following:

> The children will understand how mountains are formed. This is a "big idea" of enduring understanding because it shows young children that the Earth is not a static substance but a dynamic planet with large shifts and transformations. It resides at the heart of the discipline because it represents a process that includes many of the elements of other scientific processes—force, pressure, gravity, and so forth. It is an idea requiring uncoverage because the formation of mountains is not something that young children can easily grasp without hands-on activities that make the process more tangible. It engages students because it is a dramatic occurrence that young children will naturally love. It is an idea that integrates well with other subjects because children can approach it in different ways; they can identify with the mountain and explain the process, design or sketch each phase of a mountain's evolution, or create a timeline that indicates how long a mountain takes to form.

The learning "destination" should be something that gives young children a fundamental understanding about a phenomenon, an object, or a living thing. In the above example, the destination is that students understand how mountains form, rather than what mountains are. The latter is too general and difficult for young children to grasp. The former enables them to explore the exciting and dynamic process of moving plates, pressure, and the gradual buildup of rock and earth. It is a destination that—in its articulation—suggests a variety of ways of demonstrating, communicating, and engaging young minds.

IDENTIFY EVIDENCE OF UNDERSTANDING (STEP 3)

The third step is to clearly establish what sort of evidence (in the form of assignments, projects, behaviors, etc.) will confirm that the students understand what you intended. As brought out in previous chapters, this is an area that sometimes gets hazy in the conventional classroom. Teachers are taught to clarify learning goals and assess students to see if they reached these goals, but the assessment (formal or informal) will probably not target understanding unless the goals do. Frequently, learning goals will state what students will do, but the questions that teachers need to ask themselves are the following: Do these activities necessarily lead to understanding? Where do I want my students to be in terms of understanding essential science content? What skills do I want them to master through this "journey?"

If you intend children to understand how different kinds of clouds form, you can target this understanding by having students

- explain how the process works in their own words,
- diagram each phase in a series of sketches,
- translate cloud formation into movement and narration,
- compare how one kind of cloud (e.g., cumulus) forms versus another (stratus).

The above list provides different ways for children to demonstrate understanding. Without the writing skills to express an idea on paper or the confidence to express themselves verbally, some young students may show their mastery of certain concepts by sketching, diagramming, constructing, or even discussing their perceptions informally. Without this variety, there is a danger of underestimating what children know simply because they cannot express it in one particular way. Young children are particularly susceptible to this. For example, you might ask a student what trees need to live and she might answer "dirt," not realizing that you want to know *all* the elements a tree needs to stay alive and grow. That same child may respond differently if asked to *show* what trees need on paper—through her own sketches and explanations.

PLAN THE JOURNEY (STEP 4)

Science instruction grows from the sources that you gather together at the beginning of a unit or lesson. Sometimes, teachers have students bring materials or do their own research (in the form of observations, notes in journals, sketches) as a springboard into a new subject. The teacher who began a new unit by having her students observe clouds and record their observations is an example of this. An activity such as this should target the "destination" you've identified and the different learning needs of your students. It's conceivable that you could create a stimulating catalyst that won't necessarily serve your objectives or meet the students where they need the most support.

Let us take the example of the mountains. If your objective is that students understand how a mountain range was formed, consider what smaller "understandings" are necessary—the moving plates on the earth, the substance of the rocks, the pressure and friction between plates, and so on. What sorts of activities and materials would best introduce this subject and involve students in a learning process? One possibility, for example, might be to give groups of students flat rocks of different sizes and experiment with pushing the flat rocks against each other, piling up smaller rocks along the edges—thus creating a mountain range. Students can also extend this by creating a diagram of how it works. From here, students can generate questions about the process, and different groups can explore how it applies to different regions of the world. Some children may look into the Himalayan range, formed when the Indian plate and Eurasian plate collided (fossils of ocean creatures ended up on top of Mount Everest in the upheaval). Others may explore the Rocky Mountains and the fact that this range begins in Alaska and extends down to Central America.

Introduce a New Unit to Preassess

As with other subjects, you need to know what level of preparedness your students should have to engage in the concepts and skills of the new unit. What background do they need in terms of knowledge and experience? In a class of young children, the range of ability, experience, and skill is often greater than in the higher grades when discrepancies between high and low even out somewhat. Deciding on the form of assessment depends on what you need to know. If you are beginning a unit on the solar system and it relates to an earlier unit you did several months ago, some students will need review; others will not. You might, for example, hand them some art paper and ask them to draw and/or describe the following: what an orbit is, how the Earth and Moon move in the solar system, and what the *inner planets* and the *outer planets* refer to.

Science allows for a variety of ways to assess knowledge, skill, and ability. Some examples include the following:

- a simple experiment conducted by a child and explained by her or him,

- notes on observations made by the child supporting a science fact she learned,

- illustrations of a process (such as how volcanoes erupt),

- charts that show the relationship between changes in the tides and changes in the Moon's orbit around the Earth.

Another way to assess is to observe students in an introductory activity. Many teachers feel that they already know what different students need and can make adjustments based on how they respond to an initial process.

> I always start my insect unit with an ant colony in a terrarium. The children have a diagram of the different parts of the ant ahead of time and what these parts do. They then observe the ants and write down their observations based on the following questions: Can you tell what the ants are doing? Is there a reason to their activity? Name times you think they used their antenna. Follow the actions of one ant and write down what this one ant did. Follow the actions of a group of ants and describe what they do. From the students' responses, I can gauge differences in observation skills and also levels of thinking. One of my students wrote this: "The ants move around carrying crumbs. They like to climb over each other." Another wrote this: "Some ants carry crumbs and the crumbs are bigger than they are. How can they carry them? Other ants were carrying building stuff. Maybe they're in charge of the anthill. It's like an army. Who's the boss?" The second student saw more and posed questions. Another student didn't really follow my instructions but became intrigued by the industry and activity of the ants. He just asked questions on his paper. Does each ant have a job of his own? Is this like a factory for ants? How do the ants figure out who does what and what is it for? He drew sketches of the ants and imagined what the ant world looked like under the hole.
>
> —*Second-grade teacher*

All of this provided useful information about how to proceed with the unit. None of the children knew much about ants, but all came to the table with different abilities, skills, and interests. Equipped with the knowledge of what these differences are, the teacher can adjust *how* and *at what level* the children learn about ant biology and its relation to food gathering, home building, and social interactions.

Sequence Teaching Strategies and Learning Activities

Examples of how you can sequence learning activities to meet a wider range of needs and abilities follow.

- *Destination*: The children will understand that different kinds of rocks tell stories about how the Earth was formed and the plants and animals that lived a long, long time ago.

  Standards: (a) Know and apply the concepts, principles, and processes of scientific inquiry. (b) Know and apply concepts that describe the features and processes of the Earth and its resources.

  Evidence: Children can identify and group different types of rocks—sedimentary, metamorphic, and igneous—and tell how they were made. They can make diagrams of the different layers of the Earth (crust, mantle, outer core, inner core) and how rocks (such as basalt) start as liquid rock (magma) deep in the Earth. They can explain what fossils are and how the images of small animals and plant life become imprinted in rocks.

  Teaching strategy: Inquiry and guided questioning. The classroom has a picture of the different layers of the Earth and diagrams of the main categories of rocks. You can introduce a subject by reading a book such as Stuart Murphy's *Dave's Down-to-Earth Rock Shop*. Ask questions: "How were Dave's rocks grouped (color, size, hardness)? How did Josh and Amy sort their rock collection?" You can select a rock (e.g., igneous) and pass out enough for all the children to have turns feeling and examining them. Then point to the diagram of the Earth's layers, showing where this rock came from and how it was formed. Provide the class with samples of fossils, which they can feel and examine closely. Ask, "What kind of living thing is this? How do you think it was formed?"

  Learning activity: Provide a box full of different kinds of rocks, divide the class into groups, and ask them to create at least two different systems for grouping their rocks and to justify their systems. Then pose the following question: "What are the different ways you can think of to divide the rocks (size, shape, weight, color, texture, etc.)?" The students can create a scale such as "Moh's Scale of Hardness" in *Dave's Down-to-Earth Rock Shop*. They can look up the different rocks to discover what they are made of and how they were formed, as well as make entries and sketch diagrams in "rock journals."

Resources: Rocks, identification books, stories, diagrams and displays, poems about rocks, little notebooks for keeping records of rocks the children find.

Grouping: Tiered and interest groups. More advanced children work with a larger variety of rocks, identify and classify the rocks, and create diagrams of how they were formed. Children with specific interests or abilities can spend more time in a related activity (e.g., creating a timeline, learning more about the minerals in the rocks).

Adjustments: Young children may need a more personal connection to the material presented. An option would be to read Byrd Baylor's *Everybody Needs a Rock* and give them an opportunity to select a special rock in a collection (or they can find one from home and bring it to the class). Ask, "Why did you choose this rock as your special rock? What do you like about the shape, color, size, and feeling of your rock?" From here, you can enter the subject of the story of the rock—how it began and where it's traveled. Other students—those who are more scientifically inclined—may be ready for more challenging projects (e.g., creating a series of pictures and text explaining how a rock is formed).

- *Destination:* The children will understand that animals in different environments (desert, polar region, rainforest, etc.) depend on their own habitats and on each other to survive.

  Standard: Know and apply concepts that explain how living things function, adapt, and change and that describe how living things interact with each other and with their environment.

  Evidence: Children can identify the habitat of different kinds of animals. They can list the characteristics of these animals that are designed for specific environments (e.g., fur and fat on polar bears, padded feet of camels, etc.). They can explain why a polar bear would not survive in a rainforest or why a camel could not tolerate living at the North Pole.

  Teaching strategy: Direct instruction; demonstration; guided questioning. Introduce the different habitats—ocean, polar region, desert, grassland, mountains, freshwater, temperate forests, and tropical forests. Show a video that explores animal life in different regions. Use a source (e.g., Patricia Lauber's *Fur, Feathers, and Flippers*) to demonstrate the relationship between a region and fauna. Pose questions such as the following: "Can a camel live at the North Pole? Can a kangaroo live in the Rocky Mountains? Why or why not?" Guide a brainstorming session focused on what animals need to survive and ask for examples of the special features animals have to survive in their habitats. As the children offer ideas, ask what each characteristic is for (e.g., if a child says "fur," ask what a bear needs fur for; then discuss a fundamental need all living things have for protection from the elements, whatever they may be).

Learning activity: Children divide into groups according to regions that interest them. Using books, pictures, and diagrams, they can draw different parts of an animal from this region. Ask the following questions: "When you look at the different parts of the animals, what parts help them to survive in this habitat (e.g., the padded feet of a camel, the feathers of geese, the shell of a turtle)? How do they protect themselves from the elements? From predators? How do they survive the temperatures? How do they get food and water? How do they relate to other creatures/plants?" Have a wall that displays charts/pictures for different needs: protection from climate and weather, protection from predators, shelter, and food. The children can focus on these areas as they draw maps of where their animals live and sketch the kind of environments (mountainous, desert, etc.) they inhabit. They can imitate the movements of their animals and what their animals do to get food, shelter, and so on. They can imagine that they are these animals and write stories about one day in their lives— what they did and what they liked about being a hawk, camel, fish, lizard, and so on.

Resources: Posters, maps, designs, art materials, books, magazines, notebooks.

Grouping: Interest groups. Children can work in groups according to habitats or individually.

Adjustments: Independent study options for advanced children. If the children have a definable range of skills, tiered assignments would allow those with more advanced reading and writing ability to use more difficult sources and do more in-depth research.

• *Destination:* The children will understand that every part of a tree has a special purpose that helps it to grow and adapt to its environment.

Standards: (a) Know and apply concepts that explain how living things function, adapt, and change. (b) Know and apply concepts that describe how living things interact with each other and with their environment.

Evidence: The children can identify each part of the tree and explain how it interacts with the environment and helps the tree live and grow. They can diagram or sketch how trees get the "food" they need to grow, how they reproduce themselves, and how seasons or changes in weather and climate affect them.

Teaching strategy: Inquiry; demonstration; guided questioning. Using photographs, drawings, or paintings (e.g., Thomas Locker's *Sky Tree Portfolio* [Sky Tree Press, 1995]), ask children what the different parts of a tree are. Have the students identify themselves with trees: "What part of the tree is like your feet? What part is like your middle and legs? What part is like your arms? Your hands?" Diagram and sketch as you ask questions. While drawing the trunk as it extends down to the earth, ask, "Does the tree go beneath the earth? What do you think it looks like? Why do the roots go down and how long do you think they are?" Draw some branches on the board and ask, "What's missing? What should I put on these branches? What do the leaves look like? What shape?" Step by step, you provide instruction by asking the children leading questions while sketching. Have them stand up and be trees. Describe how their feet (roots) pick up the moisture and good nourishment in the soil. The children bend over and make a movement to indicate how the tree draws this nutriment up from the earth. They hold an arm out to an imaginary sun and make a move to show the sun hitting the leaves (their hands) and the leaves carrying energy to the tree. Show the children different samples of leaves and have them look the trees up and identify them. They can examine leaves from different trees and feel the samples of rough bark and the lichen that grows on it. If possible, they can go outside to look at the trees nearby, sketch what they see, and take notes on what the tree looks like, smells like, and feels like up close. They can pose questions for the class to explore.

Learning activity: Children choose a species of tree from books and pictures. They explore the following: What is the environment like (hot, cold, dry, wet)? What seasons does it have—winter, summer, spring, fall; wet seasons and dry seasons; or no seasons? What special problems does the tree face in its environment, and how does it cope? An example might be the baobab tree in Africa, which, to survive the dry season, has a huge barrel-shaped trunk to store water and protect it from evaporation. Through questioning, the children write about themselves as the tree. They explore questions such as the following: "Where do I live? What climate do I live in? What kind of land surrounds me (woods, fields, desert, hills, etc.)? How tall am I? What do my leaves look like? What kinds of animals live around me and crawl over me? How do I make the sugars that become food for me? What is the most beautiful or wonderful thing about me?" They sketch their responses.

Resources: Samples of leaves that you can put into categories according to families of trees—pine, willow, elm, walnut, beech, birch, rose, and maple; samples of bark and branches; pictures; prints; art materials; stories; poems.

Grouping: Interest and ability groups.

Adjustments: Cluster students who are already familiar with the parts of the tree. Design more complex projects that still focus on the learning "destination." For example, the children could create prints from leaves they've collected and write a life story or a poem about the leaves. Compare trees in their environment with those in another climate and explore the following question: Would they survive in each other's habitats? Why or why not? For children with little exposure to the natural world, allow more time for them to touch, observe, and improvise with leaves and bark and also to make their own spontaneous observations about what they feel, smell, and see.

- *Destination:* The children will understand that the oceans next to the United States differ from all freshwater sources in size, temperature, salinity, and the life systems they support.

  Standards: (a) Know and apply concepts that describe the features and processes of the Earth and its resources. (b) Know and apply concepts that describe how living things interact with each other and with their environment.

  Evidence: The children can compare the ocean and a lake, pond, river, or stream in terms of its size, temperature, salinity, and the plants and animals that live in it. They can show, on a map, what oceans the United States has on its shores and identify and sketch the plant and animal life there. They can describe the special conditions that each ocean offers to support specific plants and animals.

  Teaching strategy: Inquiry; questioning. Engage their senses. Begin by finding out who among your students has experienced the sea and who has spent time at rivers, streams, ponds, or lakes. Pose questions: What is the water like? How salty is it? Did you go in it? Was the water still or moving (waves, river current, etc.)? What did you see by the shore (weeds, fish, birds, shells, rocks)? If any children have experienced *both* ocean and freshwater places, ask them to say what they felt was different. Experiment with table salt and water to give them opportunities to experience some of the qualities of seawater. Ask who has visited the aquarium and the salt-water environments displayed there. Present a video or read a story about the ocean. Play audiotapes of sounds by the sea and tell the children to close their eyes and imagine that they are walking along the shore. What do they hear (waves, seagulls, sea lions)? Provide samples of shells and other sea objects (bits of crab claws, dried seaweed, kelp, etc.) for the children to touch, smell, feel, and sketch. What does it smell like? What do they notice about the objects (roughness of the surface, the sharpness of the claws, the colors, etc.)? Have children brainstorm all the things that make the ocean different from freshwater places.

Learning activity: Focus on a specific sea habitat and engage students in exploring the life there. An example: the kelp forest. Expose the children to videos about kelp forests, otters, sea lions, sea birds, and so on and provide picture books and prints. Have students choose two species of animals or plants and create a list of questions to explore. They make observations, speculate, and then look up the answers to their questions in books and magazines. They sketch and create a story about how their animals eat, how they rest, and what they do with others and their own species (travel together or alone?). The children construct a kelp forest with a variety of materials. Different groups assume responsibility for specific areas of the underwater scene—for example, the kelp species, anemones, sea urchins, fish species, seals, otters, birdlife, and so on. Around the edges of the kelp forest, they pin up paragraphs they wrote on specific animals or plant life. They create detailed diagrams of the food chain. They compose free verse poems and autobiographical stories of themselves as seals, otters, school fish, and so forth.

Resources: Art materials, books and pictures on the sea, fictional stories and poems, ocean maps, videos, shells, dried seaweed, and kelp.

Grouping: Interest groups to work on assigned areas of the aquarium; pairs.

Adjustments: A project such as this is ideal for children with different learning styles. Those who thrive in the arts can focus more on observation and re-creating the details of a kelp forest through a mural or some other kind of model kelp forest. Those who prefer science can investigate the kelp habitat in more depth (e.g., they can create a kelp forest food web or study predator-prey relationships in this delicate ecosystem). Children who love drama can assume roles of the sun, plants, and animals to demonstrate a variety of food chains in the kelp forest.

- *Destination:* The children will understand what insects are and how their structure is different from people.

  Standards: (a) Know and apply concepts that explain how living things function, adapt, and change. (b) Know and apply concepts that describe how living things interact with each other and with their environment.

  Evidence: Children can name and diagram the different parts of an insect. They can explain differences between insects and people, what insects eat, and how the insects get their food, move, and grow.

  Teaching strategy: As an introduction, build a terrarium for crickets. Involve children in setting up the space with potting soil, pebbles, and plants. Add moss for the baby crickets to hide in and show the children the fruit, vegetables, and dry rabbit food that they eat; add a place for water. Using the cricket (or any other insect of your choice), have students diagram the different parts and name the major parts. The children can keep checking their diagrams against the crickets they see in the terrarium. Ask, "What is different between you and an insect such as a cricket? What is the same?" Allow them to speculate: "What major parts or segments of the cricket (or any other insect) can you see?" Gradually introduce the exoskeleton and how this differs from the human skeleton. Through books, prints, and videos, expose students to more information on the unique physical characteristics of insects—the head, thorax, and abdomen.

  Learning activity: Students choose an insect. They ask questions that interest them about their insect and write them down. They explore resources in the classroom—books, magazines, diagrams, pictures, and the Internet—and sketch the different parts of their insect and label them. They construct a large version of an insect, using materials from their homes (e.g., plastic bottles, boxes, wire, etc.) and art materials. The children can also create an exhibit of insects with as many parts attached and visible as possible. They can write a short essay on what insects have that people don't have and how the different parts work. They can address questions they themselves have about insects: How do they smell? How do they protect themselves from predators? How do they find food? How do they see? How do they feel? They can imagine they are their insect and write a "Day in the Life" autobiography.

Resources: Videos, pictures, diagrams of parts of insects, stories, art materials, assorted instruction materials, hand lenses to examine insects.

Grouping: Independent.

Adjustments: Some children may already know about insects and, consequently, may need to explore a more challenging project (e.g., explore insects that help people— either by providing food or pollinating, etc.). Kinetic learners may need to construct an insect, using, perhaps, cardboard, colored paper, blocks, wire, or other materials. Using Chris Van Allsburg's story, *Two Bad Ants*, creative students can write a similar adventure story. Or, they can choreograph or mime the different stages of an insect—for example, a caterpillar metamorphosing from a cocoon to a butterfly with music or sound.

- *Destination:* The children will understand that the Earth revolves around the Sun, the Moon revolves around the Earth, and these orbits create day and night.

    Standards: (a) Know and apply concepts that describe force and motion and the principles that explain them. (b) Know and apply concepts that explain the composition and structure of the universe and Earth's place in it.

    Evidence: The children can demonstrate how the Earth moves around the Sun and the Moon around the Earth by acting it out. They can explain why it looks like the Sun comes from the east and disappears in the west. They can describe what orbit means and can draw a diagram (or make a model) of the Earth's orbit and the Moon's orbit.

    Teaching strategy: Inquiry; direct instruction; guided questioning. Read a book to introduce the main concepts (e.g., Joanna Cole and Bruce Degen's *The Magic School Bus: Lost in the Solar System*). Ask questions such as the following: "Where does the Sun rise and set? What is an orbit? Does the Sun go around the Earth or the Earth around the Sun? How does the Moon move?" Use children to demonstrate the movement of Earth, Sun, and Moon and also other planets (if time allows). The child who is the Earth rotates in one place, the one who is the Moon moves around the Earth, and the one who plays the Sun holds a flashlight and points it at the Earth. The children playing the Moon and the Earth rotate from east to west (counterclockwise). Ask the class questions: "Is it day or night on this side of the Earth? Why do you say so?" You can further demonstrate this by using a flashlight with a globe, rotating the globe slowly, and asking, "Where is it nighttime? Where is it daytime?"

Learning activity: Children create a mobile of the Sun, Earth, Moon, and other planets. Different students take on specific tasks. Using a chart of the solar system and your guidance, one group prepares the Sun, another the Earth, and so on. They can do artistic representations on cutouts. Some students can help hang the planets, measure distances, and make comparisons with the chart. All of the students use the mobile as a reference and aid in learning more about the solar system. They demonstrate how the Earth's revolution around the Sun and the Moon's revolution around the Earth create day and night. With these activities and other sources (e.g., Terence Dickinson's *Exploring the Night Sky* and Robin and Sally Hirst's *My Place in Space*), students can further their understanding through a range of options. Examples might be the following: (a) Write a free verse poem or autobiography about self as the Earth, Sun, Moon, or another planet and express how the other planets look, how it travels, and what it sees as it turns and moves. (b) Create a chamber theater piece with a narration of an eclipse using a group of students to dramatize the orbiting planets. (c) Choose several places on a globe, put a piece of masking tape on each place, and in a dark room, shine a flashlight on the globe and note whether or not all the places are in daylight at the same time. (d) On the playground, one child stands with a sign of the Earth; the other children use a meter tape to count 38 centimeters, and a child with the Moon sign stands there. Next, the children count 150 meters from the Earth sign, and a child with the Sun sign stands there. They then compare the distances and write their observations in notebooks. You can rotate the children holding the signs so that everyone has a chance to observe the distances. This can be extended by having some children interpret "light"; they move out from the sun as rays. Others go to the Moon and bounce off to the Earth, and that is how we see moonlight.

Resources: Books, pictures, photographs of planets in space, solar charts, construction materials, art materials, picture books, videos, stories, poems.

Grouping: Interest groups and ability groups.

Adjustments: You can easily adapt instruction when you have a range of resources and activities planned ahead of time. Provide clear instructions that allow those who are kinetic learners to act out the movements of planets, others to chart them, and so forth (see Chapters 1 and 3 for managing activities such as this). Make sure the children have a structure to follow so that those who "dramatize" the movements of the solar system don't spin like tops. The group has to figure out the following: Which way should they turn? How long is one rotation for the four inner planets? Each activity should have specific instructions and criteria for completing it satisfactorily.

ASSESS AND ADAPT INSTRUCTION (STEP 5)

As explained in the last chapter, you can best measure the progress of your students by having clearly stated criteria for assignments. In order for assessment to provide direction for future learning and build consistently on understanding and skill, try to focus on *specific strengths* the students bring to science and to the assignment at hand, the criteria for the assignment, the *areas of need* that they and you see in their work, and a *plan* for adjusting the students' assignments if necessary.

Let us say that a group of children are constructing a mobile of the solar system. Give them the criteria for this activity *before* they do it, so they have a clear understanding of what's expected of them. It might look something like this:

Learning Goal: Children will demonstrate understanding of the movements of the Earth and Moon as well as the "inner planets" around the Sun through a mobile.

Criteria:

- The Moon is placed so that it can orbit around the Earth.
- Mercury, Venus, Earth, and Mars are strung in the correct places in relation to the Sun.
- The four "inner planets" are approximately the right size in relation to each other.
- The children can demonstrate how the planets move around the Sun.

Notes:

_____

_____

With criteria clearly identified, you can determine the adjustments that specific students will need as they continue on their learning "journey." What special experiences and strengths do the children bring to this unit? Are they ready for a more challenging assignment? Do they need more time to practice or apply what they've learned? Or do they need a different process altogether? Remember that those who don't complete the project correctly or seem not to understand the concept may be struggling with the form of the assignment rather than the assignment itself.

> I have some students who go blank when it comes to anything visual. I know better than to have them work with diagrams or maps or anything like that when I'm introducing a new concept. They can apply their knowledge to a map or some kind of visual design, but that's only *after* they understand the concept. A couple of these kids are dancers, and so I often have them physicalize new concepts as much as possible. When we were learning about plant life, for example, they created a dance-mime piece about how the rays of the sun, the earth, the rain, etc. nourish a tree. They created a

sequence of movements that helped them internalize the basic concepts.

—First-grade teacher

Most classrooms have at least a few children who finish their assignments quickly and need more advanced work. It's not enough to provide an extension or enrichment activity for such children. Gifted science students need authentic challenges that involve accelerated learning and higher level thinking. If any of your students already know a fair portion of the content you intend to teach, compacting may offer the best solution for adjusting the pace and level of an assignment. The following is a way to monitor the children's progress:

Student: Rita Hernandez

Content to be compacted: Content on local geological formations

Adjusted assignment: Apply knowledge to a study of volcanoes

Criteria   **Rating Scale (1–3):**

1. Diagram of volcanic eruption shows how process happens. _____

2. One-paragraph description explains the diagram. _____

3. Autobiography of volcano is imaginative and expresses the science of volcanic activity in a vivid way. _____

Science provides many opportunities for children to work together while they speculate, experiment, test, retest, and make observations. Assessment can become part of this experience if, again, the students have a list of what's required. Here are a few examples:

Assignment: Show the migration of whooping cranes.

1. Make a map of a migratory route used by the whooping cranes.

2. Mark where they nest in the summer and where they go in winter.

3. In two paragraphs, explain why these birds migrate.

4. Draw a sketch of the whooping crane and label the parts.

Assignment: Create a drama about how the Rocky Mountains formed.

1. Write a "script" for what the narrator will say and directions on how the mountains will move.

2. Stage the actions of the plates that cause rock and earth to build up.

3. Choreograph and practice these movements.

4. Pretend you are the plates, the mountain, or a tree who watched the mountains form, and write two paragraphs about it.

Assignment: Create a drawing that shows how photosynthesis works.

1. Include arrows to show the sources of energy and "food" for the plant.

2. Attach notes to explain each step.

3. Explain why trees grow higher in a forest than in a field.

If the students are assessing their own group project where, for example, they have staged a drama about the food chain in a kelp forest, they can take turns using their "script" and playing the different roles. After they finish the assignment, they can check off each requirement and share ideas on how they can change or improve it. Young students generally enjoy assessing each other's work if they have a clear structure for it. As you supervise the process—noting your own observations and providing guidance where needed—you will find that they become more skilled at targeting what's most important in assigned work.

> I have my kids assess each other within a very defined window. What I do is have them check each other's work to see that all the pieces are there. When it comes to examining quality, I usually do that with the child. For right now, this works for me, and it saves me time. I can continue working with different groups knowing that my kids are checking each other to be sure that their work is complete. This means that they are completing things on their own, which is a big step. So, when I evaluate the assignment with the kids, incomplete work is not an issue. We can get straight to the substance of their work.
>
> *—Second-grade teacher*

When necessary, you can also design a rating scale for any of the assignments just mentioned and gauge specific strengths and needs of individual students. The following is an example:

Assignment: Create a display of the migration of whooping cranes from Wisconsin to Florida.

Learning Objectives:

- To understand the challenges faced by whooping cranes.

- To show how a foundation in Baraboo, Wisconsin, has helped a new population find wintering grounds in Florida.

- To understand the habitat needs of whooping cranes.

Criteria   **Rating Scale (1–3)**

1. Create a map that shows the birds' route clearly. ____

2. In two paragraphs, explain what the whooping cranes need for habitat when they migrate north (for nesting) and when they migrate south to winter. ____

3. Sketch the whooping crane and label the parts. ____

Comments: _____

_____

From rating scales such as these, you can target specific areas where a child may need more practice or instruction. For example, you might have a group of children whose writing skills hamper their ability to explain a process or phenomenon. In future sessions, a group of these students could do projects that give them more opportunity to write about science.

Another group of students may show their true potential through visual means—either through a drawing, a chart, or a map. Some children have a hard time understanding a new concept until they've had time to "see" it. These would be children who, for example, might get lost on a trip if given directions audibly but who could seize on the route immediately if shown a map. Other students have to manipulate things or dramatize a phenomenon in order to understand how it works. Assessments that show you where your students have genuine talent and where they need more support or experience are critical to meeting their needs.

LOOKING AHEAD

The next chapter applies the five-step planning process to mathematics. It provides specific strategies for ensuring that all students reach essential learning goals and enables you to create more flexibility in adapting lessons or units when needed. Numbers, shapes, lines, and patterns have intrigued children from their earliest years of life. Chapter 8 draws on that early curiosity and drive to discover the patterns and properties of the world around them.

SAMPLE OF STATE GOALS AND STANDARDS (ILLINOIS)

Goal 1: Understand the processes of scientific inquiry and technological design to investigate questions, conduct experiments, and solve problems

Standards:

- **Know and apply the concepts, principles, and processes of scientific inquiry.** (Early elementary: Describe an observed event. Develop questions on scientific topics. Collect data for investigations using measuring instruments and technologies. Arrange data into logical patterns and describe the patterns. Compare observations of individual and group results.)

- **Know and apply the concepts, principles, and processes of technological design.** (Early elementary: Given a simple design problem, formulate possible solutions. Design a device that will be useful in solving the problem. Build the device using the materials and tools provided. Test the device and record results using given instruments, techniques, and measurement methods. Report the design of the device, the test process, and the results in solving a given problem.)

Goal 2: Understand the fundamental concepts, principles, and interconnections of the life, physical, and earth/space sciences

Standards:

- **Know and apply concepts that explain how living things function, adapt, and change.** (Early elementary: Identify and describe the component parts of living things and their major functions. Categorize living organisms using a variety of observable features—for example, size, color, shape, and backbone.)

- **Know and apply concepts that describe how living things interact with each other and with their environment.** (Early elementary: Describe and compare characteristics of living things in relationship to their environments. Describe how living things depend on one another for survival.)

- **Know and apply concepts that describe properties of matter and energy and the interactions between them.** (Early elementary: Identify and compare sources of energy.

Compare large-scale physical properties of matter—for example, size, shape, color, texture, and odor.)

- **Know and apply concepts that describe force and motion and the principles that explain them.** (Early elementary: Identify examples of motion—for example, moving in a straight line, vibrating, and rotating. Identify observable forces in nature—for example, pushes, pulls, gravity, and magnetism.)

- **Know and apply concepts that describe the features and processes of the Earth and its resources.** (Early elementary: Identify components and describe diverse features of the Earth's land, water, and atmospheric systems. Identify and describe patterns of weather and seasonal change. Identify renewable and nonrenewable natural resources.)

- **Know and apply concepts that explain the composition and structure of the universe and Earth's place in it.** (Early elementary: Identify and describe characteristics of the Sun, Earth, and Moon as familiar objects in the solar system. Identify daily, seasonal, and annual patterns related to the Earth's rotation and revolution.)

Goal 3: Understand the relationships among science, technology, and society in historical and contemporary contexts

Standards:

- **Know and apply the accepted practices of science.** (Early elementary: Use basic safety practices. Explain why similar results are expected when procedures are done the same way. Explain how knowledge can be gained by careful observation.)

- **Know and apply concepts that describe the interaction between science, technology, and society.** (Early elementary: Explain the uses of common scientific instruments—for example, ruler, thermometer, balance, probe, and computer. Explain how using measuring tools improves the accuracy of estimates. Describe contributions that men and women have made to science and technology. Identify and describe ways that science and technology affect people's everyday lives—for example, transportation, medicine, agriculture, sanitation, and communication occupations. Demonstrate ways to reduce, reuse, and recycle materials.)

Differentiated Instruction Applied to Mathematics

The Center for Gifted, National-Louis University, Evanston, Illinois

Get the habit of analysis—analysis will in time enable synthesis to become your habit of mind. "Think simples" as my old master used to say— meaning to reduce the whole of its parts into the simplest terms, getting back to first principles.
—Frank Lloyd Wright

Children first encounter mathematics when they begin counting and grouping objects around the house—forks and spoons assembled from the dinner table, shoes arranged in pairs, or a group of family members painstakingly drawn, counted, and named on paper. Some parents encourage this with counting books, but in most cases, the children develop a sense of numbers on their own and often seem eager to share this knowledge with anyone willing to listen. A child will seize upon a pile of oranges or potatoes and pull one out at a time, pronouncing the number with great gusto. She may further her learning in the supermarket by counting boxes of rice or calculating the number of shopping bags it took to carry all the groceries to the car.

When children begin learning how to shape the numbers as figures on paper, it is only after they've had a world of meaningful experience. Preschoolers can be very adept at dividing up a small pile of leftover cookies so that everyone has the same amount. Yet these same children may not know how to write the numbers well or explain division. They only know that when each counted what they had, a few had more than the others, and so they cut up the extras to make it fair. These young students may be oblivious to the fact that they're learning key math lessons over a small pile of cookies, and sadly, many of them may never have this kind of real-life situation in arithmetic lessons they later receive in school.

When differentiating the math curriculum, the first step must be to create situations that inspire observation, reasoning, and imagination. Providing lively contexts where young children can explore the properties of different objects, seek patterns, and calculate quantities makes mathematics a process of discovery and invention. Mathematics doesn't come to young children from textbooks but from the world around them. They acquire a sense of patterns by rhythms they hear in music, the visual display of squares on the tile floor, the pairs of feet standing in line waiting for recess, the intricate lines threading through a maple leaf. Patterns, shapes, quantities, lines, and measures surround their everyday living. A differentiated classroom should draw on the mathematical universe to inspire mathematical thinking and learning in young children.

THE BIG PICTURE: MATHEMATICS

Because of the pressure to ensure that all students master a certain level of skill in arithmetic every year, teachers often spend a great deal of time on paper-and-pencil drill. The result is a situation where children know how to perform the rules of arithmetic but don't have a clear sense of what they're doing.

> Learning to do paper-and-pencil arithmetic on isolated examples does nothing to ensure that children will truly understand the algorithms or develop the ability to use them when needed. This fact is obvious to teachers when addition problems are assigned and a child asks, "Do I have to carry on this page?" It's obvious when word problems are assigned and a child asks, "Do I need to add or subtract?" It's clear when a

child makes a division error, omitting a zero in the quotient so the answer is ten times too small, and the child doesn't even notice. All of these examples indicate students' lack of understanding and are substantiated by research findings. (Burns, 1992, p. 6)

A growing priority in mathematics teaching today is to give students real-world experience with mathematical concepts so that they can make meaningful connections to word problems and understand what they are asking. Math is a language for exploring patterns, functions, and measures and for solving problems. Like any other language, children need to learn what the numbers and symbols stand for. To see a number as an abstract object hanging out there is useless and misleading. The "2" that a child sees on paper stands for two *of something*. Numbers refer to the real world and should be explored in the world.

The class had spent a number of sessions adding and subtracting double-digit numbers and using marbles, paper clips, and other objects. They kept groups of 10 to the left of the 1s and became comfortable with the concept of what numbers meant in the two digits. When we shifted from working with things to working with the numbers on paper, the kids had slightly different ways of calculating—all perfectly valid. Some students worked from right to left as I showed, but because I let them discover their own way of making calculations, they didn't feel that this was a "rule." One child subtracted the 10s first. When he got to the 1s and saw that there were not enough 1s to subtract, he reduced the answer in the 10s column by 1, subtracted from 10, and then added the 1s from the upper number to reach his answer. It was clear that he knew what he was doing. Another child came up with another solution: He explained in a problem that subtracted 59 from 83, "Since I need 6 more to give me 9 to subtract my 9 from, I can subtract the 3 in the upper figure from 9 to give me 6 and subtract 6 from one of the 10s in the 10s column, which will give me 4 in the 1s column. Then since I lost 10 in the 10s column, I have 7 minus 5. So the answer is 24."

—Second-grade teacher

Clearly, these students understand the mathematical process of subtracting double digits and can arrive at the answer in different ways. Once children can make sense of mathematical operations through manipulating and experimenting with objects, they can solve more difficult problems by building on the skills and knowledge they gained from this experience.

Solving problems is the essence of mathematics, and for young children, early lessons should build on the students' emergent understanding of mathematical concepts. The students should "discover" solutions to puzzling problems by manipulating materials and testing their ideas. When they actively engage in a process and apply reason to what they already understand, a number of them will arrive at solutions in different ways, and this is the ideal. As the example just cited shows, a teacher who sees this happening knows that the children are not following a formula but are actively working through each problem with a clear sense of what the problem is in real-world terms.

In many cases, young children use strategies for solving problems intuitively. They read a problem about a raccoon stealing 1/4 of a gingerbread cake and a dog making off with 1/2 of what is left, and they draw the cake, thinking about the best way to show 1/4. Should they make a round cake with four sections or a square one sliced in half on both sides? Or, they might prefer to find four small blocks, push them together, and pretend each block is 1/4 of the cake. The child who does this may raise her hand and say, "1/2 of what's left means you can put 1/4 side by side, and then you need to get a saw and saw this other in half, so it's 1/4 and 1/2 of 1/4." Although the child may not know yet how to convert this answer to "3/8," she understands what she's doing and has solved the problem!

With support and guidance, many students can create their own solutions to problems such as this. But they also need to become familiar with a range of useful math strategies and learn when and how to apply them. Examples (Burns, 1992, p. 19) include the following:

- look for a pattern,
- construct a table,
- make an organized list,
- act it out,
- draw a picture,
- use objects,
- guess and check,
- work backward,

- write an equation,

- solve a simpler (or similar) problem,

- make a model.

Other strategies may occur to you as you teach. Some teachers post problem-solving strategies on the wall so that students can refer to them before they begin working on a problem. A display such as this becomes useful when the class discusses and shares what strategies they used. It also expands the range of processes children can apply to the problem at hand. For young children who often need to experience mathematical concepts in creative ways, you can add strategies such as these:

- listen to, record, and tap out the rhythms of music, percussion, or any sounds;

- paint a math problem on one sheet and then paint the solution on another sheet;

- choreograph geometric patterns;

- estimate distances between points by regular steps, hops, and skips;

- create a physical action to represent such symbols as "+, −, =, >, <," and so forth;

- measure the ratio between an object in a poster and its shadow;

- draw three- and four-sided patterns from nature;

- express the phenomena of gravity, force, momentum, and pressure through dance and mime.

If the larger purpose of math instruction is to enable young students to solve problems and to reason, test, explore, and discover solutions, teachers need to find many different ways for them to do this. A differentiated classroom varies not only the pace and level of math content but also the "intelligences" involved (e.g., visual-spatial, bodily-kinesthetic, verbal-linguistic, logical-mathematical). It enables advanced students to attempt more challenging applications and those who need to spend more time practicing a skill or concept to do so, using the materials that work best for them.

To be successful, this kind of classroom typically includes three components. The first component is direct instruction, whereby a teacher introduces the new concept or skill to be learned, gives directions for an initial activity and shows where the materials are. The second component is exploration, whereby the children work on problems to solve. In some cases, they may all work on a similar problem but at different levels (depending on experience and mastery). In other cases, the teacher may have a "menu" of activities that vary in process, level of difficulty, and materials involved. The children can select different activities according to their needs but still focus on the same concept (e.g., place value or measuring and comparing perimeters). The third component is sharing, where the teacher and students come together and evaluate the strategies they used. They raise questions about the process and how a particular strategy worked and then brainstorm other ways of solving the problem.

CHOOSE THE LEARNING "DESTINATION" (STEP 2)

Previous chapters have explored the importance of beginning all curriculum planning (i.e., the "journey") with an understanding of the "travelers"—that is, the students (Step 1). Obviously, selecting an appropriate "journey" can only take place if you know what sort of experience, skill, special strengths, and weaknesses the travelers bring with them. During the first few months of teaching, try to find an opportunity to explore the experiences children have had. Counting to a high number, though impressive to some adults, does not signify mathematical understanding. But direct experiences in a variety of contexts may reveal intuitive understandings or skills that a parent or even the child would not think to mention.

> When I start my first math lessons for the year, I try to connect what we're about to learn with the kids' lives. I ask them about many different domains where mathematics applies—building things with blocks and other materials, dancing, playing music, shopping, measuring, etc. I ask if any of them have been involved in these activities. Kids' who love telling you anything about their lives, soon volunteer, and as they talk, I scribble and sketch their stories on the board. They can't read much but are intrigued that I've written down what they've said. It also helps me because this is useful information that I will copy down into a notebook later on. I draw things from their everyday lives. "How many of you put your own shoes on?" After they raise their hands, I ask, "How do you know which shoe goes on which foot?" From

there we talk a little about shape and size. Then I move on to other things. "How many of you were shorter last year than you are this year?" Usually, most hands go up. I explain that this is math too. I had one child from Serbia whose father owned a grocery store, and he said that he likes to watch his older sister make change at the cash register. "That's math!" I exclaimed. The kids love this activity because they see all the math that they have in their lives. What I love about this is that I can make immediate links between specific math concepts and their experiences.

—Kindergarten teacher

When you develop your math units, you can create a vibrant link between your students' abilities and experiences and the most important content of the discipline. As shown in the last three chapters, choosing an appropriate learning "destination" should focus on the following (Wiggins & McTighe, 1998, pp. 10–11):

- a "big idea" of enduring understanding;
- an idea, topic, or process that resides at the heart of the discipline;
- an idea, topic, or process that requires uncoverage;
- an idea, topic, or process that engages students.

An example of a "destination" that meets these requirements in math might be the following:

The children will understand that many things around them appear in patterns and groups. This is a "big idea" of enduring understanding because it shows young children that patterns in twos, threes, fours, and so on describe things in nature and all around them. It resides at the heart of the discipline because finding patterns is an essential part of mathematics and a core understanding for arithmetic. It is an idea requiring uncoverage because although toddlers group blocks and books and other objects together, conceptualizing a pattern is a more advanced step, requiring you to begin with what is closest to their experience. It engages young children because of the versatility of the subject; patterns exist in so many media—from the rhythms in a favorite song to the pattern in the kitchen tile to the petals of an open flower. It is an idea that integrates well with other subjects, such as science, language arts, and visual and performing arts: the rhythms of a drumming sequence, the lines and points of a choreographed dance, the drama of an addition story, the calculation of an orbit, or the probability of rain.

For early mathematics instruction, a key part of any "destination" must be to give young children an understanding that numbers, patterns, quantities, and shapes exist *in the world*. Math is a way of observing and exploring this world and giving students the tools and experiences they need to discover hidden patterns and principles. Knowing how to add or how to identify shapes only becomes significant in real contexts, which is why any "destination" must focus on actual situations or phenomena. For example, identifying tree species requires some understanding of numbers and patterns. A young child can examine numbers and patterns by comparing a simple leaf and a compound leaf or a feather compound (where leaflets grow on either side of a twig) and a fan compound (where leaves shoot out at the end of a stem in a fan shape). To identify anything in nature, you need to pay attention to shape, size, pattern, and number. How do ornithologists know if a bird is in the finch family or the warbler family? They look, among other things, at the thickness and length of the beak and the general size of the two families of birds.

IDENTIFY EVIDENCE OF UNDERSTANDING (STEP 3)

After you know what your "destination" is, you need to decide what evidence (in the form of assignments, projects, behaviors, etc.) will prove that the students have reached the goal (i.e., *understand* the concepts intended). Carefully consider the different abilities, special needs, and unique learning styles of your students. If you have several bilingual children, a couple of students with learning disabilities, and several advanced students, you can adjust the form that this "evidence" takes. For example, if the "destination" involves understanding how to calculate the area of an object or shape, you could establish the following as "evidence":

- explain the meaning of *area* in their own words;
- create a unit of measure (a sheet, a book, a block) and demonstrate how to figure out the area of a table, a room, and so forth;
- show how to compare the area of two similar things by lining them up;

- measure the length and width of a geometric shape and multiply (an advanced student might do this).

These are just four examples of how you might have children express their understanding. Students should be given many opportunities to explain what they're doing—how they solved the problem and why they chose the method they did. They should also have *time* to show what they have mastered because young children are more likely to have trouble understanding what you want to know or expressing themselves clearly.

> I wanted the kids to perform the mathematical process I created in a story. It was about mice dividing up a piece of cheese. First, there were two of them, and so they split the piece in half; then six more came and they wanted some. I asked the class how many different ways they could divide the cheese up for eight mice. They each had a good-sized piece of cheese made of cardboard and a pair of scissors. There's always a chance, in group work, that some of the kids will just do what the other kids are doing rather than take the time to work it out for themselves. So, to avoid this, I asked each of them to write down what they did and why. They could also create a sketch to show the process—even drawing the eight hungry mice and how each one got an equal piece of the cheese. In another group, I had a situation where the kids had to figure out how three caterpillars would divide up a feathered compound that had eight leaflets on it (this was related to a science unit we were also doing). "What would you do with the two extra leaflets to make this fair?" I asked. Some kids decided they should just throw them out so no one would have them. Someone else said that each one could take turns taking a bite until the two leaflets are gone. Some students, though, said that if you divided each of the two leaves into three bits, it would mean that each caterpillar got two whole leaflets and an extra two thirds of a leaf. Observing the kids work, I learned the value of providing different ways for them to do a math process. I can observe what they really understand, rather than what they've managed to copy from each other.
>
> *—Third-grade teacher*

This kind of activity enables you to see how well your students understand the concepts you're teaching and also what processes they use as they work through the assignment.

PLAN THE JOURNEY (STEP 4)

From their earliest years, young children are measuring and calculating things. From a pile of family boots in the closet, they choose the ones that look like the right size for their feet. They try on their mittens and realize they're too big. They delight in wearing their parents' clothes that hang loosely about them and drag along the floor. When thinking of catalysts to begin a unit, try to draw on the everyday experiences of young children and include commonplace objects they're used to handling such as shoes, combs, utensils, cardboard boxes, and so on.

> How do you teach kindergarteners to compare sizes? They can tell me if their foot is larger or smaller than their parents. But they can't tell me how they know this. One child will say, "My foot is only this big (holding up his hands to demonstrate), and my dad has a much bigger foot—like this! (holding hands out widely)." Then I ask, "Is my hand bigger or smaller than yours?" They answer "bigger," and I invite different children to prove it to me. It's interesting how many different ways they come up with to show me. One kid will draw around his hand and around my hand and compare the two sizes. Another one will place her hand flat on the desk and mine right next to hers and show me how my fingers go way beyond hers. A couple of kids will think of lining our two hands up together. From here, I can arrange a number of activities for different groups to calculate relative sizes. A couple of kids may even be ready to create a unit of measurement, like a large paper clip, and measure the lengths of different objects and compare them.
>
> —*Kindergarten teacher*

Introduce a New Unit to Preassess

Many teachers already have an idea of what their students can do based on prior lessons. In mathematics, where units often build on concepts sequentially, assessment should focus on how well students apply these concepts to real contexts. This is particularly important because young children can't always explain their thinking process or why they chose a particular strategy to solve a problem.

If your students are learning how to add, you might preassess by

- asking them to explain what addition is;
- having them give an example of addition in a way that they prefer—using manipulatives, drawing or diagramming an addition problem, or showing the process by moving bodies or by acting out an addition situation;
- showing what the symbols of an addition problem mean;
- creating an addition problem from a painting, using objects in that painting;
- adding the petals of one flower to the petals of another flower.

Sometimes, a pretest will provide enough information to gauge a child's skill and understanding. But some students may not understand the format of the test. Other students may know addition in an algorithm form—that is, they can add two figures when it's written, "5 + 3 = "—but may not see how it applies to a word problem. Hence, preassessments such as those suggested above can go further in showing specific areas where children have mastered a concept and where they need more instruction or support.

If you're introducing completely new material and want to know how prepared your students are, you can design an experience such as the following:

Children may know how to add and subtract when presented with "6 + 8" or "9 – 4," but they often have a difficult time connecting this with an actual situation. For young children, it helps to tell a story and add and subtract numbers on the blackboard. For example: "Once upon a time, 5 kangaroo moms hopped out into the field. Each had a baby in her pouch. The babies were happy while their moms were hopping, but when they stopped, the baby roos got bored. The kangaroo moms found 3 friends to talk to in the field and they couldn't stop talking. So the baby roos jumped out and went off to play. When the 3 friends left, the 5 moms found their babies, put them back in their pouches, and hopped home together." While telling a story like this, you can sketch little figures and also write what's happening in algorithms. Five kangaroo moms plus the 5 babies equal 10 kangaroos (5 + 5 = 10). Then they meet their 3 friends (10 + 3 = 13). For a while, there are 13 kangaroos. Five roos leave (13 − 5 = 8). Later, the 3 friends leave (8 − 3 = 5). Then the kangaroo moms found their little roos and put them back in their pouches (5 + 5 = 10). As you progress in the story, you can ask, "How would I write that? How many kangaroos did we have before this happened? How many are there now?" Invite the children to add more to the story. This demonstration quickly gives students an idea of how to translate a tale into an algorithm and vice versa.

You can discover useful information through this sort of activity. By student responses to and participation in the story, you can gauge their level of understanding and style of thinking. Imaginative processes help young children to visualize mathematical scenarios and solutions.

Sequence Teaching Strategies and Learning Activities

Examples of how you can sequence learning activities to meet a wider range of needs and abilities follow.

- *Destination:* The children will understand that addition increases the number and subtraction decreases the quantity.

    Standard: Demonstrate knowledge and use of numbers and their representations in a broad range of theoretical and practical settings.

    Evidence: Children can act out simply worded addition and subtraction "stories," find the answer, and record them symbolically. They can depict addition and subtraction problems through visual means.

    Teaching strategy: Guided inquiry. Focus on the process of adding and subtracting in different ways. For example, you could start out with a group of large index cards with dramatic scenarios written down, such as this: "You are all animals in a zoo. Three animals are locked in a large area outside—two rhinos and one monkey. Three new ones join them—another monkey, an elephant, and a gazelle. At night, when everyone has fallen asleep, the two monkeys scale the wall and escape. How many animals are left? What will happen next? Will the monkeys be returned? Will they unlock the gate and let all the animals escape? Write out the different scenarios in math symbols."

Learning activity: The children work on their math dramas and write the scenarios in the form of algorithms. For more practice, they receive addition and subtraction problems written as algorithms, create a story from them, and present their math stories to each other. You can reinforce their learning through a variety of situations: Use paintings or prints to create addition and subtraction problems. Use old photographs of the children to show how they can prove each other's present age ("if the photo was taken 2 years ago and she was 4 years old then, how can you figure out how old she is now?").

Resources: Books, art materials, numbers and symbols written in large letters and displayed.

Grouping: Tiered groups. Young children often express different levels of understanding, and tiered instruction allows you to vary the complexity.

Adjustments: More advanced children should have an opportunity to extend their math stories to create more complex situations. Children with specific learning styles can acquire new concepts through appropriate means (kinetic learners manipulate objects, dramatize mathematical situations, etc.).

- *Destination:* The children will understand the concept of multiplication and division in terms of patterns and repetitions.

    Standard: Investigate, represent, and solve problems using number facts, operations (addition, subtraction, multiplication, division), and their properties, algorithms, and relationships.

    Evidence: Children can explain that multiplication involves adding a number (such as 4) a specified number of times (e.g., three times) and that division involves subtracting a number (such as 2) from another number (such as 8) until there's nothing left. They can explain that 2×4 means adding four 2s together. They can show that 8 divided by 2 means finding out how many 2s are in 8. They can give real-life examples of these operations.

Teaching strategy: Inquiry; guided questioning. Lean a mirror against the front wall and place two stuffed animals in front of it. Ask, "How many pairs of animals do you see?" Then add two more. "How many pairs of animals can you see now? Four pairs of animals means how many animals altogether?" Have the children write down how they added up the pairs. Then ask the class to draw a diagram of a mirror with many different stuffed animals standing in front of it in groups of three, then in groups of four. Ask, "How many stuffed animals in a group of three? In a group of four?" They can write the solution in sketches and symbols.

Learning activity: Children practice working with 2s until they become comfortable with the concept using this number. Activities could include situations such as the following: A child has a bag of eight objects, which he takes out two at a time, and says, "2 plus 2 plus 2, etc.," keeping each group of 2 separate. Ask, "How many times did you pull the 2s out of the bag?" Because multiplying involves repeated actions with the same number, students can extend this in different ways. Example: Children work in pairs. One of them chooses a small number (preferably 4 and below). This child hops out the number and then stops, hops out the same number again and stops, and so on (not too many times!). The other child counts out loud the number of times the child hops, counts the number with paper clips, and puts them in a pile. He repeats this process however many times the child hops and places each pile next to the one before. The two look at the results and conclude, "Three hops six times over." Now reverse this for division. The children count the paper clips, knowing that each one is a hop, and work out how many groups of the same number of hops they can get out of this number. They record their findings.

Resources: Manipulatives (paper clips, marbles, or other math materials), paper, pencils.

Grouping: Ability or tiered groups; independent study.

Adjustments: Independent study options for advanced children. If the children have a definable range of skills, tiered assignments would allow those with a strong grasp of multiplication and division to work on more challenging assignments. Students who find math symbols too abstract should not use symbols at all for a while. When they begin to use them, have the students explain the symbols in real-life terms.

- *Destination:* The children will understand that measurement is a way to figure out the ratio of one object to another.

  Standard: Measure and compare quantities using appropriate units, instruments, and methods.

  Evidence: Children can compare two objects using their own standard of measurement and write it in their own way. Children can record the ratio on paper and explain what they are doing.

  Teaching strategy: Inquiry; guided questioning. Read a book such as Stuart Murphy's *Bigger, Better, Best!* Guide the class through two steps: (a) making comparisons between objects by matching and (b) comparing objects with nonstandard units. Have two children stand next to each other. Who is taller? Students offer their answers. Continue with other things—books, shoes, or pens. Children offer their own things to match up and take turns telling which one is larger, longer, and fatter. Next, have children use an object as *a measuring unit*—a hand, a book, or a pen—and then measure two objects. They share results: "This book is two hands; this book is two hands and part of my hand. This desk is three books long; the teacher's desk is seven books long." Allow plenty of time for children to share their findings and system of measurement.

  Learning activity: Students apply their initial measuring experiences to learn about ratios. Pose questions such as, "How much bigger is your body than your foot?" Guide children in using string to measure the length of each other's bodies, toe to head; cut the string. Then, they count the number of times they can extend the string from toe to heel. You can show them how to express this: Foot/Height = 1:6. Children break up into groups to explore other ratios with their body (hand to leg, head to body, etc.).

Resources: Collected objects for measuring, books, art materials, art books, string.

Grouping: Ability groups.

Adjustments: Cluster children who already understand simple ratios; they could work on more challenging ratios or begin using standard measurements or explore ratios through creative writing or the visual arts. Make adjustments for children who are not visual learners or who may need to tackle mathematical concepts within an interest area. For example, you could find out what they collect and encourage them to do ratios within a collection.

• *Destination:* The children will understand that shapes, angles, lengths, lines, sizes, and proportions are attributes that identify what something is in nature (species or type).

Standard: Identify, describe, classify, and compare relationships using points, lines, planes, and solids.

Evidence: The children can list differences between shapes based on how many sides and corners the shape has, whether the lines are curved or straight, and the size and proportion of different parts of the shape. They can make different kinds of shapes and describe differences between two species of leaves or animals on the basis of shape, proportions, angles, lines, and so on.

Teaching strategy: Inquiry, guided questioning. Read Leonard Fisher's *Look Around! A Book About Shapes* and explore with students the real-world shapes around them. Ask, "Where do you see circles in this room—even tiny ones? Curves? Straight lines? Rectangles, squares?" Ask the children to compare them. "How is the shape of the door different from the shape of the table?" As a creative alternative, have the children brainstorm how many ways they can use circular and four-sided shapes. Do a drawing of a scene with the children. List all the things you want to put in the drawing (kids, animals, trees, mountains, etc.) and ask, "How do we make a person out of these shapes? How should we make arms or feet?" Have different children contribute to the drawing. Ask questions about the lengths of lines, the pointiness of the corners, and the fatness of different parts. For example, "What is the difference between this four-sided shape here and that one there?" Ask for differences in length, width, breadth, and so on. Give the students cutout circles, squares, rectangles, and triangles and prints or paintings of different scenes (both rural and urban). Ask, "Are any of the shapes you have like any of the shapes you see in these prints and paintings?" Have the children move the shapes around on the artwork and explore where the circular, curved, and pointed shapes are.

Learning activity: Children transfer what they've learned in these introductory experiences about shapes, sizes, angles, lines, and so forth to examine specific patterns in nature. Use identification books on trees and animals (or you can photocopy shapes or enlarge and duplicate them). Children compare a "simple leaf" with a "compound leaf," as well as the patterns and shape of the simple leaf and "leaflets." They then fold them over to determine if they're symmetrical; if not, they determine why not. Include real leaves from outside as much as possible. The students can create lists of observations, focusing on size, angles of pointy areas of the leaf, and a comparison with other shapes they learned—circles, oblongs, triangles, and so forth. They determine a species based on attributes of the shapes (wide leaves with many points such as the eastern sycamore vs. the long, slender leaves of the common elderberry); patterns (wavy-edged, toothed—including single-toothed, double-toothed, lines of the veins); and number (e.g., the "feather-compound" with leaves in twos and the "fan-compound" with leaves in the shape of a star). Children can do a similar process with animal life. They can examine the different shapes of starfish, shellfish, and regular fish.

Resources: Identification books; photocopies of trees, plants, and animals that show the shapes; examples of real leaves; art materials; rulers or some nonstandard unit of measurement.

Grouping: Tiered groups.

Adjustments: Adjust level of difficulty so that children who are comfortable with more complex patterns can explore these; those who need more time with simply shaped leaves or animals can explore fewer differences, inconsistencies, and so on.

- *Destination:* The children will understand that triangles can be combined with other triangles to make a wide variety of shapes with more than three sides.

  Standard: Demonstrate and apply geometric concepts involving points, lines, planes, and space.

  Evidence: Children can draw lines inside squares, rectangles, hexagons, octagons, and so on to make triangles. They can take cutouts of triangles and make a variety of shapes, including the shapes of animals, furniture, and landscapes. They can solve problems such as making a rectangle from two, three, four, and five triangles.

  Teaching strategy: Guided questioning, demonstration. Read an imaginative book about triangles such as Marilyn Burns and Gordon Silveria's *The Greedy Triangle.* Introduce a problem: "You are visiting an alien world made of triangles. You are the first person to visit this alien world who is not triangular. You can't stay at their hotel because the bed is triangular, and every time you try to walk through the door, you bump your head. (The teacher could have large sheets of cardboard to put together so that the children can see the problem that people would have getting through a triangular door.) So, you have to make your own place to stay. But the builders can only give you materials made of triangles." Give the students triangular shapes to experiment with or have them draw triangles on paper to sketch their ideas. Pose problems: "Can you make doors, beds, and desks out of triangles? How would you design a little house for you to stay using only triangles? How would you make the triangular windows? Is it possible to make a car and a wheel out of triangles?"

  Learning activity: After the above exploration, children tackle a complete environment. They could begin with the classroom. Ask, "Is there a way you could make a table out of triangles? What kinds of triangles would you need to make walls that look like our walls? How can you construct a door out of triangles? Can you make something round—like a doorknob—out of triangles? If we had a plant in this room, what would it look like? Can you make the plant's leaves look more like leaves even though you use triangles? Can you make three-sided windows into another shape? Can you make a person—you, me, or another student—out of triangles? Can you make the person look like an ordinary human being rather than a triangular one? What would you have to do to change the triangular being with the little pinhead and wide body into something more like us? Can you draw a human face out of triangles?" Children can refer to Picasso's cubist paintings and some surrealist work to see how artists have experimented with shape. Children may use a wide variety of materials to construct models, draw, graph, or create a collage that expresses their ideas of the hidden triangles in other objects.

Resources: Cutout triangles, art materials, sketchpads, rulers for measuring, art books and prints, design books.

Grouping: Independent.

Adjustments: Keep this process simple for students who need practice putting triangles together to make a variety of shapes with more than three sides. The students can focus on different ways to put sides together and how the arrangements enable them to see more triangles inside the larger shape. Advanced students often love assignments such as this and can be guided into different directions depending on particular strengths and learning preferences. Mathematical students may investigate perimeters of the shapes they create and compare perimeters of two sets of six triangles arranged differently; artistically gifted students may become intrigued by design possibilities.

- *Destination:* The children will understand what place value means in real-life situations involving adding or subtracting double-digit numbers.

  Standard: Solve problems using systems of numbers and their properties.

  Evidence: The children can group materials by 10s and explain why 20 is two 10s, 30 is three 10s, and so on. They can subtract other numbers from these piles and express this operation physically (e.g., they can remove one 10 and two 1s from four groups of 10 and show what is left).

They can read a story involving double-digit numbers, perform these operations concretely, and also write them down in algorithms.

Teaching strategy: Inquiry; guided questioning. Tell a story as a way of expressing the concept of place value. An example: "A mouse family called Billings moved into a large house. They had 6 mouse children. [Teacher draws the house.] Now, this house could only take 9 mice because the Mouse Mayor said, 'This is a House of 1s and it can take only 9 mice. No more!' So, after about a year, the mother had twins, which makes how many mice? [Children answer "10."] So what do they do? Father Mouse called the mayor, and he hired other mice to come and build a mouse condo to the left of them with 9 floors for 9 families. [Teacher draws large high-rise with 10 floors.] The Mouse Mayor said, 'This shall now be the House of 10s, and only families with 10 mice can live here.' So, the Billings family moved next door, and a new mouse family of 7 moved into the House of 1s. As soon as they got 10 mice, they would move into the second floor of the House of 10s, and another smaller family would move into the House of 1s." Stories such as this captivate young children and provide another way of learning place value. You can present many problems within a story, and the children will enjoy inventing scenarios of their own. What happens if you have a mouse family of 14? What happens if 5 mice from the House of 10s move away? You can apply this to place value with any double-digit number by drawing a line between the 2 and 8 of 28, for example, and drawing a house around each number so that the students can see the House of 10s and the House of 1s.

Learning activity: Children explore placement based on the above story. The rules have to be clear for the children to use mathematical reasoning. They should be written on the wall: (a) the House of 10s—the mouse condo with nine floors—is always to the left of the single-family home of 1s; (b) the single-family House of 1s can have no more than 9, but it can have any number below it; (c) the condo House of 10s must have exactly 10 mice per floor—no more, no less; (d) if 1 or more mice move out of the House of 10s, the rest of the mice have to move back to the single-family home. Another option is for the children to dramatize this, subtracting a single digit from a double digit (e.g., $15 - 8$). Ten children stand in the House of 10s, and 5 stand in the House of 1s. The class discusses different ways they can do this. For example, one is to remove 8 mice from the House of 10s, forcing the 2 remaining to move to the House of 1s and add onto the 5. Or, they can remove the 5 that are already in the House of 1s and then 3 more that are from the House of 10s. Because this is a "story," children will express different reasons for both. For example, a child might say, "We should let the 5 go because then at least the 8 that go to the House of 1s will still all be from the same mouse family." Remember that although we often teach children to perform double-digit subtraction from right to left, there's no reason why they cannot subtract from left to right as long as they understand what they're doing. Children can work on adding and subtracting double-digit numbers in groups. Then they can draw the operations or create groups of mice that they can move around and rearrange.

Resources: Boxes for House of 1s and House of 10s, egg cartons, art and construction materials (to make mice), paper with the House of 10s condo drawn to the left of the single-family House of 1s.

Grouping: Tiered groups.

Adjustments: Place value is definitely a subject that should not be rushed. Therefore, children should only move on to more difficult problems when they're ready. It's important to avoid having children follow a rule without understanding what they're doing. Most young children are kinetic learners (some more than others), and they need time to play around with this process. Advanced math students can move on to more challenging material. For example, they can deal with three-digit numbers or create word problems for each other by writing creative mouse stories.

ASSESS AND ADAPT INSTRUCTION (STEP 5)

At the end of your "itinerary" (math unit), you may find that most of the students understand the basic concept but not necessarily at the same level or in the same way. As described previously in this book (see Chapters 2 and 5–7), you should try to give your students opportunities to evaluate their own work, focusing on

1. the specific strengths they bring to mathematics and to the assignment at hand,

2. the criteria by which they and you should assess their work,

3. the areas of need (evident in their assignment), and

4. a plan for adapting the assignment to create a better bridge between the students and the curriculum.

Giving the children practice in reviewing their own work—seeing what they have mastered and where they got lost—is an important part of the learning "journey." The field of mathematics involves trial and error at its most advanced levels, and young children can become involved in this trial-and-error process if they understand the criteria by which they should evaluate their assignments. For example, let us say that you want your first-grade students to understand, in real terms, what "more expensive" and "less expensive" mean and be able to figure this out by understanding the value of pennies, nickels, dimes, and quarters. You could create a criteria list to guide their assessments:

Learning Goal: Children understand the value of pennies, nickels, dimes, and quarters and can calculate differences in expense.

Criteria:

- The children can show how many pennies are in a nickel, dime, and quarter.

- The children can order a group of objects (labeled "1 quarter, 2 dimes, 1 dime, and 1 nickel," etc.), from most to least expensive.

- The children can calculate the expense of one group of objects versus another group by adding the money from each and comparing (the change should have different combinations so children can identify value based on something more than the number of coins).

- Children can explain the expense of a thing by translating the currency into the number of pennies.

With criteria clearly identified, you and the children can observe areas of mastery and other areas where they need more practice. A child may tell you how many pennies are in a nickel, a dime, and a quarter and explain that things that cost two quarters are more expensive than things that cost two dimes. But he may also become confused when he sees 20 pennies and a nickel for one thing and three dimes for another. He might decide that, because the first thing has so many more coins, it costs more. If this happens, the child may require more practice with the coins, especially in converting money such as 20 pennies into two dimes or 2 quarters into 5 dimes. If he's a kinetic learner, he may benefit from a shopping scenario where he has a certain amount of play money and practices buying things with different combinations of cash. Soon, he will become more adept at instantly knowing that nickels—even when he has more of them and they are larger than dimes—never exceed 5 pennies.

Almost every class has some math whizzes who come to class already knowing a fair amount of the content you intend to teach. If one of your students, for example, already understands that multiplying three by four means adding three four times, you may want to introduce division to create a more challenging problem that will still involve grouping numbers in a repeated sequence. Example:

> Give the student a broken telephone receiver from a cordless phone. Tell her to look at each letter of her name and write down the corresponding number for each letter. She could then choose the lowest number and work out how many times this number can be found in all the other ones. Have her write this down. What's left over? If these leftover numbers are added together, how many times does the lowest number go into the leftover numbers? By the end, she should have the total number of times the lowest number goes into the total of all the other numbers. Ask her to explain and diagram her process.

You could use a rubric such as the following to assess the suitability of the assignment and monitor the child's progress:

Student: _Amanda Deering_

Content mastered: _Understands that multiplication means adding a number over and over, and can apply it to different situations_

Adjusted assignment: _Examine numbers of her first name (each letter corresponds to a number from the phone receiver), note repeated numbers, and figure out how many times one of the small numbers can be found in all the larger numbers combined. Create a diagram._

Criteria	Incomplete	Fair	Excellent
Write out each number of name.	Only half of the numbers included.	Almost all of the numbers present.	All numbers included.
Choose smallest number and figure out how many times this number can be found in the rest of the numbers in the name.	Chose number; strategy is weak and expresses student's confusion, especially about numbers left over.	Chose number; strategy shows that student understands process but still has kinks to work out.	Chose number; strategy works and enables student to solve problem quickly.
Create a diagram on paper that shows each step taken.	Drawing is incomplete and unclear.	Drawing shows that student understands process, but misses some steps.	Drawing is detailed and clear.

Notes:_____

_____

In mathematics, where you are attempting to expand the children's repertoire of problem-solving strategies, it's often helpful to have them compare their work with their peers. You can create a variety of scenarios that focus on specific math concepts. Here are examples:

Assignment: Show how four kids who found one quarter, one dime, and one penny can divide the money equally.

1. Convert each coin into pennies and add.

2. Choose a strategy for dividing the money between four.

3. Create a diagram, sketch, or small dramatization to show the process.

Assignment: Write an algorithm that expresses the action in a story and use characters in a story to create a new algorithm.

1. Identify number of characters in the book (e.g., in *The Three Little Pigs*, there are four: three pigs and one wolf).

2. Diagram or draw a sequence, focusing on the scenes when the numbers change.

3. Create a new algorithm as a plot for a different three pigs story.

4. Invent a new story expressing the new algorithm.

Assignment: Measure a ratio based on an object and its shadow in the sun.

1. Put a stick in the earth on a sunny day and measure its length with ruler.

2. Measure the length of stick and compare it to the length of its shadow.

3. Measure the shadow of a person and create a strategy for figuring out how to calculate the original size from the shadow.

Working in tiered groups, the students can tackle projects at more or less the same level of knowledge and ability. They can write up a list of the different methods they used to solve a problem, switch papers, and try each other's strategies. Some teachers have students compare the different methods they used in their group and then report which one worked best for a particular problem and why.

You can take each of these three assignments and create a rating scale to gauge each child's strengths and weaknesses. An example:

Assignment: Measure the average distance that migrating whooping cranes travel each day from Baraboo, Wisconsin, to Florida.

Learning Objectives:

- To understand what information is needed to solve this kind of problem.
- To understand the mathematical operation required to come up with an average daily distance.
- To be able to try different methods for solving the problem.

Criteria   **Rating Scale (1–3)**

1. Create a map that shows the birds' route, number of miles, and number of days. _____

2. Add the total number of miles; then add total number of traveling days. _____

3. Divide miles by days and explain why in own language. Or, if child knows only a little division, figure out another way to find average. _____

Comments: _____

_____

From rating scales such as these, you can identify where a child may need more practice or instruction and make adjustments in the following ways.

1. *Design an identical problem or process that is simpler and more accessible to the students.* An example of the above whooping crane assignment would be as follows: "A couple of lazy cranes traveled a total of 10 miles in 2 days. What was the average number of miles they traveled each of the 2 days?" The children can think about the process more easily in this example because you have simplified the problem. For a gifted math student, you could either introduce new content or a more challenging application of a concept.

2. *Design alternative means for solving the problem—a means that reflects the strengths or learning styles of the children.* An example of this might be to have the children reproduce the migratory route on the floor with yarn and masking tape, create a scale for measuring distances, and construct models of the whooping cranes. Many children—especially young ones—cannot think through a process without first doing it. Other students may prefer to begin by reading a story about migration or by creating a story of their own that focuses on a single crane's adventures traveling south.

In each of these cases, you improve a student's access to specific concepts and skills by varying the level of difficulty and responding to his or her interests and learning styles. Differentiating gives you the flexibility to create diverse assignments within a larger curriculum goal. You might have an advanced child working with fractions and another child just beginning to divide, yet both are focused on grouping smaller numbers within larger ones. Some of these children may learn best by designing a visual display and others by dramatizing different scenarios of buying and selling in a store.

For young students, stories, drawing, and dramatizations are as important as math manipulatives in helping them understand fundamental concepts and apply these to solving problems. There is a high level of motivation when they have an imaginative context to explore math processes. A child may be bored using manipulatives to find the common denominator of two fractions. But this changes when he's faced with the problem of dividing four large brownies among six hungry trolls who held up a bakery. Drawing sketches of the six trolls and the four brownies, he will say, "Each of these trolls has to have some of each of these brownies to be fair."

In this sort of context, the child becomes invested in the creative scene and wants to solve the problem. With coaching and questioning from you, he begins to find ways to solve the problem mathematically. How much of each brownie should he give each troll? How should he divide it?

Some children will see that you can divide each brownie three ways; others will have to divide each one six times first in order to discover, by the pattern they have created, that they could have divided it three ways. Young children often show much more persistence in solving mathematical puzzles when they can invest their imagination and creative thinking in this way.

LOOKING AHEAD

In the next section, you will find an extensive list of sources for primary teachers. We have included books on general topics as well as lists of sources within specific subject areas. We hope that you will find them useful in designing educational alternatives that better meet your students' needs.

SAMPLE OF STATE GOALS AND STANDARDS (ILLINOIS)

Goal 1: Demonstrate and apply a knowledge and sense of numbers, including numeration and operations (addition, subtraction, multiplication, division), patterns, ratios, and proportions

Standards:

- **Demonstrate knowledge and use of numbers and their representations in a broad range of theoretical and practical settings.** (Early elementary: Identify whole numbers and compare them using the symbols <, >, or = and the words less than, greater than, or equal to, applying counting, grouping, and place value concepts. Identify and model fractions using concrete materials and pictorial representations.)

- **Investigate, represent, and solve problems using number facts, operations (addition, subtraction, multiplication, division), and their properties, algorithms, and relationships.** (Early elementary: Solve one- and two-step problems with whole numbers using addition, subtraction, multiplication, and division.)

- **Compute and estimate using mental mathematics, paper-and-pencil methods, calculators, and computers.** (Early elementary: Select and perform computational procedures to solve problems with whole numbers. Show evidence that whole-number computational results are correct and/or that estimates are reasonable.)

- **Solve problems using comparison of quantities, ratios, proportions, and percents.** (Early elementary: Compare the numbers of objects in groups.)

Goal 2: Estimate, make, and use measurements of objects, quantities, and relationships and determine acceptable levels of accuracy

Standards:

- **Measure and compare quantities using appropriate units, instruments, and methods.** (Early elementary: Measure length, volume, and weight/mass using rulers, scales, and other appropriate measuring instruments in the customary and metric systems. Measure units of time using appropriate instruments— for example, calendars, clocks, and watches. Identify and describe the relative values and relationships among coins and solve addition and subtraction problems using currency. Read temperatures to the nearest degree from Celsius and Fahrenheit thermometers.)

- **Estimate measurements and determine acceptable levels of accuracy.** (Early elementary: Given a problem, describe possible methods for estimating a given measure. Compare estimated measures taken with appropriate measuring instruments.)

- **Select and use appropriate technology, instruments, and formulas to solve problems, interpret results, and communicate findings.** (Early elementary: Determine perimeter and area using concrete materials—for example, geoboards, square tiles, grids, and measurement instruments.)

Goal 3: Use algebraic and analytical methods to identify and describe patterns and relationships in data, solve problems, and predict results

Standards:

- **Describe numerical relationships using variables and patterns.** (Early elementary: Identify, describe, and extend simple geometric and numeric patterns. Solve simple number sentences.)

- **Interpret and describe numerical relationships using tables, graphs, and symbols.** (Early elementary: Solve problems involving pattern identification and completion of patterns.)

- **Solve problems using systems of numbers and their properties.** (Early elementary: Describe the basic arithmetic operations orally and in writing, using concrete materials and drawings.)

- **Use algebraic concepts and procedures to represent and solve problems.** (Early elementary: Find the unknown numbers in whole-number addition, subtraction, multiplication, and division situations.)

Goal 4: Use geometric methods to analyze, categorize, and draw conclusions about points, lines, planes, and space

Standards:

- **Demonstrate and apply geometric concepts involving points, lines, planes, and space.** (Early elementary: Identify related two- and three-dimensional shapes, including circle-sphere, square-cube, triangle-pyramid, rectangle-rectangular prism, and their basic properties. Draw two-dimensional shapes.)

- **Identify, describe, classify, and compare relationships using points, lines, planes, and solids.** (Early elementary: Identify and describe characteristics, similarities, and differences of geometric shapes. Sort, classify, and compare familiar shapes. Identify lines of symmetry in simple figures and construct symmetrical figures using various concrete materials.)

- **Construct convincing arguments and proofs to solve problems.** (Early elementary: Draw logical conclusions and communicate reasoning about simple geometric figures and patterns using concrete materials, diagrams, and contemporary technology.)

Goal 5: Collect, organize, and analyze data using statistical methods; predict results; and interpret uncertainty using concepts of probability

Standards:

- **Organize, describe, and make predictions from existing data.** (Early elementary: Organize and display data using pictures, tallies, tables, charts, or bar graphs. Answer questions and make predictions based on given data.)

- **Formulate questions, design data collection methods, gather and analyze data, and communicate findings.** (Early elementary: Formulate questions of interest and design surveys or experiments to gather data. Collect, organize, and describe data using pictures, tallies, tables, charts, or bar graphs. Analyze data, draw conclusions, and communicate the results.)

- **Determine, describe, and apply the probabilities of events.** (Early elementary: Describe the concept of probability in relationship to likelihood and chance. Systematically list all possible outcomes of a simple one-stage experiment—for example, the flip of one coin, the toss of one die, the spin of a spinner.)

Bibliography

I. RESOURCES FOR TEACHERS

General Topics

Armstrong, D. G. (2003). *Curriculum today.* Upper Saddle River, NJ: Merrill/Prentice Hall.

Bigge, M. L., & Shermis, S. S. (1999). *Learning theories for teachers.* New York: Longman.

Burke, K., Fogarty, R., & Belgrad, S. (1994). *The portfolio connection.* Palatine, IL: IRI/Skylight.

Clayton, M., & Forton, M. B. (2001). *Classroom spaces that work.* Greenfield, MA: Northeast Foundation for Children.

Discovery Channel, instructional ideas that tie into programming offered, *Classroom Activities,* www.school.discovery.com

Edwards, C., Gandini, L., & Forman, G. (1998). *The hundred languages of children* (2nd ed.). Norwood, NJ: Ablex.

Elkind, D. (1998). *Reinventing childhood, raising and educating children in a changing world.* Rosemont, NJ: Modern Learning Press.

Erickson, E. (1993). *Childhood and society* (Rev. ed.). New York: Norton.

Flack, J. (1993). *TalentEd: Strategies for developing the talent in every learner.* Englewood, CO: Teacher Ideas Press.

Fogarty, R., & Stoehr, J. (1995). *The mindful school: Integrating curricula with multiple intelligences.* Palatine, IL: IRI/SkyLight.

Forsten, C., Grant, J., & Hollas, B. (2002). *Different strategies for different learners.* Peterborough, NH: Crystal Springs Books.

Garcia, R. (1991). *Teaching in a pluralistic society: Concepts, models, strategies* (2nd ed.). New York: HarperCollins.

Gardner, H. (1993). *Multiple intelligences: The theory in practice.* New York: Basic Books.

Gardner, H. (1999). *Intelligence reframed: Multiple intelligences for the 21st century.* New York: Basic Books.

Good, T. L., & Brophy, J. E. (2000). *Looking in classrooms* (8th ed.). Boston: Longman.

Grant, J. (1998). *Developmental education in an era of high standards.* Rosemont, NJ: Modern Learning Press.

Gregory, G. H., & Chapman, C. (2002). *Differentiated instructional strategies: One size doesn't fit all.* Thousand Oaks, CA: Corwin Press.

Heacox, D. (2002). *Differentiating instruction in the regular classroom: How to reach and teach all learners, Grades 3–12.* Minneapolis: Free Spirit Press.

Katz, L., & McClellan, D. (1997). *Fostering children's social competence: The teacher's role.* Washington, DC: National Association for the Education of Young Children.

Kitano, M. K., & Petersen, K. S. (2002). Action research and practical inquiry: Teaching gifted English learners. *Journal for the Education of the Gifted, 26*(2), 132–147.

Kitano, M. K., & Petersen, K. S. (2002). Multicultural content integration in gifted education. *Journal for the Education of the Gifted, 25*(3), 269–289.

Knopper, D. (1994). *Parent education: Parents as partners.* Boulder, CO: Open Space Communications.

Ladson-Billings, G. (1994). *Dreamkeepers: Successful teachers of African American children.* San Francisco: Jossey-Bass.

Lazear, D. (2001). *Pathways of learning: Teaching students and parents about multiple intelligences.* Tucson, AZ: Zephyr.

Linder, T. (1993). *Transdisciplinary play-based assessment.* Baltimore: Brookes.

McNeely, S. (1997). *Observing students and teachers through objective strategies.* Boston: Allyn & Bacon/Longman.

Moll, L. C. (1992). Funds of knowledge for teaching: Using a qualitative approach to connect homes and classrooms. *Theory Into Practice, 31*(2), 132–141.

Morrison, G. S. (1993). *Contemporary curriculum K–8.* Boston: Allyn & Bacon.

Morrison, G. S. (2000). *Teaching in America* (2nd ed.). Boston: Allyn & Bacon.

Paley, V. G. (1999). *The kindness of children.* Cambridge, MA: Harvard University Press.

Piirto, J. (1998). *Understanding those who create.* Scottsdale, PA: Gifted Psychology Press.

Renzulli, J., & Smith, L. (1978). *The learning styles inventory.* Mansfield Center, CT: Creative Learning Press.

Risko, V. J., & Bromley, K. (2001). *Collaboration for diverse learners: Viewpoints and practices.* Newark, DE: International Reading Association.

Roberts, P. L., & Kellough, R. D. (1999). *A guide for developing interdisciplinary thematic units* (2nd ed.). Upper Saddle River, NJ: Merrill/Prentice Hall.

Rolheiser, C., Bower, B., & Stevahn, L. (2000). *The portfolio organizer.* Alexandria, VA: Association for Supervision and Curriculum Development.

Ross, E. W. (1998). *Pathways to thinking: Strategies for developing independent learners K–8.* Norwood, MA: Christopher-Gordon.

Ruggiero, V. R. (1997). *The art of thinking: A guide to critical and creative thought* (5th ed.). New York: Longman.

Sisk, D. (2003). Maximizing the high potential of minority economically disadvantaged students. In J. F. Smutny (Ed.), *Underserved gifted populations: Responding to their needs and abilities* (pp. 239–259). Cresskill, NJ: Hampton.

Smutny, J. F. (2003). *Differentiated instruction: Fastback.* Bloomington, IN: Phi Delta Kappa Educational Foundation.

Smutny, J. F. (2003). *Gifted education: Promising practices.* Bloomington, IN: Phi Delta Kappa Educational Foundation.

Smutny, J. F. (Ed.). (2003). *Underserved gifted populations: Responding to their needs and abilities.* Cresskill, NJ: Hampton.

Strickland, K., & Strickland, J. (2000). *Making assessment elementary.* Portsmouth, NJ: Heinemann.

Tomlinson, C. A. (1999). *The differentiated classroom: Responding to the needs of all learners.* Alexandria, VA: Association for Supervision and Curriculum Development.

Tomlinson, C. A., & Eidson, C. C. (2003). *Differentiating in practice: A resource guide for differentiating curriculum (Grades K–5).* Alexandria, VA: Association for Supervision and Curriculum Development.

Tomlinson, C. A., Kaplan, S. N., Renzulli, J. S., Purcell, J., Leppien, J., & Burns, D. (2002). *The parallel curriculum: A design to develop high potential and challenge high-ability learners.* Thousand Oaks, CA: Corwin Press.

Torrance, E. P. (1977). *Discovery and nurturance of giftedness in the culturally different.* Reston, VA: Council for Exceptional Children.

Torrance, E. P., & Safter, T. (1990). *Incubation model of teaching: Getting beyond aha!* Buffalo, NY: Bearly Limited.

Torrance, E. P., & Sisk, D. A. (1998). *Gifted children in the regular classroom.* Buffalo, NY: Creative Education Foundation.

Treffinger, D., Hohn, R., & Feldhusen, J. (1979). *Reach each you teach.* East Aurora, NY: D.O.K. Publishers.

Udall, A., & Daniels, J. (1991). *Creating the thoughtful classroom: Strategies to promote student thinking.* Tucson, AZ: Zephyr.

Understanding Our Gifted: Differentiation (Vol. 15–1). (2002, Fall). Boulder, CO: Open Space Communication.

Wiggins, G., & McTighe, J. (1998). *Understanding by design.* Alexandria, CA: Association for Supervision and Curriculum Development.

Winebrenner, S. (1997). *Teaching kids with learning difficulties in the regular classroom: Strategies and techniques every teacher can use to challenge and motivate struggling students.* Minneapolis, MN: Free Spirit Publishing.

The Early Years

Beaty, J. J. (1996). *Skills for the preschool teacher.* Upper Saddle River, NJ: Merrill/Prentice Hall.

Billman, J., & Sherman, J. (2003). *Observation and participation in early childhood settings: A practicum guide* (2nd ed.). Boston: Allyn & Bacon/Longman.

Burns, M. S., Griffin, P., & Snow, C. E. (Eds.). (1999). *Starting out right: A guide to promoting children's success.* Washington, DC: National Academy Press.

Cadwell, L. B. (1997). *Bringing Reggio Emilia home: An innovative approach to early childhood education.* New York: Teachers College Press.

Cuffaro, H. K. (1995). *Experimenting with the world: John Dewey and the early childhood classroom.* New York: Teachers College Press.

De Gaetano, Y., William, L. R., & Volk, D. (1998). *Kaleidoscope: A multicultural approach for the primary school classroom.* Upper Saddle River, NJ: Merrill.

De Vries, R., & Zan, B. (1994). *Moral classrooms, moral children: Creating a constructivist atmosphere in early education.* New York: Teachers College Press.

De Vries, R., Zan, B., Hildebrandt, C., Edmiaston, R., & Sales, C. (2002). *Developing constructivist early childhood curriculum: Practical principles and activities.* New York: Teachers College Press.

Derman-Sparks, L., & ABC Task Force. (1989). *Anti-bias curriculum, tools for empowering young children.* Washington, DC: National Association for the Education of Young Children.

Dodge, D. T., & Colker, L. J. (1992). *The creative curriculum for early education* (3rd ed.). Washington, DC: Teaching Strategies.

Edwards, C., Gandini, L., & Forman, G. (Eds.). (1998). *The hundred languages of children: The Reggio Emilia approach—advanced reflections.* Greenwich, CT: Ablex.

Fisher, M. D., & Fisher, E. (1981). *The early education connection: An instructional resource for teachers and parents of pre-school and kindergarten children.* Manassas, VA: Gifted Education Press.

Grace, C., & Shores, E. F. (1992). *The portfolio and its use: Developmentally appropriate assessment of young children.* Little Rock, AR: Southern Association on Children Under Six.

Helm, J. H., & Beneke, S. (Eds.). (2003). *The power of projects: Meeting contemporary challenges in early childhood classrooms—strategies & solutions.* New York: National Association for the Education of Young Children.

Hohman, M., & Weikert, D. P. (1995). *Educating young children: Active learning practices for preschool and child care programs.* Ypsilanti, MI: High Scope Press.

Hughes, F. P. (1999). *Children, play, and development* (3rd ed.). Boston: Allyn & Bacon.

Jablon, J. R., Marsden, D. B., Meisels, S. J., & Dichtelmiller, M. L. (1994). *The work sam-

pling system omnibus guidelines: Preschool through third grade (3rd ed.). Ann Arbor, MI: The Work Sampling System.

Johnson, J., Christie, J., & Yawkey, T. (1999). *Play and early childhood development.* New York: Addison Wesley Longman.

Kaiser, B., & Rasminsky, J. S. (1999). *Meeting the challenge: Effective strategies for challenging behaviors in early childhood program.* Ottawa, Ontario: Canadian Child Care Federation.

Katz, L. G. (1995). *Talks with teachers of young children: A collection.* Norwood, NJ: Ablex.

Kendall, F. (1996). *Diversity in the classroom: New approaches to the education of young children.* New York: Teachers College Press.

Kostelnik, M., Onaga, E., Rohde, B., & Whiren, A. (2002). *Children with special needs: Lessons for early childhood professionals.* New York: Teachers College Press.

Kranor, L., & Kuschner, A. (Eds.). (1996). *Project exceptional—exceptional children: Education in preschool techniques for inclusion, opportunity-building, nurturing, and learning.* Sacramento: California Department of Education.

Meisels, S. (1987). *Developmental screening in early childhood: A guide.* Washington, DC: National Association for the Education of Young Children.

Montessori, M. (1964). *The Montessori method.* New York: Schocken.

Montessori, M. (1966). *The secret of childhood.* South Bend, IN: University of Notre Dame.

Morrison, G. (2001). *Early childhood education today* (8th ed.). Upper Saddle River, NJ: Merrill/Prentice Hall.

Morrison, G. S. (2000). *Fundamentals of early childhood education* (2nd ed.). Upper Saddle River, NJ: Merrill.

National Association for the Education of Young Children. (1996). *Responding to linguistic and cultural diversity: Recommendations for effective early childhood education.* Washington, DC: Author.

Odom, S. (Ed.). (2002). *Widening the circle: Including children with disabilities in preschool programs.* New York: Teachers College Press.

Piaget, J. (1977). *The development of thought: Equilibration of cognitive structures.* New York: Viking.

Piaget, J. (1980). *Adaptation and intelligence: Organic selection and phenocopy.* Chicago: University of Chicago Press.

Preschool curriculum framework and benchmarks for children in preschool programs. (1999, May). Hartford: Connecticut State Department of Education.

Roopnarine, J. L., Johnson, J. E., & Hooper, F. H. (Eds.). (1994). *Children's play in diverse cultures.* Albany: State of New York University Press.

Seefeldt, C. (Ed.). (1999). *The early childhood curriculum: Current findings in theory and practice* (3rd ed.). New York: Teachers College Press.

Smutny, J. (Ed.). (1998). *The young gifted child: Potential and promise, an anthology.* Cresskill, NJ: Hampton.

Smutny, J., Veenker, K., & Veenker, S. (1989). *Your gifted child: How to recognize and develop the special talents in your child from birth to age seven.* New York: Ballantine.

Smutny, J. F., Walker, S. Y., & Meckstroth, E. A. (1997). *Teaching young gifted children in the regular classroom: Identifying, nurturing, and challenging ages 4–9.* Minneapolis, MN: Free Spirit Publishing.

Vygotsky, L. S. (1962). *Thought and language* (E. Hanfmann & G. Vakar, Trans.). Cambridge: MIT Press.

Wolfgang, C. H., & Wolfgang, M. E. (1999). *School for young children: developmentally appropriate practices* (2nd ed.). Boston: Allyn & Bacon/Longman.

Wright, J. L., & Shade, D. D. (Eds.). (1994). *Young children: Active learners in a technological age.* Washington, DC: National Association for the Education of Young Children.

Creativity and the Arts

Bany-Winters, L. (1997). *On stage: Theatre games and activities for kids.* Chicago: Chicago Review Press.

Beal, N. (2001). *The art of teaching art to children in school and at home.* New York: Farrar, Straus, & Giroux.

Blizzard, G. S. (1990). *Come look with me: Enjoying art with children.* Charlottesville, VA: Thomasson-Grant.

Braman, A. N. (2000). *Traditional Native American arts and activities.* New York: John Wiley.

Cassidy, J., & Hurd, T. (1992). *Watercolor for the artistically undiscovered.* Palo Alto, CA: Klutz Press.

Cavalier, D. (Ed.), & Perez, Z. (1997). *Folk dances from around the world* (The World Dance Series). Miami, FL: Columbia Pictures Publications.

Christensen, J. (1994). *The art of James Christensen: A journey of the imagination* (Retold by R. St. James). Shelton, CT: The Greenwich Workshop.

Cole, J. (1989). *Anna Banana: 101 jump rope rhymes.* New York: Beech Tree Books.

Cook, C., & Carlisle, J. (1985). *Challenges for children: Creative activities for gifted and talented primary students* (D. Dillon, Illus.). West Nyack, NY: Center for Applied Research in Education.

Corsi, J. (1995). *Leonardo Da Vinci: A three-dimensional study.* Rohnert Park, CA: Pomegranate Artbooks.

Delafosse, C., & Gallimard, J. (1993). *Landscapes.* New York: Scholastic.

Delafosse, C., & Gallimard, J. (1993). *Paintings.* New York: Scholastic.

Delafosse, C., & Gallimard, J. (1993). *Portraits.* New York: Scholastic.

Dissanayaka, E. (1992). *Where does art come from?* Seattle: University of Washington Press.

Duckworth, E. (1996). *"The having of wonderful ideas" and other essays on teaching and learning* (2nd ed.). New York: Teachers College Press.

Duckworth, E. (2001). *"Tell me more": Listening to learners.* New York: Teachers College Press.

Edwards, L. C. (1990). *Affective development and the creative arts: A process approach to early childhood education.* Upper Saddle River, NJ: Merrill/Prentice Hall.

Engel, B. S. (1995). *Considering children's art: Why and how to value their works.* Washington, DC: National Association for the Education of Young Children.

Englebaugh, D. (1994). *Art through children's literature: Creative art lessons for Caldecott books.* Englewood, CO: Teacher Ideas Press.

Eyewitness Books. (Categories: art, science, music). New York: Dorling Kindersley.

Flack, J. (1997). *From the land of enchantment: Creative teaching with fairytales.* Englewood, CO: Teacher Ideas Press.

Gallas, K. (1994). *The languages of learning: How children talk, write, dance, draw, and sing their understanding of the world.* New York: Teachers College Press.

Gardner, H. (1982). *Art, mind, and brain: A cognitive approach to creativity.* New York: Basic Books.

Gee, K. (2000). *Visual arts as a way of knowing.* York, ME: Stenhouse.

Goertz, J. (2003). Searching for talent through the visual arts. In J. F. Smutny (Ed.), *Underserved gifted populations: Responding to their needs and abilities* (pp. 459–467). Cresskill, NJ: Hampton.

Goodnow, J. (1977). *Children drawing.* Cambridge, MA: Harvard University Press.

Graham, T. (1982). *Let loose on Mother Goose: Activities to teach math, science, art, music, life skills, and language development.* Nashville, TN: Incentive Publications.

Herman, G., & Hollingsworth, P. (1992). *Kinetic kaleidoscope: Exploring movement and energy in the visual arts.* Tucson, AZ: Zephyr.

Isenberg, J., & Jalongo, M. R. (2001). *Creative expression and play in early childhood.* Upper Saddle River, NJ: Merrill/Prentice Hall.

Khatena, J., & Khatena, N. (1999). *Developing creative talent in art: A guide for parents and teachers.* Stamford, CT: Ablex.

Lasky, L., & Mukerji, R. (1980). *Art: Basic for young children.* Washington, DC: National Association for the Education of Young Children.

Massalski, D. (1997). Petrouska performs in pre-school: A teacher's analysis through the lens of Vygotsky psychology. *Illinois Association for Gifted Children Journal, 13,* 87.

Meador, K. (1998). *Creative thinking and problem solving for young learners.* Englewood, CO: Libraries Unlimited.

Mettler, B. (1970). *Children's creative dance book.* Tucson, AZ: Mettler Studios.

Multicultural Education Series. [Let's Dance Series; My Beautiful House Series]. Miami, FL: M-DCPS Video and Film Library.

Orozco, J. L. (1994). *De Colores and other Latin-American folk songs for children.* New York: Puffin.

Perry, S. (1995). *If . . . .* Venice, CA: Children's Library Press.

Prelutsky, J. (Comp.). (1999). *The 20th century children's poetry treasury* (M. So, Illus.). New York: Knopf.

Schmidt, G. D. (1994). *Poetry for young people: Robert Frost* (H. Sorensen, Illus.). New York: Sterling.

Smith, N. R. (1993). *Experience and art.* New York: Teachers College Press.

Solga, K. (1991). *Draw!* Cincinnati, OH: North Light Books.

Spolin, V. (1986). *Theater games for the classroom: A teacher's handbook.* Evanston, IL: Northwestern University Press.

Striker, S. (1982). *The anti-coloring book of masterpieces: Creative activities for ages 6 and up.* New York: Henry Holt.

Sullivan, C. (Comp.). (1989). *Imaginary gardens: American poetry and art for young people.* New York: Harry N. Abrams.

Thane, A. (1967). *Plays from famous stories and fairy tales: Royalty-free dramatizations of favorite children's stories.* Boston: Plays.

Torrance, E. P. (1980). *Thinking creatively in action and movement.* Bensenville, IL: Scholastic Testing Service.

Torrance, E. P. (1984). *Mentor relationships: How they aid creative achievement, endure, change, and die.* Buffalo, NY: Bearly.

Torrance, E. P. (1997). Growing up creatively gifted: A 22-year longitudinal study. *Creative Child and Adult Quarterly, 5*(1), 148–158.

Torrance, E. P., & Safter, H. T. (1999). *Making the creative leap beyond . . . .* Buffalo, NY: Creative Educational Foundation Press.

Voyages of Discovery Series. (Categories: arts and sciences). New York: Scholastic.

Wheeler, L., & Raebeck, L. (1985). *Orff and Kodaly adapted for the elementary school* (3rd ed.). Dubuque, IA: William C. Brown.

Zakakai, J. D. (1997). *Dancing as a way of knowing.* York, ME: Sternhouse.

Language & Literacy

Ada, A. F. (2003). *A magical encounter: Latino children's literature in the classroom.* Boston: Allyn & Bacon.

Adams, M. J. (1998). *Beginning to read: Thinking about print.* Cambridge: MIT Press.

Barton, R. M., & Booth, D. (1990). *Stories in the classroom: Storytelling, reading aloud and role playing with children.* Portsmouth, NH: Heinemann.

Beaty, J. J. (1994). *Picture book storytelling: Literature activities for young children.* Fort Worth, TX: Harcourt Brace.

Bedard, M. (1992). *Emily* (B. Cooney, Illus.). New York: Doubleday Books for Young Readers.

Bernhardt, E. (1988). *ABCs of thinking with Caldecott books* (With an introduction by N. Polette). O'Fallon, MO: Book Lures.

Blakemore, C. (2002). *Faraway places: Your source for picture books that fly children to 82 countries.* Albany, WI: Adams-Pomeroy.

Carter, P., McNeer, M., Faber, D., & Faber, H. (1992). *Exploring biographies.* New York: Scholastic.

Davidson, J. (1995). *Emergent literacy and dramatic play in early childhood education.* Albany, NY: Delmar.

Despain, P. L. (1993). *Thirty-three multicultural tales to tell.* Little Rock, AR: August House.

Dyson, A. H. (1997). *Writing superheroes: Contemporary childhood, popular culture, and classroom literacy.* New York: Teachers College Press, Columbia University.

Finney, S. (2000). *Keep the rest of the class reading . . . while you teach small groups: 60 high-interest reproducible activities—perfect for learning centers—that build comprehension, vocabulary, and writing skills.* New York: Scholastic.

Finney, S. (2001). *Using guided reading and literacy centers to help your students become better readers: Resource handbook.* Bellevue, WA: Bureau of Education and Research.

Flack, J. D. (1990). *Mystery and detection: Thinking and problem solving with the sleuths.* Englewood, CO: Teacher Ideas Press.

Harvey, S., & Goudvis, A. (2000). *Strategies that work: Teaching comprehension to enhance understanding.* Portland, ME: Stenhouse.

Heath, S. B., & Mangiola, L. (1991). *Children of promise: Literate activity in linguistically and culturally diverse classrooms.* Washington, DC: National Education Association.

Jackman, H. L. (1999). *Sing me a story! Tell me a song! Creative curriculum activities for teachers of young children.* Thousand Oaks, CA: Corwin Press.

Koch, K. (1973). *Rose, where did you get that red? Teaching great poetry to children.* New York: Random House.

Leimbach, J., & Eckert, S. (1996). *Primary book reporter: Independent reading for young learners* (E. Ahlin, Illus.). San Luis Obispo, CA: Dandy Lion.

Livingston, M. C. (1992). *I never told and other poems.* New York: Margaret K. McElderry.

Magsamen, S. (2001). *The story of the heart.* New York: Rizzoli International Relations.

McGowan, M. (1994). *Appreciating diversity through children's literature: Teaching activities for the primary grades.* Englewood, CO: Teacher Ideas Press.

Meier, D. (2000). *Scribble, scrabble: Learning to read and write.* New York: Teachers College Press.

Moll, L. C. (1992). Literacy research in community and classrooms: A sociocultural approach. In R. Beach, J. Green, M. Kamil, & T. Shanahan (Eds.), *Multidisciplinary perspectives in literacy research* (pp. 211–244). Urbana, IL: National Conference on Research in English.

Myers, R. E. (2002). *Word play: Language lessons for creative learners.* Marion, IL: Pieces of Learning.

National Center on Education and the Economy. (1999). *Reading and writing grade by grade.* Washington, DC: National Center on Education and the Economy and the University of Pittsburgh.

National Center on Education and the Economy. (1999). *Reading and writing in every grade: New standards primary literacy standards.* Washington, DC: National Center on Education and the Economy.

Newman, S. B., & Bredekamp, S. (2000). *Learning to read and write: Developmentally appropriate practices for young children.* Washington, DC: National Association for the Education of Young Children.

Newman, S. B., & Roskos, K. A. (Eds.). (1998). *Children achieving: Best practices in early literacy.* Newark, DE: International Reading Association.

Norton, D. E. (2001). *Multicultural children's literature: Through the eyes of many children.* Upper Saddle River, NJ: Merrill/Prentice Hall.

Ortiz, M. (Ed.). (1998). *Literacy instruction for culturally and linguistically diverse students.* Newark, DE: International Reading Association.

Owacki, G. (2001). *Make way for literacy! Teaching the way young children learn.* Washington, DC: National Association for the Education of Young Children.

Polette, N. (1989). *The best ever writing models from children's literature* (P. Dillon, Illus.). O'Fallon, MO: Book Lures.

Polette, N. (2000). *Gifted books, gifted readers: Literature activities to excite young minds.* Englewood, CO: Libraries Unlimited.

Pratt, L., & Beaty, J. J. (1999). *Transcultural children's literature.* Upper Saddle River, NJ: Merrill/Prentice Hall.

Robinson, V. B., Ross, G., & Neal, H. C. (2000). *Emergent literacy in kindergarten: A review of the research and related suggested activities and learning strategies.* San Mateo: California Kindergarten Association.

Roskos, K., & Christie, J. (Eds.). (2000). *Play and literacy in early childhood: Research from multiple perspectives.* Mahwah, NJ: Lawrence Erlbaum.

Schenk de Regniers, B., Moore, E., White, M. M., & Carr, J. (1988). *Sing a song of popcorn: Every child's book of poems.* New York: Scholastic.

Schickedanz, J. A. (1999). *Much more than ABC's: The early stages of reading and writing.* Washington, DC: National Association for the Education of Young Children.

Sky-Peck, K. (Ed.). (1991). *Who has seen the wind? An illustrated collection of poetry for young people.* New York: Rizzoli International Publications.

Smutny, J. F. (1996). Enhancing linguistic gifts of the young. *Understanding Our Gifted, 8*(4), 1, 12–15.

Snow, C., Burns, M. S., & Hewitt, D. (1998). *Preventing reading difficulties in young children.* Washington, DC: National Academy Press.

Steele, L. (1989). *Primarily poetry: Poetry lessons for Grades K–3* (J. Thornley, Illus.). San Luis Obispo, CA: Dandy Lion Publications.

Sullivan, C. (Comp.). (1989). *Imaginary gardens: American poetry and art for young people.* New York: Harry N. Abrams.

Wayman, J. (1995). *If you promise not to tell.* Marion, IL: Pieces of Learning.

Social Studies

Bartok, M., & Ronan, C. (1996). *Indians of the Great Plains.* Glenview, IL: GoodYear Books.

Berman, S., & La Farge, P. (Eds.). (1993). *Promising practices in teaching social responsibility.* Albany: State University of New York Press.

Bruchac, J., & Locker, T. (1996). *Between earth and sky: Legends of Native American sacred places.* New York: Harcourt Brace & Co.

Cech, M. (1991). *Globalchild: Multicultural resources for young children.* New York: Addison-Wesley.

Corsaro, W. A. (1985). *Friendship and peer culture in the early years.* Norwood, NJ: Ablex.

Cortes, C. (2000). *The children are watching: How the media teach about diversity.* New York: Teachers College Press.

Cox, P. (2002). *Tell me the continents.* Marion, IL: Pieces of Learning.

Csikszentmihalyi, M. (1993). *The evolving self: A psychology for the third millennium.* New York: HarperCollins.

Daniels, R. (1990). *Coming to America: The history of immigration and ethnicity in American life.* New York: HarperCollins.

Dyson, A. H. (1993). *Social worlds of children learning to write in an urban school.* New York: Teachers College Press.

Giddens, A. (2000). *Runaway world: How globalization is reshaping our lives.* New York: Routledge.

Glew, M. (2002). *American government.* Ann Arbor: University of Michigan Press.

Goodwin, M. (1990). *He-said-she-said: Talk as social organization among Black children.* Bloomington: Indiana University Press.

Jones, J. J. (1998). *Chalk stories of extraordinary African-Americans* (Portraits by J. Steele; chalk story drawings by P. Bleidorn). Marion, IL: Pieces of Learning.

Kindersley, B., & Kindersley, A. (1995). *Children just like me: A unique celebration of children around the world.* New York: DK Publishing/United Children's Fund.

Kreidler, W., & Wittall, S. T. (1999). *Adventures in peacemaking* (2nd ed.). Cambridge, MA: Educators for Social Responsibility.

Levine, E. (1993). *If your name was changed at Ellis Island* (W. Parmenter, Illus.). New York: Scholastic.

Mattson, M. (1993). *Environmental atlas of the United States.* New York: Scholastic.

National Women's History Project. (1986). *101 wonderful ways to celebrate women's history.* Windsor, CA: National Women's History Project.

Norton, D. (2003). *Through the eyes of a child: An introduction to children's literature* (6th ed.). Upper Saddle River, NJ: Merrill/Prentice Hall.

Paley, V. G. (1992). *You can't say you can't play.* Cambridge, MA: Harvard University Press.

Paley, V. G. (1995). *Kwanzaa and me: A teacher's story.* Cambridge, MA: Harvard University Press.

Risby, B., & Risby, R. (1994). *Map activities for primary students.* San Luis Obispo, CA: Dandy Lion Publications.

Risinger, C. F. (1992). *Current directions in social studies.* Boston: Houghton Mifflin.

Roberts, J. L. (1995). *Nelson Mandela: Determined to be free*. Brookfield, CT: Millbrook.

Savage, T., & Armstrong, D. (2004). *Effective teaching in elementary social studies*. Upper Saddle River, NJ: Pearson, Merrill/Prentice Hall.

Seefeldt, C. (2001). *Social studies for the preschool/primary child*. Upper Saddle River, NJ: Merrill/Prentice Hall.

Selwyn, D. (1995). *Arts and humanities in the social studies* (Bulletin 90). Washington, DC: National Council for the Social Studies.

Sewall, M. (1986). *The pilgrims of Plimoth*. New York: Atheneum.

Sewall, M. (1990). *People of the breaking day*. New York: Atheneum.

Starkey, D. (1993). *Atlas exploration*. New York: Scholastic Reference.

Varley, C., & Miles, L. (1993). *The Usborne geography encyclopedia*. London: Usborne.

Wade, R. C. (1991). *Joining hands*. Tucson, AZ: Zephyr.

Science

Althouse, R. (1988). *Investigating science with young children*. New York: Teachers College Press.

Bowden, M. (1989). *Nature for the very young: A handbook of indoor and outdoor activities* (M. Rishel, Illus.). New York: John Wiley.

Carin, A. A., & Bass, J. E. (2001). *Teaching science as inquiry* (9th ed.). Upper Saddle River, NJ: Merrill/Prentice Hall.

Casey, S. (1997). *Women invent! Two centuries of discoveries that have shaped our world*. Chicago: Chicago Review Press.

Cliatt, M. J. P., & Shaw, J. M. (1992). *Helping children explore science: A sourcebook for teachers of young children*. Upper Saddle River, NJ: Merrill/Prentice Hall.

Cole, J., & Degen, B. (1990). *The magic school bus: Lost in a solar system*. New York: Scholastic. [See also other books in the Magic School Bus series]

Cook, J. G., & The Thomas Alva Edison Foundation. (1988). *The Thomas Edison book of easy and incredible experiments*. New York: Dodd, Mead & Company.

Cornell, J. (1989). *Sharing the joy of nature: Nature activities for all ages*. Nevada City, CA: Dawn Publications.

Dickinson, T. (1987). *Exploring the night sky: The equinox astronomy guide for beginners* (J. Bianchi, Illus.). Buffalo, NY: Firefly Books.

Doris, E. (1991). *Doing what scientists do: Children learn to investigate their world*. Portsmouth, NH: Heineman.

Dunn, A. (1997). *The children's atlas of scientific discoveries and inventions*. Brookfield, CT: Millbrook.

Eyewitness Books. (Categories: art, science, music). New York: Dorling Kindersley.

Fromboluti, S., & Seefeldt, C. (1998). *Early childhood: Where learning begins—Geography*. Washington, DC: National Institute on Early Childhood Development and Education, Office of Educational Research and Improvement, U.S. Department of Education.

Full Option Science System (FOSS), Lawrence Hall of Science, U.C. Berkley. (2002). *Air and weather*. Hudson, NH: Delta Education.

Full Option Science System (FOSS), Lawrence Hall of Science, U.C. Berkley. (2002). *Balance and motion*. Hudson, NH: Delta Education.

Full Option Science System (FOSS), Lawrence Hall of Science, U.C. Berkley. (2002). *Pebbles, sand and silt*. Hudson, NH: Delta Education.

Gates, P. (1995). *Nature got there first: Inventions inspired by nature*. New York: Larousse Kingfisher Chambers.

Gibson, G. (1996). *Science for fun experiments.* Brookfield, CT: Copper Beech Books.

Great Expectation in Mathematics and Science (GEMS), Lawrence Hall of Science. (1996). *Ant homes underground.* Berkeley: Regents, University of California, Berkley.

Great Expectations in Mathematics and Science (GEMS), Lawrence Hall of Science. (1997). *Treasure boxes.* Berkeley: Regents, University of California.

Haber, L. (1970). *Black pioneers of science and inventions.* New York: Harcourt Brace & World.

Hammerman, E., & Musial, D. (1995). *Classroom 2061: Activity-based assessments in science, integrated with mathematics and language arts.* Palatine, IL: IRI/Skylight Training and Publishing.

Haugland, S., & Wright, J. (1997). *Young children and technology: A world of discovery.* New York: Allyn & Bacon.

Henderson, S. K. (1998). *African-American inventors* (Vols. 2, 3). Mankato, MN: Capstone Press.

Herriot, J. (1992). *James Herriot's treasury for children.* New York: St. Martin's.

Hill, D. M. (1977). *Mud, sand, and water.* Washington, DC: National Association for the Education of Young Children.

Holt, B. G. (1993). *Science with young children* (Rev. ed.). Washington, DC: National Association for the Education of Young Children.

Karasov, N., Field, C., & Hunkel, C. (1991). *Discovering wolves: A nature activity book.* Middleton, WI: Dog-Eared Publications.

Kellough, R. D. (1996). *Integrating mathematics and science for kindergarten and primary children.* Upper Saddle River, NJ: Merrill/Prentice Hall.

Liem, T. (1992). *Turning kids on to science in the home: Our environment.* Chino Hills, CA: Science Inquiry Enterprises.

Locker, T. (2002). *Walking with Henry: Based on the life and works of Henry David Thoreau.* Golden, CO: Fulcrum Publishing.

Locker, T. (1995). *Sky tree portfolio* (paintings by Thomas Locker on 14 posters). Text by C. Christiansen. New York: Sky Tree Press.

Locker, T. (1997). *Water dance.* San Diego: Harcourt Brace.

Locker, T. (2000). *Cloud dance.* San Diego: Harcourt Brace.

Locker, T. (2001). *Mountain dance.* San Diego: Harcourt Brace.

Lowery, L. F. (1985). *The everyday science sourcebook: Ideas for teaching in the elementary and middle school.* Palo Alto, CA: Dale Seymour Publications.

Martin, D. (2000). *Elementary science methods: A constructivist approach* (2nd ed.). Belmont, CA: Wadsworth/Thompson Learning.

National Association for the Education of Young Children. (1996). *Technology and young children: Position statement on technology and young children—ages three through eight.* Washington, DC: Author.

National Science Resources Center. (1996). *Resources for teaching elementary school science.* Washington, DC: National Academy Press.

National Science Resources Center. (1997). *Science for all children: A guide to improving elementary science education in your school district.* Washington, DC: National Academy Press.

Nickelsburg, J. (1976). *Nature activities for early childhood.* Menlo Park, CA: Addison-Wesley.

Overbeck, C. (1982). *The world of ants.* Minneapolis, MN: Lerner.

Perdue, P. K. (1991). *Science is an action word!* Glenview, IL: Scott, Foresman.

Piaget, J. (1965). *The child's conception of physical causality.* Totowa, NJ: Littlefield, Adams.

Poppe, C. A., & Van Matre, N. A. (1988). *K–3 science activities kit* (N. A. Van Matre, Illus.). West Nyack, NY: Center for Applied Research in Education.

Saul, W., & Newman, A. R. (1986). *Science faire: An illustrated guide & catalog of toys, books and activities for kids.* New York: Harper & Row.

Seefeldt, C., & Galper, A. (2002). *Active experiences for active children: Science.* Upper Saddle River, NJ: Merrill/Prentice Hall.

Sipiera, P. P. (1987). *I can be an oceanographer.* Chicago: Children's Press.

Smith, J. C. (1988). *What color is Newton's apple? Inquiry science for young children.* Monroe, NY: Trillium.

Wasserman, S., & Ivany, J. W. G. (1996). *The new teaching elementary science: Who's afraid of spiders?* (2nd ed.). New York: Teachers College Press.

Wilkes, A. (1996). *The amazing outdoor activity book.* New York: Dorling Kindersley.

Wood, J. N. (1993). *Woods and forests: Nature hide and seek book* (M. Silver, Illus.). New York: Knopf.

Mathematics

Andrews, A. G., & Trafton, P. R. (2002). *Little kids, powerful problem solvers: Math stories from a kindergarten classroom.* Portsmouth, NH: Heinemann.

Baroody, A. J. (with Coslick, R. T.). (1998). *Fostering children's mathematical power: An investigative approach to K–12 mathematics instruction.* Mahwah, NJ: Lawrence Erlbaum.

Burns, M. (1993). *Math and literature (K–3): Book One.* Sausalito, CA: Math Solutions Publications.

Burns, M. (2000). *About teaching mathematics: A K–8 resource* (2nd ed.). Sausalito, CA: Math Solutions Publications.

Charlesworth, R. (2000). *Experiences in math for young children.* Albany, NY: Delmar.

Copley, J. V. (Ed.). (1999). *Mathematics in the early years.* Washington, DC: National Council of Teachers of Mathematics and National Association for the Education of Young Children.

Donlon, C. (Ed.). (1998). *The development of mathematical skills.* East Sussex, UK: Psychology Press.

Eckert, S., & Leimbach, J. (1993). *Primarily math: A problem solving approach* (A. Palouda, Illus.). San Luis Obispo, CA: Dandy Lion Publications.

Fisher, L. (1987). *Look around! A book about shapes.* New York: Viking Kestrel.

Freeman, C. (2003). *Drawing stars: Building polyhedra.* San Luis Obispo, CA: Dandy Lion Publications.

Greenes, C. (1989). *Math Games: Sparkling activities for early childhood classrooms.* Allen, TX: DLM Teaching Resources.

Hamilton, O. (2002). *Super 7—Daily exercises in problem-solving: Number sense, computation, measurement, geometry, problem solving, patterns* (S. O'Shaughnessy, Illus.). San Luis Obispo, CA: Dandy Lion Publications.

Hirsch, E. S. (1996). *The block book* (3rd ed.). Washington, DC: National Association for the Education of Young Children.

Hugel, B. (1998). *Secret-code math: Kids solve math problems to crack secret codes and reinforce essential math skills.* New York: Scholastic.

Johnson-Foote, B. (2001). *Cup cooking.* Beltsville, MD: Gryphon House.

Kamii, C. (1982). *Number in preschool and kindergarten: Educational implications of Piaget's theory.* Washington, DC: National Association for the Education of Young Children.

Kamii, C., & DeVries, R. (1980). *Group games in early education.* Washington, DC: National Association for the Education of Young Children.

Kamii, C. K. (with Houseman, L. B.). (2000). *Young children reinvent arithmetic: Implications of Piaget's theory* (2nd ed.). New York: Teachers College Press.

Kamii, C. K., & DeVries, R. (1993). *Physical knowledge in preschool education.* New York: Teachers College Press. (Original work published in 1978)

Kenda, M., & Williams, P. S. (1995). *Math wizardry for kids* (T. Robinson, Illus.). New York: Scholastic.

Kimble-Ellis, S. (1997). *Math puzzlers: 25 reproducible puzzles, games, and activities that boost the math skills and up the fun!* New York: Scholastic.

Ma, L. (1999). *Knowing and teaching elementary mathematics.* Hillsdale, NJ: Lawrence Erlbaum.

Martin, L., & Miller, M. (1999). *Great graphing.* New York: Scholastic.

McCracken, J. (1990). *More than 1, 2, 3: The real basics of mathematics.* Washington, DC: National Association for the Education of Young Children.

Pappas, T. (1989). *The joy of mathematics.* San Carlos, CA: Wide World Publishing/Tetra.

Patterson, C. (1991). *Let's celebrate math.* Marion, IL: Pieces of Learning.

Payne, J. N. (1990). *Mathematics for the young child.* Reston, VA: National Council of Teachers of Mathematics.

Piaget, J. (1965). *The child's conception of number.* New York: Norton.

Piaget, J. (1969). *The child's conception of time.* New York: Basic Books.

Piaget, J., Inhelder, B., & Szeminska, A. (1960). *The child's conception of geometry.* London: Routledge.

Polonsky, L. (Ed.). (2000). *Math for the very young: A handbook of activities for parents and teachers.* New York: John Wiley.

Principles and standards for school mathematics. (2000). Reston, VA: National Council of Teachers of Mathematics.

Rasmussen, G. (1995). *Play by the rules: Creative practice in direction-following.* Eugene, OR: Tin Man Press.

Scales, B. (2000). *Math: The missing learning center.* Sacramento: California Association for the Education of Young Children.

Shaw, J. M., & Blake, S. (1998). *Mathematics for young children.* Upper Saddle River, NJ: Merrill/Prentice Hall.

Upitis, R., Phillips, E., & Higgenson, W. (1997). *Creative mathematics: Exploring children's understandings.* London: Routledge.

Van De Walle, J. (1994). *Elementary school mathematics: Teaching developmentally* (2nd ed.). White Plains, NY: Longman.

VandeCreek, B. (2001). *Math rules! 1st–2nd grade enrichment challenge.* Marion, IL: Pieces of Learning.

Washington, M. F. (1995). *Real life math mysteries: A kid's answer to the question, "What will we ever use this for?"* Waco, TX: Prufrock.

Westley, J., & Randolph, M. (1987). *Money and time* (Windows on Mathematics Series). Sunnyvale, CA: Creative Publications.

II. RESOURCES FOR CHILDREN

Creativity and the Arts

Anholt, L. (1994). *Camille and the sunflowers.* Hauppauge, NY: Barron's Educational Series.

Anholt, L. (1996). *Degas and the little dancer.* Hauppauge, NY: Barron's Educational Series.

Avery, M. W., & Avery, D. M. (1995). *What is beautiful?* Berkeley, CA: Tricycle.

Blizzard, G. S. (1990). *Come look with me: Enjoying art with children.* Charlottesville, VA: Thomasson-Grant.

Creative Kids: The National Voice for Kids. Waco, TX: Prufrock.

Delafosse, C., & Gallimard, J. (1993). *Portraits.* New York: Scholastic.

Delafosse, C., & Jeunesse, G. (1993). *Landscapes.* New York: Scholastic.

Delafosse, C., & Jeunesse, G. (1993). *Paintings.* New York: Scholastic.

Devine, D. (Producer, Director). (1992). *Beethoven lives upstairs* [Video]. (Available from Video Finders 1–800–343–4727)

Ehlert, L. (1988). *Planting a rainbow.* San Diego: Harcourt Brace.

England, L. (1998). *The old cotton blues.* New York: Simon & Schuster.

First Discovery Books. (Categories: art and atlas books). New York: Scholastic.

Frey, L. A. (2001). *The story of Van Gogh and Gauguin: A color and learn book.* Quoque, NY: Starshell Press.

Freyman, S. (1999). *How are you peeling? Foods with moods.* New York: Scholastic.

Gage, A. G. (1996). *Pascual's magic pictures.* Minneapolis, MN: Carolrhoda.

Grifalconi, A. (1994). *The bravest flute.* Boston: Little, Brown.

Hayes, A. (1991). *Meet the orchestra.* New York: Harcourt Brace.

Hayes, A. (1995). *Meet the marching Smithereens.* New York: Harcourt Brace.

Hearn, L. (1972). *The boy who drew cats.* San Marino, CA: Huntington Library and Art Gallery.

Heller, R. (1995). *Color.* New York: Putnam and Grosset.

Ho, M. (1996). *Hush! A Thai lullaby.* New York: Orchard.

Hoffman, M. (1991). *Amazing grace.* New York: Dial.

Hubbard, P. (1996). *My crayons talk.* New York: Holt.

Jeunesse, G. (1994). *Musical instruments.* New York: Scholastic.

Jeunesse, G. (1994). *Paint and painting.* New York: Scholastic.

Jonas, A. (1985). *The trek.* New York: Mulberry.

Kids' art. (Series; available: Kids' Art, P.O. Box 274, Mount Shasta, CA 96067; www.kidsart.com)

King-Smith, D. (1982). *Pigs might fly.* New York: Viking.

Kraus, R. (1974). *Owliver.* New York: Dutton.

La Pierre, Y. (1994). *Native American rock art: Messages from the past.* Charlestonville, VA: Thomasson-Grant & Lickle.

Locker, T. (1995). *Sky tree: Seeing science through art.* New York: HarperCollins.

Marzollo, J. *I spy books* (Series; W. Wick, Illus.). New York: Scholastic.

McDermott, G. (1994). *Coyote: A trickster tale from the American Southwest.* San Diego: Harcourt Brace.

Micklethwait, L. (1993). *I spy two eyes: Numbers in art.* New York: Greenwillow.

Namioka, L. (1992). *Yang the youngest and his terrible ear.* Boston: Little, Brown.

Peterson, J. W. (1994). *My mama sings.* New York: HarperCollins.

Pinkney, B. (1994). *Max found two sticks.* New York: Simon & Schuster.

Rascha, C. (1992). *Charlie Parker played be bop.* New York: Orchard.

Seeger, P. (1986). *Abiyoyo.* New York: Macmillan.

Sendak, M. (1963). *Where the wild things are.* New York: Harper & Row.

Shange, N. (1994). *I live in music* (R. Bearden, Illus.). New York: Welcome Enterprises.

Sheenan, P. (1993). *Kylie's concert.* Kansas City, MO: Marshmedia.

Sloat, R. (1998). *There was an old lady who swallowed a trout!* New York: Holt.

Steiner, J. (1998). *Look-alikes* (T. Lindley, Photography). Boston: Little, Brown.

Strohm, B., & National Wildlife Federation. (1992). *Patterns in the wild* (J. Nuhn, Photography). Washington, DC: National Wildlife Federation.

Tinus, A. W. (1994). *Young goat's discovery.* Santa Fe, NM: Red Crane.

Venezia, M. (1990). *Monet.* Chicago: Children's Press.

Walsh, E. (1989). *Mouse paint.* San Diego: Harcourt.

Warren, S. (1992). *Arlie the alligator.* Strongsville, OH: Arlie Enterprises.

WeeBee tunes travel adventures [Music and animations on geography and culture]. Chicago: Girdwood Partners.

Weitzman, J. (1998). *You can't take a balloon into the Metropolitan Museum* (Pictures by R. P. Glasser). New York: Puffin.

Welton, J. (1993). *Eyewitness art book: Impressionism.* London: Dorling Kindersley.

Williams, K. (1990). *Galimoto.* New York: Mulberry.

Winch, J. (1996). *The old man who loved to sing.* New York: Scholastic.

Wolkstein, D. (1981). *The banza.* New York: Dial.

Wyeth, S. D. (1998). *Something beautiful* (C. K. Soentpiet, Illus.). New York: Bantam, Doubleday Dell.

Language and Literacy

Ada, A. F. (1994). *Dear Peter Rabbit.* New York: Maxwell Macmillan International.

Baylor, B. (1975). *The desert is theirs.* New York: Scribner's.

Bedard, M. (1992). *Emily* (B. Cooney, Illus.). New York: Doubleday Books for Young Readers.

Cannon, J. (1993). *Stellaluna.* New York: Harcourt Brace.

Chanko, P. (1999). *Writing places.* New York: Scholastic.

Cimo, S. (1989). *The Egyptian Cinderella* (R. Heller, Illus.). New York: HarperCollins.

Cronin, D. (2000). *Click, clack, moo: Cows that type.* New York: Simon & Schuster.

cummings, e. e. (1983). *Hist whist and other poems for children* (D. Calsada, Illus.). New York: Liveright.

Dakos, K. (1990). *If you're not here please raise your hand: Poems about school.* New York: Four Winds Press.

Der Manuelian, P. (1991). *Hieroglyph from A to Z: A rhyming book with ancient Egyptian stencils for kids.* Boston: Museum of Fine Arts.

Edwards, M. (1992). *Alef-bet: A Hebrew alphabet book.* New York: Lothrop, Lee & Shepard.

Ernst, L. C. (1995). *Little red riding hood: A newfangled prairie tale.* New York: Simon & Schuster Books for Young Readers.

Fantasia. (1940). Walt Disney (1-800-343-4727).

Frank, J. (1990). *Snow toward evening: A year in a river valley* (T. Locker, Illus.). New York: Dial Books.

Gilman, P. (1992). *Something from nothing.* New York: Scholastic.

Havill, J. (1998). *Jamaica tag-along* (A. S. O'Brien, Illus.). Boston: Houghton Mifflin.

Hearn, E. (1984). *Good morning Franny, Good night Franny.* Toronto: Women's Press.

Hort, L. (2000). *The Seals on the bus.* New York: Holt.

Keats, E. J. (1968). *A letter to Amy.* New York: HarperCollins.

Lee, D. (1992). *The ice cream store: Poems.* New York: HarperCollins.

Mak, K. (2002). *My Chinatown: One year in poems.* New York: HarperCollins.

Martin, R. (1992). *The rough-face girl* (D. Shannon, Illus.). New York: Putnam.

Martin, R. (1993). *The boy who lived with the seals* (D. Shannon, Illus.). New York: Putnam.

Mora, P. (2002). *Maria paints the hills* (Paintings by M. Hesch). Santa Fe: Museum of New Mexico Press.

Olsen, M. (2001). *Native American sign language.* Mahwah, NJ: Troll Communications.

Prelutsky, J. (1990). *Something big has been here.* New York: Greenwillow.

Prelutsky, J. (1993). *The dragons are singing tonight.* New York: Greenwillow.

Raffi. (1988). *The wheels on the bus* (S. Wickstrom, Illus.). New York: Crown.

Rankin, L. (1991). *The handmade alphabet.* New York: Dial.

Samton, S. W. (1991). *Jenny's journey.* New York: Viking.

Schwartz, A. (1992). *And the green grass grew all around: Folk poetry from everyone.* New York: HarperCollins.

Scieska, J. (1989). *The true story of the three little pigs! By A. Wolf* (L. Smith, Illus.). New York: Viking Penguin.

Silverstein, S. (1974). *Where the sidewalk ends: The poems and drawings of Shel Silverstein.* New York: Harper & Row.

Silverstein, S. (1981). *A light in the attic.* New York: Harper & Row.

Slobodkina, E. (1998). *Caps for sale.* New York: Scholastic.

Southgate, V. (1970). *The enormous turnip* (Retold). Loughborough, England: Wills & Hepworth.

Speed, T. (1993). *One leaf fell* (M. McIntyre, Illus.). New York: Steward, Tabori and Chang.

Teague, M. (1994). *Pigsty.* New York: Scholastic.

Tapahonso, L., & Schick, E. (1995). *Navajo ABC.* New York: Simon & Schuster.

Thomas, J. C. (1993). *Brown honey in broomwheat tea* (F. Cooper, Illus.). New York: HarperCollins.

Viorst, J. (1995). *Sad underwear and other complications: More poems for children and their parents.* New York: Atheneum Books for Young Readers.

Wells, R. (1997). *Bunny cakes.* New York: Dial.

White, E. B. (1952). *Charlotte's web* (G. Williams, Illus.). New York: Harper.

Young, E. (1989). *Lon Po Po.* New York: Philomel.

Social Studies

Aardema, V. (1975). *Why mosquitoes buzz in people's ears.* New York: Dial.

Aardema, V. (1981). *Bringing the rain to Kapiti plain: A Nandi tale* (B. Vidal, Illus.). New York: Dial.

Aliki. (1976). *Corn is maize: The gift of the Indians.* New York: Harper Trophy.

Altman, L. J. (1993). *Amelia's road.* New York: Lee & Low Books.

American Girls Collection (Books and activity kits). Middleton, WI: Pleasant Company.

Ancona, G. (1991). *Powwow.* San Diego: Harcourt Brace.

Anderson, W. (1998). *Pioneer girl: The story of Laura Ingalls Wilder* (D. Andreasen, Illus.). New York: HarperCollins.

Ballard, R. (1990). *The lost wreck of the Isis.* New York: Scholastic/Madison.

Bartok, M., & Ronan, C. (1996). *Indians of the Great Plains.* Glenview, IL: GoodYear Books.

Baylor, B. (1975). *The desert is theirs.* New York: Scribner's.

Bentley, J. (1990). *Harriet Tubman.* Danbury, CT: Franklin Watts.

Blos, J. W. A. (1979). *A gathering of days.* New York: Scribner's.

Brewer, C., & Grinde, L. (Eds.). (1995). *Many people, many ways.* Tucson, AZ: Zephyr.

Bruchac, J., & Locker, T. (1996). *Between earth and sky: Legends of Native American sacred places.* San Diego: Harcourt Brace.

Bunting, E. (1995). *Dandelions* (G. Shed, Illus.). San Diego: Harcourt Brace.

Christiansen, C. (1992). *Calico and the tin horns* (T. Locker, Illus.). New York: Dial.

Clifford, M. L. (1993). *When the great canoes came* (J. Haynes, Illus.). Gretna, LA: Pelican.

Cole, C. K., & Kobayhashi, K. (Eds.). (1996). *Shades of L.A.: Pictures from ethnic family albums.* New York: New Press.

Cooney, B. (1988). *Island boy.* New York: Puffin.

dePaola, T. (1983). *The legend of the bluebonnet.* New York: Putnam.

dePaola, T. (1996). *Bill and Pete go down the Nile.* New York: Putnam.

Dorris, M. (1992). *Morning girl.* New York: Hyperion Books for Children.

Durrell, A., & Sachs, M. (Eds.). (1990). *The big book for peace.* New York: Dutton Children's Books.

First Discovery Books. (Categories: art and atlas books). New York: Scholastic.

Flack, M. (1958). *Ask Mr. Bear.* New York: Simon & Schuster.

Garland, S. (1998). *My father's boat* (T. Rand, Illus.). New York: Scholastic.

Garza, C. L. (1993). *Family pictures.* San Francisco: Children's Book Press.

Gleiter, J., & Thompson, K. (1985). *Pocahontas.* Chicago: Rand McNally.

Goble, P. (1978). *The girl who loved wild horses.* New York: Aladdin Books.

Graham, B. (1992). *Rose meets Mr. Wintergarten.* Cambridge, MA: Candlewick Press.

Greenfield, E. (1977). *Mary McLeod Bethune* (J. Pinkney, Illus.). New York: HarperCollins.

Hogan, L. (1995). *Solar storms.* New York: Touchstone.

Hunt, I. (1966). *Across five Aprils.* New York: Tempo.

Knight, J. (1982). *Jamestown: New world adventure.* Mahwah, NJ: Troll Associates.

Jonas, A. (1982). *When you were a baby.* New York: Lerner.

Jonas, A. (1983). *Round trip.* New York: Greenwillow.

Jonas, A. (1984). *The quilt.* New York: Greenwillow.

Jonas, A. (1986). *Now we can go.* New York: Greenwillow.

Joosse, B. M. (1991). *Mama, do you love me?* (B. Lavallee, Illus.). San Francisco: Chronicle Books.

Keats, E. J. (1967). *Peter's chair.* New York: Harper & Row.

Kindersley, A. (1997). *Children just like me: Celebrations* (B. Kindersley, Photography). New York: DK Publishing.

Lorbiecki, M. (1998). *Sister Anne's hands* (K. W. Popp, Illus.). New York: Dial.

Mak, K. (2002). *My Chinatown: One year in poems.* New York: HarperCollins.

McGuire, M. E. (1997). *The Oregon trail.* Chicago: Everyday Learning Corporation.

McKissack, P. C. (1997). *Ma dear's aprons* (F. Cooper, Illus.). New York: Atheneum.

Miles, M. (1971). *Annie and the old one.* Boston: Little, Brown.

Mora, P. (2000). *The night the moon fell/La noche que se cayo la luna.* Toronto: Groundwood.

Munch, R., & Askar, S. (1995). *From far away* (M. Martchenko, Illus.). Toronto: Annick Press.

Musgrove, M. (1976). *Ashanti to Zulu: African traditions* (L. Dillon & D. Dillon, Illus.). New York: Dial Books for Young Readers.

Penner, L. R. (1991). *Eating the plates.* New York: Macmillan.

Pinkney, A. D. (1994). *Dear Benjamin Banneker* (B. Pinkney, Illus.). San Diego: Harcourt Brace.

Roberts, J. L. (1995). *Nelson Mandela: Determined to be free.* Brookfield, CT: Millbrook.

Rylant, C. (1985). *The relatives came* (S. Gammell, Illus.). New York: Bradbury.

Say, A. (1993). *Grandfather's journey.* New York: Houghton Mifflin.

Scullar, S. (1991). *The great round-the-world balloon race.* New York: Dutton Children's Books.

Sheldon, D. (1993). *Under the moon* (G. Blythe, Illus.). New York: Dial Books for Young Readers.

Skipping Stones: A Multicultural Magazine. Eugene, OR.

Snyder, D. (1988). *The boy of the three-year nap* (A. Say, Illus.). Boston: Houghton Mifflin.

Steiner, B. (1988). *Whale brother* (G. W. Mayo, Illus.). New York: Walker & Co.

Stevens, C. (1992). *Lily and Miss Liberty.* New York: Scholastic.

Temple, L. (Ed.). (1993). *Dear world: How children around the world feel about our environment.* New York: Random House.

Thomas, J. C. (1998). *I have heard of a land* (F. Cooper, Illus.). New York: HarperCollins.

Trottier, M. (1998). *Prairie willow* (L. Fernandez & R. Jacobson, Illus.). New York: Stoddart Kids.

Tworkov, J. (1998). *The camel who took a walk* (R. Duvoisin, Illus.). New York: Dutton.

Waters, K. (1989). *Sarah Morton's day: A day in the life of a pilgrim girl* (R. Kendall, Photography). New York: Scholastic.

Williams, V. B. (1982). *A chair for my mother.* New York: Greenwood.

Winter, J. (1988). *Follow the drinking gourd.* New York: Knopf.

Science

Adshead, P. (1990). *Puzzle island.* Martinez, CA: Discovery Toys.

Appelhof, M. (1997). *Worms eat my garbage: How to set-up and maintain a worm composting system* (2nd ed.). Kalamazoo, MI: Flower Press.

Ashby, R. (1990). *Jane Goodall's animal world: Sea otters.* New York: Macmillan.

Barber, A. (1995). *The monkey and the panda.* New York: Macmillan Books for Young Readers.

Barton, B. (1990). *Bones, bones, dinosaur bones.* New York: HarperCollins.

Baylor, B. (1985). *Everybody needs a rock* (P. Parnall, Illus.). New York: Aladdin Paperbacks.

Bender, L. (1991). *Inventions.* New York: Knopf.

Branley, F. M. (1986). *What the moon is like* (T. Kelley, Illus.). New York: HarperCollins.

Brett-Surman, M., & Holtz, T. (1998). *James Gurney: The world of dinosaurs.* Shelton, CT: Greenwich Workshop.

Carle, E. (1987). *A house for hermit crab.* New York: Scholastic.

Cherry, L. (1990). *The great kapok tree: A tale of the Amazon rain forest.* San Diego: Harcourt Brace.

Cherry, L. (1993). *A river ran wild.* San Diego: Harcourt Brace.

Cherry, L. (1994). *The armadillo from Amarillo.* San Diego: Harcourt Brace.

DePaola, T. (1975). *The cloud book.* New York: Scholastic.

Donahue, M. (1988). *The grandpa tree.* Niwot, CO: Roberts Rinehart.

Fetzner, M. (2000). *The 3 pigs and the scientific wolf.* Marion, IL: Pieces of Learning.

George, J. C. (1992). *Missing gator of Gumbo Limbo.* New York: HarperCollins.

Grambling, L. G. (1995). *Can I have a stegosaurus, Mom? Can I? Please?* (H. B. Lewis, Illus.). Mahwah, NJ: BridgeWater Books.

Haven, K. (2001). *That's weird! Awesome science mysteries* (J. Lynch, Illus.). Golden, CO: Fulcrum.

Heine, H. (1983). *The most wonderful egg in the world.* New York: Atheneum.

Helldorfer, M. C. (1994). *Gather up, gather in: A book of the seasons* (V. Pederson, Illus.). New York: Lothrop, Lee & Shepard.

Heller, R. (1987). *Chickens aren't the only ones.* New York: Gosset & Dunlap.

Herriot, J. (1990). *Oscar, cat-about-town.* New York: St. Martin's.

Hirst, R., & Hirst, S. (1990). *My place in space.* New York: Orchard.

Jenkins, S. (1995). *Biggest, strongest, fastest.* New York: Ticknor and Fields Books for Young Readers.

Kent, P. (1998). *Hidden under the ground: The world beneath your feet.* New York: Dutton.

Kesselman, W. (1995). *Sand in my shoes* (R. Himler, Illus.). New York: Hyperion Books for Children.

Kovacs, D., & Madin, K. (1996). *Beneath blue waters: Meetings with remarkable sea creatures* (L. Madin, Photography). New York: Viking/Penguin Group.

Lauber, P. (1994). *Fur, feathers, and flippers.* New York: Scholastic.

Maclay, E. (1998). *The forest has eyes* (B. Doolittle, Illus.). Shelton, CT: Greenwich Workshop Press.

McNaughton, C. (1991). *If dinosaurs were cats and dogs.* New York: Four Winds Press/Macmillan.

Minasian, S. M., Balcomb, K. C., & Foster, L. (1984). *The worlds' whales.* Washington, DC: Smithsonian Books.

Minasian, S. M. (Producer). (1985). *World of the sea otters* [Video]. San Francisco: Marine Mammal Fund.

Mullins, P. (1994). *V is for vanishing: An alphabet of endangered animals.* New York: HarperCollins.

Murphy, S. (1999). *Dave's down-to-earth rock shop.* New York: HarperCollins.

Oppenheim, J. (1995). *Have you seen trees?* (J. Tseng & M. Tseng, Illus.). New York: Scholastic.

Pollock, S. (1993). *Ecology* (Eyewitness Science). New York: Teachers College Press, Columbia University.

Robinson, S. (1993). *Sea otter river otter* (G. K. Opsahl & M. C. Leggitt, Illus.). Niwot, CO: Roberts Rinehart.

Rohmann, E. (1994). *Time flies.* New York: Crown.

Sams, C. R., II, & Stoick, J. (2000). *A stranger in the woods: A photographic fantasy.* Milford, MI: Carl R. Sams II Photography.

Schimmel, S. (1994). *Dear children of the earth.* Minocqua, WI: North Word Press.

Schlank, C., & Metzger, B. (1994). *A clean sea: The Rachel Carson story.* Culver City, CA: Cascade.

Smith, J. (1988). *What color is Newton's apple? Inquiry science for young children.* Monroe, NY: Trillium.

Taylor, B. (1992). *Rain forest* (F. Greenaway, Photography). New York: Dorling Kindersley.

Taylor, B. (1993). *Forest life* (K. Taylor & J. Burton, Photography). New York: Dorling Kindersley.

Temple, L. (Ed.). (1993). *Dear world: How children around the world feel about our environment.* New York: Random House.

Terrell, S. (1995). *Roberto's rainforest.* El Cajon, CA: Interaction Publishers.

van Allsburg, C. (1988). *Two bad ants.* Boston: Houghton-Mifflin.

Whelan, F. (1992). *Bringing the farmhouse home* (J. Rowland, Illus.). New York: Simon & Schuster.

Yashima, T. (1970). *Umbrella.* New York: Viking.

Zubrowski, B. (1979). *Bubbles* (J. Drescher, Illus.). New York: Beech Tree.

Zubrowski, B. (1990). *Balloons: Building and experimenting with inflatable toys* (R. Doty, Illus.). New York: Beech Tree.

Mathematics

Adler, D. A. (1999). *How tall, how short, how faraway.* New York: Holiday House.

Anno, M. (1987). *Anno's math games.* New York: Philomel.

Anno, M. (1999). *Anno's magical seeds.* New York: Paper Star.

Anno, M., & Anno, M. (1983). *Anno's mysterious multiplying jar.* New York: Philomel.

Bang, M. (1983). *Ten, nine, eight.* New York: Mulberry.

Burns, M. (1994). *The greedy triangle.* New York: Scholastic.

Burns, M. (1996). *How many feet? How many tails?* New York: Scholastic.

Carle, E. (1969). *The very hungry caterpillar.* London: Hamish Hamilton.

Carle, E. (1986). *The secret birthday message.* New York: Harper/Trophy.

Carle, E. (1996). *The grouchy ladybug.* Old Tappan, NJ: Scott Foresman (Pearson K–12).

Clement, R. (1991). *Counting on Frank.* Milwaukee, WI: Gareth Stevens.

Dee, R. (1988). *Two ways to count to ten: A Liberian folktale.* New York: Henry Holt.

Derubertis, B. (1999). *A collection for Kate.* New York: Kane.

Dodds, D. A. (1994). *The shape of things.* Cambridge, MA: Candlewick.

Ehlert, L. (2001). *Fish eyes: A book you can count on.* New York: Harcourt Brace.

Falwell, C. (1993). *Feast for 10.* New York: Clarion.

Feelings, M. (1971). *Moja means one: A Swahili counting book.* New York: Dial.

Fitzgerald, T. (2002). *The absolutely essential math dictionary.* San Luis Obispo, CA: Dandy Lion Publications.

Gerth, M. (2001). *Ten little ladybugs.* New York: Piggy Toes Press.

Grossman, V. (1999). *Ten little rabbits.* New York: Chronicle Books.

Grover, M. (1996). *Circles and squares everywhere.* New York: Harcourt.

Haskins, J. (1991). *Count your way through the Arab world.* Minneapolis, MN: Carolrhoda.

Hopkins, L. B. (Comp.). (1997). *Marvelous math: A book of poems.* New York: Simon & Schuster Books for Young Readers.

Hutchins, P. (1986). *The doorbell rang.* New York: Mulberry Books.

Keats, J. E. (1990). *Over in the meadow.* New York: Puffin.

Keenan, S. (2001). *Lizzy's dizzy day, dizzy day.* New York: Cartwheel.

Keenan, S., & Girouard, P. (1997). *More or less a mess.* New York: Cartwheel.

Linden, A. M. (1992). *One smiling grandma.* New York: Dial.

Martin, B., Jr., & Archambault, J. (1989). *Chicka chicka boom boom.* New York: Simon & Schuster Books for Young Readers.

McKissack, P. C. (1997). *Mirandy and brother wind.* New York: Knopf.

McMillan, B. (1986). *Becca backward, Becca forward: A book of concept pairs.* New York: HarperCollins.

Meeks, S. (2002). *Drip drop.* New York: Harper/Trophy.

Micklethwait, L. (1993). *I spy two eyes: Numbers in art.* New York: Greenwillow.

Murphy, S. (1997). *Betcha!* New York: HarperCollins.

Murphy, S. (2002). *Bigger, better, best!* (M. Winborn, Illus.). New York: HarperCollins.

Myller, R. (1991). *How big is a foot?* Old Tappan, NJ: Scott Foresman (Pearson K–12).

Pinczes, E. (1993). *One hundred hungry ants.* New York: Houghton Mifflin.

Reid, M. (1990). *The button box.* New York: Dutton.

Santomero, A. C. (1998). *The shape detectives.* New York: Simon Spotlight.

Say, A. (1982). *The bicycle man.* New York: Houghton Mifflin.

Scieszka, J., & Smith, L. (1995). *Math curse.* New York: Viking/Penguin.

Seuss, Dr. (1988). *The shape of me and other stuff.* New York: Random House.

Shaw, C. G. (1988). *It looked like spilt milk.* New York: Harper/Trophy.

Stickels, T. (1995). *Think-ercises: Math and word puzzles to exercise your brain.* Pacific Grove, CA: Critical Thinking Press & Software.

Tompert, A. (1990). *Grandfather Tang's story.* New York: Crown.

Wood, J. (1992). *Moo, moo, brown cow.* New York: Gulliver.

References

Belgrad, S. (1998). Creating the most enabling environment for young gifted children. In J. F. Smutny (Ed.), *The young gifted child: Potential and promise, an anthology* (pp. 369–379). Cresskill, NJ: Hampton Press.

Bredekamp, S., & Rosegrant, T. (Eds.). (1992). *Reaching potentials: Appropriate curriculum and assessment for young children* (Vol. 1). Washington, DC: National Association for the Education of Young Children.

Burke, K., Fogarty, R., & Belgrad, S. (1994). *The portfolio connection.* Arlington Heights, IL: Skylight.

Burns, M. (1992). *About teaching mathematics: A K–8 resource.* Sausalito, CA: Math Solutions Publications.

Carson, R. (1998). *A sense of wonder* (N. Kelsh, Photography). New York: HarperCollins.

Clark, B. (2002). Assessment that empowers teachers and learners. *Gifted Education Communicator, 33*(2), 10–11, 31–32.

Cohen, L. M., & Jipson, J. A. (1998). Conceptual models: Their role in early education for the gifted and talented child. In J. F. Smutny (Ed.), *The young gifted child: Potential and promise, an anthology* (pp. 390–419). Cresskill, NJ: Hampton Press.

Coil, C., & Merritt, D. (2001). *Solving the assessment puzzle: Piece by piece.* Marion, IL: Pieces of Learning.

Cummings, C., & Piirto, J. (1998). The education of talented young children in the context of school reform. In J. F. Smutny (Ed.), *The young gifted child: Potential and promise, an anthology* (pp. 380–389). Cresskill, NJ: Hampton Press.

Eberle, B. (1996). *Scamper: Creative games and activities for imagination and development.* Buffalo, NY: D.O.K. Publishers.

Feuerstein, R. (1980). *Instrumental enrichment.* Glenview, IL: Scott, Foresman.

Gardner, H. (1993). *Frames of mind: The theory of the multiple intelligences.* New York: Basic Books.

Goertz, J. (2003). Searching for talent through the visual arts. In J. F. Smutny (Ed.), *Underserved gifted populations: Responding to their needs and abilities* (pp. 269–277). Cresskill, NJ: Hampton Press.

Gordon, W. J. (1961). *Synectics.* New York: Harper & Row.

Gregory, G. H., & Chapman, C. (2002). *Differentiated instructional strategies: One size doesn't fit all.* Thousand Oaks, CA: Corwin Press.

Guilford, J. P. (1967). *The nature of human intelligence.* New York: Harper & Row.

Harvey, S., & Goudvis, A. (2000). *Strategies that work: Teaching comprehension to enhance understanding.* Portland, ME: Stenhouse.

Heacox, D. (2002). *Differentiating instruction in the regular classroom: How to reach and teach all learners, Grades 3–12.* Minneapolis, MN: Free Spirit Publishing.

Kolb, D. (1984). *Experiential learning: Experience as the source of learning and development.* Englewood Cliffs, NJ: Prentice Hall.

Locker, T. (1997). *Water dance.* San Diego: Harcourt Brace.

Locker, T. (2000). *Cloud dance.* San Diego: Silver Whistle Harcourt.

Locker, T., & Christensen, C. (1995). *Sky tree portfolio.* Stuyvesant, NY: Sky Tree Press. (Available at the Center for Gifted, National-Louis University, 847-251-2661)

McCarthy, B. (1990). Using the 4MAT system to bring learning styles to schools. *Educational Leadership, 48*(2), 31–37.

Moll, L. C. (1992). Funds of knowledge for teaching: Using a qualitative approach to connect homes and classrooms. *Theory Into Practice, 31*(2), 132–141.

Montessori, M. (1964). *The Montessori method.* New York: Schocken.

Montessori, M. (1966). *The secret of childhood.* South Bend, IN: University of Notre Dame Press.

Morrison, G. S. (1997). *Fundamentals of early childhood education.* Upper Saddle River, NJ: Prentice Hall.

North Central Regional Educational Laboratory. (1994). Funds of knowledge: A look at Luis Moll's research into hidden family resources. *CITYSCHOOLS, 1*(1), 19–21.

Parnes, S. J. (1981). *The magic of your mind.* Buffalo, NY: D.O.K. Publishers.

Piaget, J. (1977). *The development of thought: Equilibration of cognitive structures.* New York: Viking.

Piaget, J. (1980). *Adaptation and intelligence: Organic selection and phenocopy.* Chicago: University of Chicago Press.

Piper, D. (Ed.). (1981). *Random House history of painting and sculpture.* New York: Random House.

Smutny, J. F., Walker, S. Y., & Meckstroth, E. A. (1997). *Teaching young gifted children in the regular classroom.* Minneapolis, MN: Free Spirit Publishing.

Tomlinson, C. A. (1999). *The differentiated classroom: Responding to the needs of all learners.* Alexandria, VA: ASCD.

Torrance, E. P. (1969). *Creativity.* Belmont, CA: Dimensions.

Torrance, E. P. (1977). *Discovery and nurturance of giftedness in the culturally different.* Reston, VA: Council for Exceptional Children.

Torrance, E. P. (1980). Growing up creatively gifted: A 22-year longitudinal study. *Creative Child and Adult Quarterly, 5*(3), 148–158, 170.

Vygotsky, L. S. (1962). *Thought and language* (E. Hanfmann & G. Vakar, Trans.). Cambridge: MIT Press.

wa Gacheru, M. (1985). Children of Nairobi. *Illinois Association for Gifted Children Journal, 4,* 5–7.

Wiggins, G., & McTighe, J. (1998). *Understanding by design.* Alexandria, VA: Association for Supervision and Curriculum Development.

Index

**CORWIN
PRESS**

The Corwin Press logo—a raven striding across an open book—represents the happy union of courage and learning. We are a professional-level publisher of books and journals for K-12 educators, and we are committed to creating and providing resources that embody these qualities. Corwin's motto is "Success for All Learners."